ACADEMIC ADVISING APPROACHES

Strategies That Teach Students to Make the Most of College

Jayne K. Drake, Peggy Jordan, Marsha A. Miller

EDITORS

JB JOSSEY-BASS™
A Wiley Brand

NACADA
The Global Community for Academic Advising

Published by Jossey-Bass
A Wiley Brand

One Montgomery Street, Suite 1200, San Francisco, CA 94104-4594—www.josseybass
.com

Jossey-Bass books and products are available through most bookstores. To contact Jossey-Bass directly
call our Customer Care Department within the U.S. at 800-956-7739, outside the U.S. at 317-572-
3986, or fax 317-572-4002.

Wiley publishes in a variety of print and electronic formats and by print-on-demand. Some material
included with standard print versions of this book may not be included in e-books or in print-on-
demand. If this book refers to media such as a CD or DVD that is not included in the version you
purchased, you may download this material at http://booksupport.wiley.com. For more information
about Wiley products, visit www.wiley
.com.

Library of Congress Cataloging-in-Publication Data

Drake, Jayne K.
  Academic advising approaches : strategies that teach students to make the most of college / Jayne K.
Drake, Peggy Jordan, Marsha A. Miller. – First edition.
      pages cm
  Includes bibliographical references and index.
  ISBN 978-1-118-10092-9 (hardback); ISBN 978-1-118-41876-5 (ebk.); ISBN 978-1-118-41603-7
(ebk.)
  1. Counseling in higher education–United States–Handbooks, manuals, etc. 2. Faculty advisors–
United States–Handbooks, manuals, etc. I. Title.
  LB2343.D73 2013
  378.1'94–dc23
                                    2013013535

Printed in the United States of America
FIRST EDITION
HB Printing 10 9 8 7 6 5 4 3

The Jossey-Bass Higher
and
Adult Education Series

CONTENTS

PART ONE
Foundations of Academic Advising Practice

PART TWO
A New Light: Viewing the Practice of Academic
Advising From Different Perspectives

PART THREE
A New Lens: Applying Theories From Other Disciplines to the Practice of Academic Advising

PART FOUR
A New Path: Envisioning the Future of Academic Advising

Good advising may be the single most underestimated characteristic of a successful college experience.

—Richard Light, *Making the Most of College: Students Speak Their Minds*, 2001

This book is dedicated to academic advisors across the globe whose efforts help students make the most of their college experiences.

PREFACE

The publication of this book signals a significant step forward in the evolution of academic advising as a profession. Its purpose is to expand the knowledge base of advising and link theory with practice. It provides a deep look at the scholarship that underpins advising and offers practical applications for advising contact with students. It highlights the various interdisciplinary connections between advising and other disciplines, especially the social sciences, education, and the humanities. It also challenges professional and faculty advisors, counselors, personal tutors, and advising administrators around the world to become thought leaders and scholar-practitioners (Schulenberg & Lindhorst, 2008, p. 43)—those who study the knowledge base, engage in research, explore the viability and applicability of various theories to student interactions, and assess the practical applications to their own advising practice. As Shaffer, Zalewski, and Leveille (2010) stated in "The Professionalization of Academic Advising," "academic advisors need to develop a body of theory from which to educate future advisors" (p. 73). Doing so, they maintain, "is as critical to the future of the profession as is the need for empirical research into the effectiveness of academic advising practice" (p. 73). Good practice is grounded in knowledge, research, and assessment.

To serve increasingly complex and diverse institutions of higher education around the world and their burgeoning diverse student populations, academic advising professionals need to understand that one unified theory of academic advising is neither possible nor necessary (Hagen & Jordan, 2008, p. 19). They must be able to recognize various advising approaches and adapt them to their own student populations with the expectation of enhancing student satisfaction with their academic experiences and helping students articulate and achieve their academic goals and career aspirations.

The contributors to this book provide theoretical background and practical developmental approaches to advising around the understanding that students are learners who establish a partnership of responsibility with their advisors and who ultimately take charge of their own academic, personal, and professional progress. Building relationships and encouraging this holistic development of all students are key elements in all the described approaches.

Prescriptive Advising as the Foundation

In the years following the 1972 publication of Burns Crookston's "A Developmental View of Academic Advising," in which he distinguishes between developmental and prescriptive practices, advisors have embraced a more student-centered, active-learning approach to the advising process. Attention turned from the necessity of a service orientation—the advisor as the repository and disseminator of knowledge on curricular requirements and other academic information about students' records and academic progress—to the advisor as teacher, mentor, facilitator, guide. Prescriptive advising, Crookston (1972/1994/2009) wrote, may best be seen as a largely one-way process in which the student offers little to the process. It is hierarchical in nature, "with the advisor in command of the knowledge and the advisement sessions; the advisee is passive and in receipt of advice" (1972, p. 13). His guiding metaphor is of the advisor as doctor who examines patients and prescribes the medication that will make them better. In the prevailing literature, this do-as-I-say approach has increasingly fallen on hard times and sometimes contrasts unfavorably with student development theories and approaches; some have dismissed it as a viable option for advising students.

However, all student populations, whether comprising first-year, first-generation, international, at-risk, exploratory, or military veteran students, respond well to a more prescriptive approach when direct instruction is necessary and appropriate. Students are encouraged to view their advisors as expert information and advice givers: "If you need to activate your PIN number, see your advisor." "If you need to pick several electives, see your advisor." "If you want to change your major, see your advisor." "If your GPA has slipped, see your advisor."

In the same way that classroom teachers must impart critical subject matter to their students for them to learn the discipline, so too must advisors offer key information to students as part of the learning process. Once important data, ideas, and concepts are communicated and understood, teachers incorporate the processing and application of that information as well as encourage the development of the critical and analytical thinking skills that characterize knowledge development. In both the classroom and advising settings, the prescriptive information that attracts student attention forms the basis for critical thinking and intellectual growth.

Today's practitioner knows that developmental and prescriptive advising approaches should not be seen as separate and mutually exclusive. In fact, prescriptive advising serves as the sturdy platform from which developmental advising approaches take wing. The need for information and advice often draws students into advising offices. The informational necessities of prescriptive advising create the opportunity for advisors to engage students in knowledge building and active learning—the developmental and relational components of advising. While no one will argue that a prescriptive model should be employed in isolation or adopted as the sole approach to student advising and learning, it is, nevertheless, an important and necessary element in the teaching and student-centered learning process that defines academic advising. Therefore, it warrants attention, research, and assessment.

Definition of Terms: Theories, Approaches, and Strategies

The academic approaches in this book are not considered theories. *Theories* provide the conceptual frameworks for academic advising as derived largely from social science, humanities, and education disciplines and applied to advising students. This book focuses on the variety of both *approaches* to academic advising as derived from a number of theories and *strategies* that advisors may employ to implement a particular approach.

Organization of the Book

The chapters in this book are arranged into four parts: the foundations and history of developmental advising, advising as filtered through the prism of social science disciplines, theories from other disciplines that inform advising practice, and possible futures for the profession of advising. Although the sequence of the chapters is meant to provide a reasonable ordering of the theories, approaches, and strategies that influence advising practice, it is not critical to understanding the material. Whether this book is read from cover to cover or the chapters read selectively, the chapters stand on their own as important guides that influence advising practice and student success.

The chapters in part one look at the foundations of academic advising that owe their beginnings to a developmental view of students as individual learners with their own academic, career, and personal goals. Chapter 1 invites advisors to think critically and intentionally about their professional responsibilities by becoming familiar with the scholarly research in the field, advising approaches, and strategies, and then applying those tools to enhance student success and retention. Chapter 2 views academic advising from the versatile perspective of teaching and learning and in the context of the student as learner and advisor as teacher. The *advising-as-teaching* model rests on the important connections advisors forge with students. Chapter 3 shifts from the advisor as teacher to the student as learner and explores the principles and strategies that promote learning and underpin learning-centered advising. It lays out the *teacher's dozen*—research-based, practical strategies for teaching and learning—with the caveat that advisors are not just teaching skills or values; they are teaching students. Chapter 4 carefully traces the history and principles of developmental advising as a "systematic process based on a close student–advisor relationship intended to aid students in achieving educational, career, and personal goals through the utilization of the full range of institutional and community resources . . ." (Winston, Miller, Ender, & Grites, 1984, p. 19).

The chapters in part two offer perspectives on advising from the time-honored and time-tested approaches derived from the social sciences. Chapter 5 defines and discusses the person-centered or motivational-interviewing approach that encourages positive behavior change. This approach when placed in the context of academic advising situates the advisor as the key facilitator in encouraging such change. Chapter 6 on appreciative advising, like the other chapters in this section, discusses the importance of intentional and collaborative relationships that rely on a positive, trusting advisor–student rapport. Appreciative advising is built on the practice of asking open-ended questions designed to help students think critically about their own strengths and then constructing a pathway to help their goals become a reality. Chapter 7 on strengths-based advising focuses on the talents all students bring to the academy and how advisors might use these talents to challenge and motivate students to be successful. From its deeply social science–based roots, this approach offers strong evidence of effectiveness with a wide variety of students. Chapter 8 on self-authorship theory stresses the development of students' complex decision-making skills and their capacity to balance personal beliefs and values with critical evaluation of information. Rooted in constructivist-developmental theories in cognitive psychology, self-authorship theory encourages students to learn how to learn and to develop higher order thinking skills. Chapter 9 discusses proactive (formerly intrusive) advising as purposeful outreach to students before they find themselves in academic difficulty. Using the best of both prescriptive and developmental advising approaches, proactive advising has the goal of helping students engage the institutional services and programs designed to improve their academic skills and lead to increased academic motivation and persistence. Chapter 10 on advising as coaching draws connections between leadership/personal life coaching and developmental advising approaches. It provides useful, practical coaching approaches to academic advising and outlines how to implement them to strengthen advisor–student relationships and enhance student-learning outcomes.

Part three provides a new lens, new ways of seeing, by applying theories from other disciplines not typically applied to advising—constructivism and systems theory, Socratic dialogue, and hermeneutics. Chapter 11 argues that constructivism, which defines learning as an active process of constructing knowledge rather a passive process of simply receiving it, serves as a broad foundation for nearly all advising approaches. Through the use of system theory, the chapter also offers a visual mind map of the four basic elements that underpin any advising interaction—the student, advisor, institution, and external influences. Chapter 12 delves into an exploration of the Socratic method as it applies to academic advising and the cultivation of students' critical-thinking skills. The goal of this approach is to produce a self-aware, educated citizenry who can make informed decisions, engage in self-reflection, and consider different viewpoints. Chapter 13 looks at academic advising through the perspective of hermeneutics or the art of interpretation as grounded in the humanities through the work of Martin Heidegger and Hans-Georg Gadamer. It begins by outlining and conceptualizing the process of "understanding" and ends by offering hands-on suggestions for applying a hermeneutics approach to advising practice.

In part four, Envisioning the Future of Academic Advising, chapter 14 does not presume to predict the future of academic advising, but it does describe a possible future and posits a number of ideas and goals to consider. It is a world in which advising is "the most important academic resource in higher education if only the advising community will embrace the ideas and goals set forth here and effectively articulate them to the wider academic world."

Scenarios

Students frequently ask academic advisors to help them problem solve and make decisions. To best assist them, advisors consider various approaches, often wondering which will yield the best outcomes for a specific situation or individual advisee.

To illustrate how particular advising approaches work in practice, most chapters incorporate one or both of the scenarios provided below. Each scenario features typical issues students bring to advisors. Kimball and Campbell state in their chapter that "approaches to academic advising mirror personal values and beliefs as well as the diversity of ways students learn, grow, and develop." While the scenarios are the same throughout the book, the practical strategies used to address them vary with each advising approach and thus lead to different student-learning opportunities.

Scenario I: Academic Reasons

A first-generation college sophomore, Riley, comes to Skylar, an academic advisor, and says, "I'm having trouble in two of my classes. I don't understand what the professor is talking about in one of them, but it's a required course in my major. The other is only a gen ed course, but I keep getting low grades on the writing assignments. I was always good in writing in high school. If I do poorly, this will lower my GPA, and I just got off academic probation last term. I want to stay in my major, but I don't know if I can pass this one course and that would really disappoint my family. What do you suggest I do?"

Scenario II: Nonacademic Reasons

Ali, a second-year student, comes to Drew, an academic advisor, to discuss withdrawing from school: "I'm really not doing well this term. It's not the courses or the professors—I just don't feel like I fit in. A few of my friends left after last year, and I haven't really found any new ones. My new roommates are not really like me, so they kind of stick together by themselves. I'm not in any clubs or anything like that although I do work off campus. Also, I feel my parents and I have spent lots of money, but I'm not sure it's worth spending more if I'm not that interested. Do you have any suggestions? What do you think I should do?"

Voices From the Field

In Voices From the Field articles, practicing advisors share their experiences, including successes and challenges, with the approach discussed in the accompanying chapter. We hope that the stories will encourage readers to try the featured practice with students facing a variety of academic, career, and life issues.

The Challenge

The authors and editors of *Academic Advising Approaches* challenge advisors, counselors, faculty members, personal tutors, and advising administrators everywhere to take up this book. Choose a chapter a month for a reading circle or workshop. Discuss the various strategies connected to the approach. Debate their applicability to various advising circumstances. Create the academic advising experiences that promote student growth and learning. Test them with students who will benefit most from the approach. Record your findings. Write a research article on the empirical study.

We invite everyone to interrogate the chapters in this book by using the following questions (Nutt, 2008) as guides:

- What are the key concepts that will make me a better advisor?
- What are the key concepts that will enhance the academic advising experiences of my students?
- How can I use the strategies I have learned to impact our advising program?
- What have I learned that I can use in working with my colleagues and administrators on my campus to affect change in our advising program?
- What have I learned that triggers my own thoughts for research and publication within the field? (p. xii)

The authors and editors challenge readers to use the theories, approaches, and strategies in this book to influence advising practice and help students better meet their academic goals and career aspirations.

JAYNE K. DRAKE
PEGGY JORDAN
MARSHA A. MILLER

References

Crookston, B. B. (2009). A developmental view of academic advising as teaching. *NACADA Journal, 29*(1), 78–82. (Reprinted from *Journal of College Student Personnel, 13*, 1972, pp. 12–17; *NACADA Journal, 14*[2], 1994, pp. 5–9)

Hagen, P. L., & Jordan, P. (2008). Theoretical foundations of academic advising. In V. N. Gordon, W. R. Habley, & T. J. Grites (Eds.), *Academic advising: A comprehensive handbook* (2nd ed.) (pp. 17–35). San Francisco, CA: Jossey-Bass.

Nutt, C. L. (2008). Foreword. In V. N. Gordon, W. R. Habley, & T. J. Grites (Eds.), *Academic advising: A comprehensive handbook* (2nd ed.) (pp. xi–xii). San Francisco, CA: Jossey-Bass.

Schulenberg, J. K., & Lindhorst, M. J. (2008). Advising is advising: Toward defining the practice and scholarship of academic advising. *NACADA Journal, 28*(1), 43–53.

Shaffer, L. S., Zalewski, J. M., & Leveille, J. (2010). The professionalization of academic advising: Where are we in 2010? *NACADA Journal, 30*(1), 66–77.

Winston, R. B., Jr., Miller, T. K., Ender, S. C., & Grites, T. J. (Eds.). (1984). *Developmental academic advising*. San Francisco, CA: Jossey-Bass.

ACKNOWLEDGMENTS

Good academic advising does not just happen. To be effective, be they new or veterans to the advising chair, advisors need training and development in three key components of advising—informational, conceptual, and relational (Habley, 1995, p. 76). The relational component often is the hardest area to address in effective initial advisor training and ongoing skill development for those experienced in the field.

It should surprise few familiar with the field of academic advising that the relational component was one of the key competencies delineated by a 2003 NACADA Certification Task Force chaired by Virginia Gordon. In identifying skills academic advisors must possess, that Task Force noted that academic advisors must communicate and engage students through the use of skills in interpersonal relations, communication, helping, and problem solving (para. 4). The question remained: "What curriculum can we use to teach advisors the theory and practice of various methods, or approaches, for effectively advising students?"

As recently as 2010, Shaffer, Zalewski, and Leveille noted that advising must create an acknowledged curriculum built upon accepted theories with a broad and deep research base to train advisors (p. 75). Shaffer et al. laid a challenge for advisors to create a rich and vibrant literature base to address the key components of academic advising. With this book we, as editors, take up that challenge as it applies to the relational component.

We first thank the NACADA Publications Advisory Board and NACADA Executive Director Charlie Nutt for their unqualified support of our vision for this book. We thank the scholar practitioners (listed in the Table of Contents) who accepted our challenge to document for this book the advising approaches they use successfully in working with advisees. These authors devoted considerable time and effort to this work, including submitting multiple drafts that evolved into the final manuscript. We greatly appreciate their insights and efforts.

The Content Review Panel for this book made an important contribution early in the process by asking the questions that helped authors bring clarity to the more complex aspects of advising within, and between, different approaches. We thank the members of this group for their guidance and input.

CONTENT REVIEW PANEL

○ LaDonna Bridges, Framingham State University

○ Adam Duberstein, Ohio Dominican and Bowling Green State University

○ Susan Fread, Lehigh Carbon Community College

○ David Freitag, Pima Community College

○ Julie Givans Voller, Arizona State University

- Gayle Juneau, University of Nevada, Las Vegas
- Kerry Kincanon, Oregon State University
- Nancy Markee, University of Nevada, Reno
- Holly Martin, Notre Dame University
- Pat Mason-Brown, University of Iowa
- Lisa Peck, Western Connecticut State University
- Jeanette Wong, Azusa Pacific University

We greatly appreciate and thank Nancy Vesta, NACADA copy editor extraordinaire, for her guidance and editing expertise. Nancy is able to read and review authors' work with new eyes; her experience polishes and enhances the work of each author and contributor. For that we are ever grateful. We thank Erin Null and her associates at Jossey-Bass for their faith that we could deliver what we promised: a ground-breaking addition to the literature within our field.

And finally, thanks to you, the reader, for your interest in helping students succeed. Whether you are new to advising or a veteran of the advising chair, we firmly believe that the ideas and insights shared within these pages will improve your advising practice and thus help your students make the most of their college experiences.

JAYNE K. DRAKE
PEGGY JORDAN
MARSHA A. MILLER
EDITORS

References

Gordon, V. N. (2003). National Academic Advising Association certification task force advisor competencies. Retrieved from http://www.nacada.ksu.edu/Resources/Clearinghouse/View-Articles/Academic-advisor-competencies.aspx

Habley, W. R. (1995). Advisor training in the context of a teaching enhancement center. In R. E. Glennen & F. N. Vowell (Eds.), *Academic advising as a comprehensive campus process* (Monograph No. 2) (pp. 75–79). Manhattan, KS: National Academic Advising Association.

Light, R. J. (2001). *Making the most of college: Students speak their minds*. Cambridge, MA: Harvard University Press.

Shaffer, L. S., Zalewski, J. M., & Leveille, J. (2010). The professionalization of academic advising: Where are we in 2010? *NACADA Journal, 30*(1), 66–77.

THE EDITORS

Jayne K. Drake is the Vice Dean for Academic Affairs, Director of the Master of Liberal Arts Program, and associate professor of English in the College of Liberal Arts at Temple University in Philadelphia, Pennsylvania. As Vice Dean, she is responsible for all academic matters, student services, programs, academic advising, and curricular initiatives for the College's undergraduate and graduate students. Dr. Drake is a "lifer" at Temple and has served in a number of administrative posts over the years, including Director of Academic Advising, Associate Dean of the Graduate School, Associate Dean for Student Services, and the Director of the Teaching and Learning Center, to name a few.

Dr. Drake is a past President of NACADA and publishes broadly in the field of advising. In 2012, she was awarded the Association's highest recognition, the Virginia N. Gordon Award for Excellence in the Field of Advising. As a member of the NACADA Academic Advising Consultants and Speakers Service, Dr. Drake travels nationally and internationally to provide keynote addresses and conduct workshops on a number of advising-related topics, and she serves as a consultant and reviewer to a number of universities regarding the development and reorganization of advising services.

She earned her PhD in English at Penn State. Her teaching and publication interests include 17th- though 19th-century American literature, the history of printing and publishing in America, and literary research methods. She has published numerous articles and reviews in these fields and written books on American literary periodicals and John Greenleaf Whittier.

Peggy Jordan is a professor of psychology at Oklahoma City Community College (OCCC), where she has worked for 14 years. She is a faculty advisor for approximately 250 students, serves on OCCC's training team for Cooperative Learning, and is involved in a trial study of the use of motivational interviewing in the classroom. Dr. Jordan has served as chair of NACADA's Publications Advisory Board and Two-Year Colleges Commission. She has contributed to numerous NACADA publications and presented at numerous state, regional, and national conferences. Before working in higher education, she worked as a psychotherapist in agencies and in a private practice. Dr. Jordan received a PhD in Counseling Psychology from Oklahoma State University and a MEd and BA from the University of Central Oklahoma.

Marsha A. Miller, Kansas State University, has been a NACADA member since 1988 and serves as NACADA's Assistant Director for Resources and Services. Ms. Miller was a peer advisor at the University of Missouri–Columbia and has earned graduate degrees from the University of Iowa and Emporia State University. She advised and taught at Cloud County Community College for 14 years while working in various capacities at the college. She also chaired the committee charged with restructuring Cloud's advising and academic support services, and she was appointed as the first Director of Cloud's Advising Center, which received both the NACADA Outstanding Advising Program Award and the Noel-Levitz citation for Excellence in Student Retention while under her direction.

Ms. Miller has written extensively on academic advising issues and is the managing editor for all NACADA print-based publications. She was coeditor of NACADA's monograph *Comprehensive Advisor Training and Development: Practices that Deliver* and directs the web-based NACADA Clearinghouse of Academic Advising Resources. Ms. Miller is a frequent faculty member at the NACADA Academic Advising Summer Institute. She is the NACADA representative to the Council for the Advancement of Standards Board and answers NACADA member questions regarding advising-related issues.

Editor photos courtesy of:

○ Dr. Drake: Ryan Brandenberg, Temple University

○ Dr. Jordan: Tony Jordan

○ Ms. Miller: Gail Anne Aurand, Moments in Time Photography

THE AUTHORS

Jennifer L. Bloom, EdD, is a clinical professor and Director of the Higher Education and Student Affairs Master's Degree Program in the Department of Educational Leadership and Policy Studies at the University of South Carolina. She also is an adjunct associate professor for the Department of Internal Medicine at the University of Illinois College of Medicine at Urbana-Champaign. She previously served as the Associate Dean for Student Affairs and the Medical Scholars Program at the University of Illinois College of Medicine at Urbana-Champaign (2003–07). She was elected to the position of President of NACADA for 2007–08. Her research interests include appreciative advising, academic advising, career paths in higher education administration, leadership, and change.

Susan M. Campbell serves as University of Southern Maine's Chief Student Success Officer. She earned her BS in Speech and Theatre from Ball State University, her MS in Adult Education from the University of Southern Maine, and her EdD in Higher Education Administration from the University of Massachusetts at Amherst. Dr. Campbell also holds an adjunct appointment as associate professor in the School of Education, where she coordinates the student affairs concentration in one of the master's programs.

Dr. Campbell served as President of NACADA, has held other leadership positions within the association, and received NACADA's Virginia N. Gordon Award in 2005. Her publications include contributions to the NACADA *Guide to Assessment in Academic Advising* (2005), NACADA Monograph No. 13, *Peer Advising: Intentional Connections to Support Student Learning* (Korning & Campbell, eds.), both editions of *The Distance Learner's Guide* (1999 and 2004) published by Prentice-Hall, and the second edition of *Academic Advising: A Comprehensive Handbook* (Gordon, Habley, & Grites, eds.) published by Jossey-Bass.

Patrick Cate is the Director for the University Studies Department at Plymouth State University in Plymouth, New Hampshire. He holds a BA in Biology from Keene State College and an MEd in Educational Counseling from Plymouth State University. He is the creator of the targeted advising model and has consulted with a number of institutions on its use. He has presented a number of times at state, regional, and national conferences, winning a Best of Region 1 Award in 2009 from NACADA. Mr. Cate also published an article in the NACADA Clearinghouse and the NACADA blog. Currently, he serves as the New Hampshire state liaison for NACADA.

Sarah Champlin-Scharff earned her undergraduate degree in Philosophy and Women's Studies from the University of New Hampshire, her MA in Philosophy from Boston College, and her MEd from the Harvard Graduate School of Education. She has been at Harvard University since 1999 and is currently Director of Administration for the History of Science Department. Prior to that, she was Undergraduate

Program Administrator for the Committee on Degrees in Social Studies. She has been a member of Harvard's Board of Freshman Advisors since 2004 and an active member of NACADA since 2005. She is currently Chair of its Theory and Philosophy Commission (2012–14), a member of its Research Committee, and a regular presenter at the national conference. Her chapter, "A Field Guide to Epistemology in Academic Advising Research," appears in the 2010 NACADA Monograph No. 20, *Scholarly Inquiry in Academic Advising* (Hagen, Kuhn, & Padak, eds.), and her article, "Advising With Understanding: Considering Hermeneutic Theory in Academic Advising," was published in the Spring 2010 issue of the *NACADA Journal*.

Thomas J. Grites is Assistant Provost at The Richard Stockton College of New Jersey, where he has served in a number of capacities in his 35 years there. He was one of the founding members of NACADA and served as its President for two terms. He serves as a senior editor of the *NACADA Journal* and regularly provides other services to NACADA. Dr. Grites has written more than 60 journal articles, book chapters, and professional reports; he has delivered more than 120 conference presentations; and he has conducted academic advising workshops and program reviews on more than 100 campuses. Dr. Grites earned his BS and MS degrees from Illinois State University and his PhD from the University of Maryland. Both institutions have awarded him distinguished alumni awards, and he was inducted into the College of Education Hall of Fame at Illinois State.

Peter L. Hagen serves as Director of the Center for Academic Advising at The Richard Stockton College of New Jersey. He was the founding Chair of the NACADA's Theory and Philosophy of Academic Advising Commission, served as guest editor of the Fall 2005 issue of the *NACADA Journal*, and was a member of the task force that wrote "The Concept of Academic Advising," now widely adopted by the NACADA membership. For NACADA, he currently serves on the Publications Review Board and the *NACADA Journal's* Editorial Board. He won the 2007 Virginia Gordon Award for Service to the Field of Advising. He served as lead editor for NACADA Monograph No. 20, *Scholarly Inquiry in Academic Advising*, published by NACADA in March 2010 (Hagen, Kuhn, & Padak, eds.).

Ye He, PhD, is assistant professor in the Department of Curriculum and Instruction at the University of North Carolina at Greensboro. She holds a PhD in Curriculum and Instruction with a concentration in teacher education. As coordinator for the English-as-a-Second-Language (ESL) Teacher Education Program, Dr. He serves as faculty advisor for undergraduate and graduate students. Her research areas include ESL teacher education, diversity and equity in education, program evaluation in higher education settings, and the use of mixed methods in educational research and evaluation.

Bryant L. Hutson, PhD, is Associate Director for Student Academic Services at the University of North Carolina at Greensboro and coordinates programming and assessment for a number of student support and retention efforts. He holds a PhD in Higher Education Administration with a concentration in educational research, measurement, and evaluation. Previously, he was research associate at the Center for

Educational Research and Evaluation. His research areas include college student retention and persistence, first-generation and at-risk college student academic support, and program evaluation in higher education settings.

Judy Hughey, a national certified counselor, is an associate professor at Kansas State University in the Department of Special Education, Counseling, and Student Affairs. She earned a doctorate from the University of Missouri–Columbia. Dr. Hughey's teaching responsibilities include teaching graduate courses in counselor education and supervision and undergraduate educational psychology. She is the coordinator of the Master's Program for School Counseling and is the Chair of the College of Education Faculty Assembly and Executive Committee, a member of the University Faculty Senate and serves on the Senate Leadership Council. Her research interests include counseling and advisor skill development, learning environments, and career development. Dr. Hughey has served as assistant managing editor for the *Journal of Vocational Special Needs* and assistant to the editor for *Professional School Counseling.* Dr. Hughey has copublished in *The Handbook of Career Advising* and in *Educational Considerations, Journal of Career Development, Community College Journal, School Counselor, ASCA Counselor,* and *Academic Advising Today* as well as in ERIC publications.

Ezekiel Kimball is the Director of Institutional Research at Curry College. Prior to this appointment, he was a graduate fellow and research assistant in the Center for the Study of Higher Education at The Pennsylvania State University. His prior experience includes work related to college access and student affairs in a range of nonprofit and university settings. He earned a PhD in Higher Education with a graduate minor in Social Theory from The Pennsylvania State University, an MS in Adult Education from the University of Southern Maine, and BA in History also from the University of Southern Maine. His dissertation, *Developing a Model of Theory-to-Practice-to-Theory in Student Affairs: An Extended Case Analysis of Theories of Student Learning and Development,* examined the theory use of student affairs practitioners. His published or forthcoming works include journal articles and book chapters on social theory, college admissions, and student affairs practice.

Marc Lowenstein recently retired as Associate Provost for Personnel, Programs, and Policy at The Richard Stockton College of New Jersey, where he had served since 1976 in various roles, including seven years as Dean of Professional Studies. Past responsibilities included managing Stockton's student self-designed degree program and supervising the academic component of orientation. His academic background is in philosophy, in which he holds a bachelor's degree from Colgate University and a PhD from the University of Rochester. Dr. Lowenstein has published articles on ethics in academic advising and on the theory and philosophy of advising, and has made numerous presentations on these topics at national and regional conferences.

Holly E. Martin is the Assistant Dean for Mentoring and Student Development in the First Year of Studies College at the University of Notre Dame and a recipient of the University's Dockweiler Award for Excellence in Undergraduate Advising. She is a Co-director of the cultural competence and the e-portfolio initiatives for the First

Year of Studies, and she also co-directs the First Year of Studies conferences on advising highly talented undergraduates. Dr. Martin is the past Chair of NACADA's Advising First Year Students Interest Group and is a current member of the Steering Committee for the Advising Student-Athletes Commission. In addition to advising and administrative work at Notre Dame, she teaches courses in Shakespeare, drama, interdisciplinary approaches to the arts, student advising e-portfolios, and cultural competence.

Jeffrey McClellan is an assistant professor of Management at Frostburg State University and the former Director of Advisor Training and Development at Utah Valley State College in Orem, Utah. He has worked as an advisor, counselor, faculty member, and administrator at four different institutions over the past 11 years. He holds a PhD in Leadership Studies from Gonzaga University and is the former Chair of the Commission on the Theory and Philosophy of Advising. His research interests include servant leadership development, organizational and individual growth, development and change, academic and career advising administration and leadership, and conflict management. Dr. McClellan lives with his wife and six children in Cumberland, Maryland.

Joseph Murray has served as the Director of Academic Advising and Retention Services at Miami University's Hamilton Campus since 1992. He earned both a Bachelor of Science in Engineering and a Master of Science in Human Resource Management degrees from Purdue University. He has helped to develop and refine the *Appreciative Advising Inventory* and has been part of a national task force aimed at advancing the concept of appreciative advising. Most recently, he served on the faculty for the 2010 National Conference on Academic Advising Strategies to Increase Persistence and for the 2011 and 2012 Appreciative Advising Institutes. Mr. Murray works tirelessly to help students who are traditionally underrepresented in higher education. He has been a driving force behind Ohio Reach, a state and national effort to increase access and retention to higher education for Ohio's lower income/ disadvantaged youth and foster care alumni. He has served as the Co-chair of the First-Generation College Student Interest Group for NACADA from 2007 until 2012.

Terry Musser has worked at The Pennsylvania State University for 27 years where she also acquired two degrees in Agricultural Education and her doctorate in Instructional Systems. She has advised undecided students, coordinated the University Academic Orientation Program, and conducted research and assessment activities. Dr. Musser currently coordinates advising activities for the College of Agricultural Sciences. She has presented and published on topics related to advising undecided students, theory and philosophy of advising, research in advising, and using technology in advising. She has been active in NACADA leadership, including serving as the representative for Region 2, regional division representative to the Council, the Board of Directors, the Diversity Committee, the Reorganization Task Force, Chair of the Webinar Advisory Board, and as a mentor in the Emerging Leaders Program.

Robert Pettay, PhD, is the advising coordinator and an instructor in the Department of Kinesiology at Kansas State University. He earned his doctorate in Counselor

Education from Kansas State University. Dr. Pettay's research interests relate to the use of motivational interviewing in advising and physical activity and the relationship of health and academic behaviors and life satisfaction.

Maura M. Reynolds is associate professor of Latin and since 1988 has been the Director of Academic Advising at Hope College, Holland, Michigan. Her work with NACADA has included serving on a variety of committees, being appointed to Council, and chairing the Small Colleges and Universities Commission as well as the Publications Advisory Board. She has served on the faculty of the NACADA Administrator's Institute and the Summer Institute and has been energized by working with and learning from the staff and participants. Ms. Reynolds has been a frequent presenter at NACADA conferences and webinars, has authored book reviews, articles, and monograph and book chapters, and has served as a consultant. At Hope College, she directs a faculty-only advising program, teaches in and has supervised Hope's First Year Seminar Program, and spends lots of time working with students, families, and the faculty.

Laurie A. Schreiner is professor and Chair of the Doctoral Programs in Higher Education at Azusa Pacific University, having spent 25 years in higher education as a psychology professor and associate academic dean prior to coming to Azusa Pacific. Coauthor of *The Student Satisfaction Inventory* (1994), Dr. Schreiner is also coauthor of *Helping Sophomores Succeed* (2010) and *StrengthsQuest: Discover and Develop Your Strengths in College and Beyond* (2006), as well as numerous journal articles and book chapters on engaged learning, student satisfaction, sophomore success, faculty development, and advising. She has consulted with more than 100 colleges and universities on strengths-based education, retention, academic advising, student satisfaction, and effective teaching strategies. Her most recent publications include a three-part series on college student thriving for *About Campus* and an article on the impact of faculty and staff on high-risk students for the *Journal of College Student Development*.

Janet K. Schulenberg earned her BS in Biology and Anthropology from SUNY Geneseo and her MA and PhD in Anthropology from The Pennsylvania State University. She is a Senior Undergraduate Studies adviser in the Division of Undergraduate Studies, and Coordinator of the First-Year Testing, Consulting, and Advising Program at Penn State. She was assistant professor of anthropology and coordinator of Archaeological Studies at SUNY Potsdam before returning to Penn State in 2005. Dr. Schulenberg is active in NACADA, serving as chair of the NACADA Research Committee and as an active member of the NACADA Theory and Philosophy of Advising Commission.

Nora A. Scobie, Assistant Director for Advisor Development at the University of Louisville (UofL), received her PhD in Education Counseling and Personnel Services from UofL; her research interests include second-year students, student persistence, and academic advising. She is adjunct faculty in the College of Education and Human Development at UofL. She has worked in higher education for more than 20 years, including positions in student affairs, student services, facilities management, and academic advising. She is an active NACADA member and has served as Chair of the Advisor Training and Development Commission and incoming Chair of the Professional Development Committee. Dr. Scobie loves to spend time with her family and three Labrador retrievers: Gus, Grr-Tee, and Grizz-lee Bear.

Janet M. Spence, MEd, is the Executive Director for Undergraduate Advising Practice at the University of Louisville. She holds 35 years of higher education experience as an academic advisor and an advising administrator. In her current role, she leads eight colleges and schools at the university in developing consistent and best practice in academic advising. Before joining Undergraduate Affairs, she held the role of Assistant Dean in the College of Education and Human Development at the University of Louisville. Ms. Spence currently serves on the NACADA Council and is the representative for the Commission and Interest Group Division. She was a member of the faculty for NACADA's Advising Administration Institute (AI) in 2010 and serves on the AI Planning Committee. Ms. Spence has presented at several national and regional conferences and is an author of a chapter in NACADA Monograph No. 22, *Academic Advising Administration* (Joslin & Markee, eds.).

Jennifer Varney has been working in higher education for the past 14 years: first as a classroom instructor at Hesser College and later as an academic advisor, online instructor, and currently the Assistant Dean in the School of Business at Southern New Hampshire University (SNHU). She has written many articles on best practices in advising at-risk students. Ms. Varney has also delivered webinars for NACADA and Academic Impressions. At SNHU, she teaches in the Organizational Leadership (OL) Department and was the subject matter expert for the most recent revision of OL 500. Ms. Varney is also working on a doctorate degree in Organizational Leadership. When not in the office, she can typically be found hiking in the White Mountains of New Hampshire.

Frank Yoder has been at the Academic Advising Center at The University of Iowa since 1992. He is currently an Associate Director at the Advising Center, where he is responsible for new advisor training. In the past several years, he has been involved with NACADA by leading workshops for new advisors, copresenting a webinar on advising theory, writing monograph chapters, and presenting at sessions on training and technology and other related topics. He received his PhD in History from the University of Chicago and also serves as an adjunct professor in the History Department at The University of Iowa.

ACADEMIC ADVISING APPROACHES

FOUNDATIONS OF ACADEMIC ADVISING PRACTICE

Drawn from student development and learning theories, the chapters within part one explain and illustrate time-honored approaches to advisors' work with students.

ADVISING STRATEGIES TO SUPPORT STUDENT LEARNING SUCCESS

LINKING THEORY AND PHILOSOPHY WITH INTENTIONAL PRACTICE

Ezekiel Kimball and Susan M. Campbell

"Would you tell me, please, which way I ought to go from here?"
"That depends a good deal on where you want to get to,"
said the Cat.
"I don't much care where—" said Alice.
"Then it doesn't matter which way you go," said the Cat.
"—so long as I get SOMEWHERE," Alice added as an explanation.
"Oh, you're sure to do that," said the Cat, "if you only walk
long enough."

—Lewis Carroll, *Alice's Adventures in Wonderland*, 1865

This chapter, like this book, begins from the simple premise that students' choices and behaviors in college matter to their success (Astin, 1993; Kuh, Kinzie, Schuh, & Whitt, 2005; Light, 2001; Pascarella & Terenzini, 2005) and that through careful attention to their own practices, advisors can help to create the conditions necessary for students to achieve success. To support student success, however, academic advisors must work in a highly intentional manner. They cannot just promise that students will get "somewhere" and send them on a path alone, as did the Cheshire Cat in *Alice's Adventures in Wonderland*, but instead they must be prepared to offer direction and assistance while undertaking the journey along with students. That is, advisors must act purposefully to achieve the important goals set for their practice and students. As stated in the NACADA Concept of Academic Advising (National Academic Advising Association [NACADA], 2006, para. 6): "Through academic advising, students learn to become members of their higher education community, to think critically about their roles and responsibilities as students, and to prepare to be educated citizens of a democratic society and a global community." Such intentionality is particularly important because higher education institutions are being asked to focus on the development of the whole person (Joint Statement, 2004, 2006) and to be accountable for producing clear learning outcomes (Shavelson, 2010).

However, those charged with achieving the goals set for the profession face challenges. Advising is paradoxically a relatively new profession with a long history. Though NACADA did not form until the late 1970s (Beatty, 1991), academic advising has always been a part of higher education—first as the work of college faculty members, later of student affairs personnel, and finally of professional advisors. Likewise, though a scholarly advising journal did not appear until 1981, a long history of relevant scholarly work undergirds the profession—including clear connections to the important American intellectual traditions of pragmatism and symbolic interactionism. As an interdisciplinary field of study, academic advising also draws from many different disciplines as scholars attempt to capture the experiential nature of student learning and development (Hagen, 2005; Hagen & Jordan, 2008; Kuhn, 2008). Consequently, the problem for advisors may not be an absence of useful information but rather a surfeit.

To assist in thinking about this wealth of information, we begin this chapter with a consideration of academic advising as an intentional process shaped by several different ways of thinking about students. We next review key foundational literature linking academic advising to student persistence and success. This chapter and, indeed, this volume acknowledge that students are individuals and each exhibits a specific, personal, learning style. Likewise, each advisor uniquely interprets academic advising as an educational process. As a result, approaches to academic advising mirror personal values and beliefs as well as the diversity of ways students learn, grow, and develop. We celebrate that diversity.

The Philosophical and Sociological Basis of Advising

Philosophically, academic advising is rooted in pragmatism where, according to William James (1907/1969), "Truth . . . becomes a class-name for all sorts of definite working-values in experience" (1969, p. 54). Through one's experiences personal definitions of reality and truth emerge. Through academic advising, experiences are translated and the consequences of action, anticipated or actual, are examined, embraced, or discarded in relationship to the individual's current beliefs and future dreams. A dictionary definition of *pragmatism* (Merriam-Webster's, 2012) belies its complexity:

> An American movement in philosophy founded by C. S. Peirce and William James and marked by the doctrines that the meaning of conceptions is to be sought in their practical bearings, that the function of thought is to guide action, and that truth is pre-eminently to be tested by the practical consequences of belief.

In a fundamental aspect, pragmatism is based on actions grounded in beliefs; in turn, these actions lead to consequences, and these consequences potentially reform beliefs, including those resistant to change. The pragmatist's world constantly changes as a result of action. Some debate, which is beyond the scope of this chapter, centers on whether or not pragmatism is a philosophy or a method of analysis. However, Reynolds (1993, p. 16) provided a summary of several key characteristics of American pragmatism:

○ Humans are not passive recipients of stimuli; they are creative, active agents.

○ [Because] people inhabit a world that they . . . have helped shape, even as this self-made world limits and places constraints on the activities of its creators, the world is [repeatedly] subject to planned change.

○ Subjective experience flows from behavior and does not exist prior to it. From behavior, consciousness and meaning emerge, and an object's meaning resides in the behavior directed toward it and not in the object itself (Manis & Meltzer, 1978: 3).

○ The same basic assumptions that shore up and guide empirical science should also guide philosophical analysis.

○ The solution of practical problems and the analysis of social issues should be the prime focus of philosophical concern (Lauer & Handel, 1977: 10).

○ It is necessary and desirable to reconcile science with idealism.

○ Action is the means for checking the accuracy of a hypothesis and hence the focus of reality (Weinberg, 1962).

○ [The interest theory—that which is good satisfies an impulse or an interest—is the best theory of value.]

The first three characteristics have particular relevance to academic advising and the myriad approaches to this educational process. In sum, they suggest that human actions are shaped by one's initial interpretations of situations. In turn, the consequences of actions in those situations reinforce or change the interpretation of the initial situation.

Sociologically, academic advising draws from interactionist theory; that is, individual views are modified or reinforced through interactions with others. Furthermore, through actions and interactions, individuals influence, and are influenced by, happenings in the culture. It is a relationship-based enterprise not dominated by a single truth or reality; multiple realities coexist.

Symbolic interactionism offers a perspective with particular relevance to academic advising. Rooted in pragmatism, this perspective maintains that reality emerges from the meaning that individuals share regarding the physical, ideological, and social aspects of their environment. The crux of symbolic interactionism, with pragmatism as a guiding philosophy, lies in understanding how people interpret and experience their worlds through analyzing the ways they act.

Blumer (1986), the founder of symbolic interactionism, suggested that the essence of this sociological perspective rests in the last analysis on three simple premises. The first premise is that human beings act toward things on the basis of the meanings that the things have for them. . . . The second premise is that the meaning of such things is derived from, or arises out of, the social interaction that one has with one's fellows. The third premise is that these meanings are handled in, and modified through, an interpretive process used by the person in dealing with the things he encounters. (p. 2)

Pragmatism and symbolic interactionism portray one's reality as being socially constructed based on the meaning that one gives to situations and objects. Meaning is subjective and based on one's interpretation of events. Human beings are not passive in this regard; indeed, they are active agents both influencing and being influenced by their interactions with others as well as other experiences.

Academic Advising and Meaning Making

Academic advising facilitates the development of meaning through engagement in experiences and interaction with others. Academic advising—done well—assists students in interpreting their values, beliefs, and experiences so, unlike Alice, they get somewhere they want to go. Because all students interpret their experiences in ways particular to them, no single approach or advising strategy will sufficiently assist everyone optimally. Advisors should understand and incorporate into advising strategy the following important lesson from philosophy and sociology: Actions or behaviors reflect meaning. To influence behavior and guide action, then, advisors must understand the meaning behind actions and acknowledge them as the drivers of behavior. Furthermore, if meaning is derived from interaction with others, then to influence meaning, advisors must encourage students to be involved in experiences and contexts that support, promote, and challenge current values and beliefs. In essence, one size does not fit all with regard to academic advising. The field needs, and indeed, requires, multiple strategies so advisors effectively respond to multiple and unique audiences. The field needs flexible, eclectic practitioners able to adapt their advising strategies in accordance with the needs of their students. Being married to a single approach to academic advising, advisors potentially disregard the diverse ways in which students learn and presume a single, linear developmental path that is clearly more idealistic than realistic.

Advising as an Intentional Process

Because of the breadth of scholarship and practice, four related thoughts about student experience and advising practice shape the field (each of which we describe in more detail): a) one's own values, beliefs, and assumptions; b) scholarly theories; c) advising approaches; and d) advising strategies. Though other contributors to this book address items related to scholarly theories and advising approaches, we discuss values, beliefs, and assumptions because they shape responses to the other ways advisors think about students and can powerfully influence advising (Bensimon, 2007;

Bloland, Stamatakos, & Rogers, 1994; Parker, 1977). Thinking carefully and reflecting critically on the content and role of each of these elements, advisors develop the intentional advising practices necessary to support student success.

Pragmatism and symbolic interactionism both stress the importance of experience in shaping one's values, beliefs, and assumptions (or mental framework) as well as the importance of that framework in shaping behavior. For academic advising, these theories suggest that students should engage in experiences that allow them to test their values, beliefs, and assumptions about their present and future selves. At the same time, they also indicate that the mental frameworks employed by academic advisors matter a great deal and that advisors need to be aware of the ways these paradigms affect student success. For example, Bensimon (2007) suggested that rendering the implicit theories of student behavior held by practitioners explicit and then interrogating them through evidence helps create, in part, educational equity, and that absent this investigation they may internalize potentially problematic thinking about student experience. Likewise, Parker (1977) distinguished between formal and informal theories created by student affairs practitioners. Finally, research reveals that classroom teacher performance is largely consistent with the personal practical theories that combine personal values, beliefs, and assumptions with formal academic training (Cornett, Yeotis, & Terwilliger, 1990; Levin & He, 2008). In short, values, beliefs, and assumptions not only shape behavior directly, but they also likely influence the way that educators employ scholarly theories, advising approaches, and advising strategies.

Those in the social sciences typically regard theory as comprised of a coherent group of generalizeable conditions that have been tested and commonly held by a given community to be true and/or accurate (Jaccard & Jacoby, 2010). Once produced, theory is generally expected to influence behavior in an explanatory and often predictive manner (Godfrey-Smith, 2003); that is, theory contributes to ideas about the present as well as generates expectations about the future. The advising profession, as an interdisciplinary field, does not profess a theoretical base; instead, advising scholars borrow key theoretical insights from other disciplines to form the current knowledge base. Concerned with how students learn and develop over time, contributors to advising literature rely heavily on philosophy, anthropology, sociology, and psychology—among other disciplines—to explain the influences on the profession. In practice, effective academic advising also actively incorporates and interprets the research and scholarship on student persistence and success. At the theoretical level, some of the most important scholarship to advising comes from work on student development (e.g., Evans, Forney, & Guido-DiBrito, 1998; Evans, Forney, Guido-DiBrito, Patton, & Renn, 2010) and student experience within the campus environment (e.g., Harper & Quaye, 2009; Strange & Banning, 2001).

One's advising approach typically comes from one's philosophy of academic advising, which reflects an interpretation of relevant theories and empirical literature. Advisors further refine their approaches in conversations with colleagues and through interactions with individual students or groups of students. Thus, an advising approach emerges through a heuristic process guided by individual interpretations about how best to support the developmental needs of students. Advisors must offer intentional support, for without a clear approach or plan for purposeful action, academic advising merely consists of a series of tactics that may or may not lead to desired outcomes. Because advisors strive to facilitate student development toward a desired end, which is ultimately defined by the student in ways consistent with his or her beliefs and values, the advising approach provides the lens through which these goals might be clarified.

Ideally, every advising strategy employed is consistent with the overall approach adopted by an institution, college, or individual advisor. However, an advising strategy includes all of the specific steps or actions an advisor takes within a specific advising approach whether they are consistent with that approach or not. An advising strategy is a purposeful attempt to facilitate student learning and the development of a holistic and appropriate educational plan. An educational plan, while it may be more, is never less than a plan for purposeful action. While the structure of an educational plan may vary, all designs should serve to guide students toward learning experiences to enhance and enrich their knowledge and skills and allow them to test ideas and values that may—or may not—be incorporated into their future goals. Thought of in this way, good advising practice is a form of teaching.

The specific pedagogy or instructional method employed to facilitate student goal achievement may, and probably will, be different for each individual. For example, many advisors prefer to utilize a one-on-one approach, engaging students in conversation and reflection specifically about the content and methods of learning and how both relate to students' images of the future, particularly with respect to career interests. Others may effectively employ a group setting using a peer-led method that engages students in advisor-guided discussions with each other. Still others may use a mixed approach with one-on-one and pre-designed materials that guide the conversation toward a desired end. Academic advisors working with students taking courses online face more complexity and must address questions about effectively utilizing technologies available to connect with students and build an advising relationship. The extensive list of potential advising plans in many ways reflects the multiple approaches to academic advising proffered in succeeding chapters of this book. In the end, no singular strategy works in all situations, and no single educational plan or endgame best characterizes every student's situation. Only the strategy that works best for the individual advisor and the student with whom he or she is working can be optimally effective; only the educational plan that embraces and reflects the student's beliefs, values, and goals—as well as actions to achieve those goals—will best meet the objectives of advising.

No universal prescription applies to academic advising because each situation and the ways individuals interpret it differ. Academic advisors must first and foremost understand how a student interprets her or his situation: What has meaning? What has value? The answers inform the strategy the advisor employs. This focus on meaning leads to consideration of the philosophical and sociological underpinnings

Figure 1.1. Levels of advising knowledge

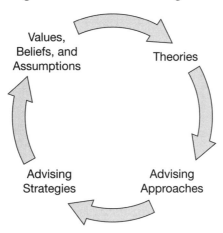

of academic advising as well as the key foundational literature that, to date, informs practice. Ultimately, the uniqueness of each advising relationship requires that the academic advisor make a series of well-informed judgments such that she or he considers more than personal values, beliefs, and assumptions and applies scholarly theories to advising strategies. The necessity of this practice reiterates the importance of Hutson, Bloom, and He's (2009) call for reflective advising. It also echoes Reason and Kimball's (2012) suggestion that advisors regard theory-to-practice translations in student development work as a form of assessment wherein they shift their attention from scholarly (formal) theory to reflective practice by carefully regarding institutional context and informal theories of student development.

When conceptualizing the relationship between the four levels of advising knowledge, as depicted in Figure 1.1, advisors initiate an assessment cycle that enhances their thinking about advising practice.

This model suggests that values, beliefs, and assumptions might lead to preference of certain theories or parts of theories above others. One's theoretical foundation dictates the sort of advising approach adopted, which shapes the strategies employed. Finally, based upon the relative success of these strategies and self-observations, a theory-to-practice model calls for a purposeful refinement of values, beliefs, and assumptions—starting the assessment cycle anew. By connecting personal experience and scholarly knowledge in this way, academic advisors can negotiate the problematic task of using scholarly theories, which are generally true but often difficult to apply in specific cases, to inform the selection of advising practices designed to be contextually appropriate to the relationship between a specific student and advisor.

The Role of Advising in Student Success

As advisors redirect their attention from the intellectual, theoretical, and practical foundations of the advising profession and toward its impact, the power of high-quality advising becomes all the more clear and with it the need to continue to expand advisor knowledge of best practices within the profession. In this section, to provide clarity regarding the kinds of experiences in which student learning thrives, we review some of the key literature that links academic advising to student persistence and success. The literature stresses the importance of relationship development in creating positive contexts to support student learning. Indeed, this literature informs practice and can help to provide a framework for intentionality.

The retention literature offers clear evidence of the importance of academic advising to a successful student experience. The pool of research about academic advising continues to grow; yet a few pieces of scholarship have been instrumental in helping to shape the direction of that research and the development of academic advising as a field and profession. In particular, the works of Bean and Eaton (2002), Kuh et al. (2005), and Tinto (1993) all point to the significant role that academic advising plays in effective retention programs and, more importantly, in the individual experiences of students.

Few would argue that Tinto (1993) provided extraordinary leadership in helping colleges and universities understand the importance of constructing educational experiences for students that support academic and social integration. His longitudinal model of student departure explains student characteristics, internal and external commitments, as well as the interaction effects of the institutional academic and social contexts on student leaving behavior. The model illustrates a college impact model of student development.

Tinto's (1993) research proved instrumental in capturing themes regarding college student voluntary leaving behavior as well as furthering educators' understanding of the college student experience. Of particular importance and relevance, Tinto suggested that retention is a by-product of a good educational experience. He also identified a set of effective principles among institutions with successful retention programs. In his words, institutions with effective, successful, retention programs demonstrate "an enduring commitment to student welfare, a broader commitment to the education, not mere retention, of all students, and an emphasis upon the importance of social and intellectual community in the education of students" (pp. 145–146).

To successfully achieve retention goals, everyone at colleges and universities must focus on intentionally defining and shaping a quality educational experience for all students. They must look holistically at the student experience and reflect the institution's commitment to the education of students. While the student educational experience may—and will—vary from institution to institution, Tinto suggested that some commonalities characterize myriad campus initiatives, and also some specific conditions influence student persistence and success.

Tinto (n.d., 1999) posited five institutional conditions that stand out as particularly supportive of student success and clearly articulated the role of academic advising in supporting student success:

○ students are more likely to persist and graduate if they are in settings in which expectations are high, clear, and consistent;

○ support is available;

○ feedback that supports early understanding of academic performance is utilized;

○ involvement with the community and, in particular, with faculty members, staff, and peers is available; and

○ learning is relevant and constitutes value added (Tinto, 1999, pp. 5–6).

With regard to academic advising, Tinto (n.d.) noted:

> Students do best in settings where expectations are clear and consistent. This is particularly evident in the domain of academic advising. Students need to be clear about what is expected of them and what is required for successful completion of both courses and programs of study. Students, especially the many who are undecided about their plans, need to understand the road map to completion and know how to use it to achieve personal goals. (p. 2)

Academic advising plays an important role in supporting student achievement, particularly in helping students reach their potential. In fact, according to Tinto (1993), effective retention programs reflect policy maker understanding that academic advising underpins student success.

Kuh et al. (2005) further affirm the role of academic advising in supporting students. These researchers suggested that "advising is viewed as a way to connect students to the campus and help them feel that someone is looking out for them" (p. 214). This connection reflects an institutional commitment to the student and his or her education, which Tinto also finds essential to effective retention programs.

Few in the field are unaware of Kuh's involvement with the National Survey of Student Engagement (NSSE) and the impact NSSE has exerted on understanding the college student experience, particularly in terms of engagement. At its basic level, *engagement* represents the intersection of institutional conditions and student behaviors over which the institution can maintain, at least, marginal control. As Tinto (1993) and others have argued, some aspects of a student's life remain out of the purview of institutional influence. External commitments of students, particularly those related to family, are not easily affected by institutional programs and services. Understanding these commitments can be important to academic advising; they are clearly important in understanding students.

To encourage engagement, effective institutions direct students toward appropriate extracurricular activities, directly addressing the challenge of getting students in venues that will optimize their learning. These high-impact efforts require student initiative, involve faculty–student interaction, and provide opportunities to apply knowledge obtained in other settings. Kuh (2008) identified the following activities as high impact:

- first-year seminars and experiences,
- common intellectual experience,
- learning communities,
- writing-intensive courses,
- collaborative assignments and projects,
- undergraduate research,
- diversity/global learning,
- service and community-based learning,
- internships, and
- capstone courses and projects (pp. 9–11).

Researchers on the psychology of leaving (Bean, 2005; Bean & Eaton, 2002) examined individual attributes that influence student persistence and retention. They found that a student's intention to leave an institution is the best predictor of actual departure, and intentions are the by-product of interactions between the student and the institution (i.e., faculty members, staff, administrators, and students). An additional layer of complexity in the psychology of leaving framework involves attitudes about attachment to the institution and being a student. Satisfaction, self-efficacy, and competence comprise important aspects of attitude. Understanding the relationship between topics of study and one's imagined future (i.e., students ask if a program will help them reach their goals) is only slightly less critical.

Bean (2005) clearly explained that good academic advising affects a student's desire to persist and graduate:

> Good advising should link a student's academic capabilities with his or her choice of courses and major, access to learning resources, and a belief that the academic pathway a student is traveling will lead to employment after college. Advising should be done well so students recognize their abilities and make informed choices. (p. 226)

By extension good advising should contribute to academic and social integration resulting from positive experiences that increase satisfaction with being a student at a given institution, confidence in one's ability, academic competence, and one's understanding about educational, career, and life goals.

How should scholarly knowledge affect academic advising practice? The works of Bean (2005), Bean and Eaton (2002), Kuh (2008), Kuh et al. (2005), and Tinto (1993) offer guidance regarding experiences that support student success and provide a framework for intentionality. Tinto instructed postsecondary personnel to focus on the education of students and the contexts, holistic in nature, in which they learn best. He stressed that students learn best when challenged with expectations that are high, clear, and consistent; they achieve more with readily available support as well as early and frequent feedback regarding their academic performance. In addition to pointing to the link between current studies and future plans, Tinto emphasized the importance of ensuring that students get involved in the institution and feel valued as community members. Academic advising helps students set expectations and connect their learning and their imagined futures.

Kuh et al. (2005) spoke directly to academic advising as a means of connecting institutions with students. Practitioners and administrators exert some level of control over the delivery of academic advising. They need to consider the ways that academic advising acts as a vehicle through which students make meaningful connections at the institutions and get involved in learning experiences that result in positive gains in learning. They need to ask about the manner in which academic advising can help students establish important relationships with faculty and staff members who can engage them in conversations about their studies and their career aspirations. They need to create and advocate for employing high-impact activities into educational plans.

Bean and Eaton (2002) turned their attention to the individual and linked beliefs, attitudes, and intentions with behavior. Their research also affirms the important role that everyone on a campus plays in supporting student persistence. As a synthesis of this work, Bean (2005) affirmed this notion: "Students evaluate their experiences and form attitudes toward the college that influence their intentions to stay enrolled and their decision to stay or leave. Anyone and everyone on campus can affect these attitudes . . ." (p. 220).

Summary

We began this chapter with a quote from *Alice's Adventures in Wonderland* in which the Cheshire Cat promises Alice that she will get "somewhere" provided she "walk long enough." In today's higher education institutions, however, getting students "somewhere" is not enough. Students, society, and the advising profession all demand that advisors do more. A key step in delivering upon a commitment to student success includes the creation of the conditions necessary to engage in intentional, purposeful advising practice. To do so, we suggest, requires not only an understanding of the history of the advising profession but also its future. With a wide array of knowledge about students coming from personal experiences, scholarly theories, advising approaches, and advising strategies, advisors have more tools at their disposal than ever before. To use them effectively, they need to use critical reflection to convert theory to practice and apply knowledge of relevant literature to garnering student success. A complex and challenging process to be sure, these efforts lead to a meaningful and intentionally charted place where the diverse needs of students are met and they receive optimal opportunities to succeed.

References

Astin, A. W. (1993). *What matters in college? Four critical years revisited*. San Francisco, CA: Jossey-Bass.

Bean, J. (2005). Nine themes of college student retention. In A. Seidman (Ed.), *College student retention: Formula for student success*. Westport, CT: Praeger.

Bean, J., & Eaton, S. B. (2002). A psychological model of college student retention. In J. M. Braxton (Ed.), *Reworking the student departure puzzle* (pp. 48–61). Nashville, TN: Vanderbilt University Press.

Beatty, J. D. (1991). The National Academic Advising Association: A brief narrative history. *NACADA Journal, 11*(1), 5–15.

Bensimon, E. M. (2007). The underestimated significance of practitioner knowledge in the scholarship on student success. *The Review of Higher Education, 30*(4), 441–469.

Bloland, P. A., Stamatakos, L. C., & Rogers, R. R. (1994). *Reform in student affairs: A critique of student development*. Greensboro: University of North Carolina Press.

Blumer, H. (1986). *Symbolic interactionism: Perspective and method*. Chicago, IL: University of Chicago Press.

Carroll, L. (1865). *Alice's adventures in wonderland*. Retrieved from http://www.gutenberg.org/ebooks/19033

Cornett, J. W., Yeotis, C., & Terwilliger, L. (1990). Teacher personal practical theories and their influence upon teacher curricular and instructional actions: A case study of a secondary science teacher. *Science Education, 74*(5), 517–529.

Evans, N. J., Forney, D. S., & Guido-DiBrito, F. M. (1998). *Student development in college: Theory, research, and practice*. San Francisco, CA: Jossey-Bass.

Evans, N. J., Forney, D. S., Guido, F. M., Patton, L. D., & Renn, K. A. (2010). *Student development in college: Theory, research, and practice* (2nd ed.). San Francisco, CA: Jossey-Bass.

Godfrey-Smith, P. (2003). *Theory and reality: An introduction to the philosophy of science*. Chicago, IL: University of Chicago Press.

Hagen, P. (2005). From the guest editor: Theory building in academic advising. *NACADA Journal, 25*(2), 3–8.

Hagen, P., & Jordan, P. (2008). Theoretical foundation of academic advising. In V. N. Gordon, W. R. Habley, & T. J. Grites (Eds.), *Academic advising: A comprehensive handbook* (2nd ed.) (pp. 17–35). San Francisco, CA: Jossey-Bass.

Harper, S. R., & Quaye, S. J. (Eds.). (2009). *Student engagement in higher education: Theoretical perspectives and practical approaches for diverse populations*. New York, NY: Routledge.

Hutson, B. L., Bloom, J. L., & He, Y. (2009). Reflection in advising. *Academic Advising Today, 32*(4), 12.

Jaccard, J., & Jacoby, J. (2010). *Theory construction and model-building skills: A practical guide for social scientists*. New York, NY: Guilford.

James, W. (1969). *Pragmatism and four essays from The Meaning of Truth*. Cleveland, OH: Meridian. (Originally published in 1907)

Joint Statement. (2004). *Learning reconsidered: A campus-wide focus on the student experience*. Washington, DC: American College Personnel Association & National Association of Student Personnel Administrators.

Joint Statement. (2006). *Learning reconsidered 2: Implementing a campus-wide focus on the student experience*. Washington, DC: American College Personnel Association, Association of College and University Housing Officers–International, Association of College Unions International, National Academic Advising Association, National Association for Campus Activities, National Association of Student Personnel Administrators, & National Intramural–Recreational Sports Association.

Kuh, G. D. (2008). *High-impact educational practices: What they are, who has access to them, and why they matter*. Washington, DC: Association of American Colleges and Universities.

Kuh, G. D., Kinzie, J., Schuh, J. H., & Whitt, E. J. (Eds.). (2005). *Student success in college: Creating conditions that matter*. San Francisco, CA: Jossey-Bass.

Kuhn, T. (2008). Historical foundations of academic advising. In V. N. Gordon, W. R. Habley, & T. J. Grites (Eds.), *Academic advising: A comprehensive handbook* (2nd ed.) (pp. 3–16). San Francisco, CA: Jossey-Bass.

Levin, B. B., & He, Y. (2008). Investigating the content and sources of preservice teachers' personal practical theories (PPTs). *Journal of Teacher Education, 59*(1), 55–68.

Light, R. J. (2001). *Making the most of college*. Cambridge, MA: Harvard University Press.

Merriam-Webster Dictionary. (2012). Retrieved from http://www.merriam-webster.com/dictionary/pragmatism

National Academic Advising Association. (2006). *NACADA concept of academic advising*. Retrieved from http://www.nacada.ksu.edu/Resources/Clearinghouse/View-Articles/Concept-of-Academic-Advising-a598.aspx

Parker, C. A. (1977). On modeling reality. *Journal of College Student Personnel, 18*(5), 419–425.

Pascarella, E. T., & Terenzini, P. T. (2005). *How college affects students: A third decade of research*, Vol. 2. San Francisco, CA: Jossey-Bass.

Reason, R., & Kimball, E. (2012). A new theory-to-practice model for student affairs: Integrating scholarship, context, and reflection. *Journal of Student Affairs Research & Practice, 49*(4), 359–376.

Reynolds, L. T. (1993). *Interactionism: Exposition and critique* (3rd ed.). New York, NY: General Hall.

Shavelson, R. J. (2010). *Measuring college learning responsibly: Accountability in a new era*. Stanford, CA: Stanford University Press.

Strange, C. C., & Banning, J. H. (2001). *Educating by design*. San Francisco, CA: Jossey-Bass.

Tinto, V. (n.d.). *Taking student retention seriously: Rethinking the first year of college*. Retrieved from http://faculty.soe.syr.edu/vtinto/Files/Taking%20Student%20Retention%20Seriously.pdf

Tinto, V. (1993). *Leaving college: Rethinking the causes and cures of student attrition*. San Francisco, CA: Jossey-Bass.

Tinto, V. (1999). Taking retention seriously: Rethinking the first year of college. *NACADA Journal, 19*(2), 5–9.

2

ADVISING AS TEACHING AND THE ADVISOR AS TEACHER IN THEORY AND IN PRACTICE

Jayne K. Drake

The lush green expanse of a lawn well tended offers a pleasing aesthetic. It is composed of individual leaves of grass, each in some way different from the other, yet, when taken together, they comprise a unified and satisfying composition. With a nod and apologies to Walt Whitman, one might also make the point that the many individual theories and philosophies of teaching and learning, with their own particular foundations and approaches, when taken together, form a broad and compelling sweep from which to view the advising-as-teaching metaphor. As the other chapters in this publication amply attest, all theoretical perspectives, no matter the field or discipline from which they are derived, offer divergent and compelling avenues from which to view advising in the context of student learning and advisor development. As Hagen and Jordan (2008) suggested in the second edition of the *Academic Advising Handbook*, multiple theories can coexist peacefully: "There is no grand unified theory of advising, just as there is no master theoretical perspective that informs practice and research in . . . other professions" (p. 19). One approach, they argued, just cannot tell the whole story: "There can and should not be one lens, but many, through which to scrutinize academic advising" (p. 18), each shedding light on the other, each lending its own perspective, each contributing to the complexity of academic advising. Leaves of grass.

By now the advising-as-teaching metaphor has become one of the most closely tended of the leaves of grass. From the time the phrase was coined by Crookston (1972/1994/2009), much has been made about the versatility and durability of viewing academic advising from teaching and learning and from student-as-learner and advisor-as-teacher perspectives. One need only scan the publications in the NACADA Clearinghouse to see the many chapters, articles, and reflection pieces written on the topic as well as NACADA webinars and pocket guides that provide a fresh perspective on student learning and advisor development. Of particular relevance, Ryan (1992) drew extensive comparisons between effective teachers and effective advisors. She is among the first advising professionals to make these comparisons and to encourage faculty members to regard advising as a fundamental element of their teaching, and conversely, to encourage advisors to regard teaching as a fundamental element of their advising. In the second edition of

Academic Advising: A Comprehensive Handbook, Appleby (2008) carefully charted those similarities along with seven additional parallels that round out the comparisons. For more information on the advising-as-teaching paradigm see also Creamer (2000), Drake, Hemwall, and Stockwell (2009), Drake and King (2010), Folsom (2007), McGillin (2000), Nutt and Campbell (2010), Reynolds (2010), and Williams (2007) among others. These publications and this book illustrate the progress made since advising was considered little more than the tedious chore of scheduling classes or signing off on course registration forms.

Many of the cited publications in this volume derive from three major areas of inquiry largely based in the social sciences: a) psychosocial identity formation (e.g., Erikson's [1959] eight stages of development, Chickering's [n.d.] seven vectors of student growth, Clifton and Anderson's [2002] strengths-based advising); b) sociocultural and developmental research and theories (e.g., Vygotsky's [1978] zone of proximal development, Crookston's [1972/1994/2009] developmental advising, and O'Banion's [1972/1994/2009] five vectors of development); and c) cognitive development theories (Piaget's [1952] four stages of cognitive development, Kohlberg's [1969] nine stages of moral development, and Perry's [1970] nine positions model of student intellectual and ethical development). These and similar theories serve as points of information and departure for other chapters in this book by providing important views for professional and faculty advisors, peer advisors, academic counselors, personal tutors, and all those who interact with various student populations.

In 2000, Creamer offered a definition of advising that appropriately characterizes it as an educational activity that "depends on valid explanations of complex student behaviors and institutional conditions to assist college students in making and executing educational and life plans" (p. 18). More specifically, when viewed as an educational activity with student learning at its core, an approach of advising as teaching encourages professional and faculty advisors to examine their roles from the perspective of classroom teachers. In a broad sweeping definition, Cuseo (2012) explained that the good advisor, like the good teacher, is one who

> helps students become more self-aware of their distinctive interests, talents, values, and priorities; who enables students to see the "connection" between their present academic experience and their future life plans; who helps students discover their potential, purpose, and passion; who broadens students' perspectives with respect to their life choices, and sharpens their cognitive skills for making these choices, such as effective problem-solving, critical thinking, and effective decision-making. (p. 15)

Regarding this point, Hemwall and Trachte (1999) asserted that

> advisors need to think about advising as if they were teachers. Curricular goals must be identified and effective pedagogies must be developed if advisors hope that advisees will learn the values and goals educators set as the main purpose of college education. (p. 9)

In his seminal 2005 article, Lowenstein echoed these observations with his statement: "If advising is teaching, and the result is learning, then the advisor must be a good teacher" (p. 72).

How might advisors, then, formulate a definition of a *good*—and therefore an effective—teacher and advisor that offers a fresh look at the advising-as-teaching models as posited by Creamer, Cuseo, Lowenstein, and the many other authors who have contributed ideas and research on student learning and developmental advising approaches? What is left to say?

Two interesting but largely overlooked areas of inquiry provide additional interesting insights on effective teaching and (therefore) advising: *instructional pedagogy* (the art and practice of teaching itself) and *student perceptions of the good teacher and good teaching*. The unlikely coupling of these two topics, when joined with the other approaches in this book, help to round out and enrich the understanding of the importance and complexity of the advising-as-teaching concept as it supports student success.

Instructional Pedagogy: The Advisor as Teacher

All theorists seem to agree that good teachers plan carefully, thoughtfully, and thoroughly; they also most effectively help students make the most gains possible in academic achievement and prepare thoroughly for both in-class instruction and out-of-class contact with students. With this general approach to instruction in mind, educational theorist Hunter, in the *Mastery of Teaching* (1982), used the term *guided practice* to refer to specific instructional practices used by the most effective teachers and presented a sequenced lesson plan (the Hunter method) for both cultivating the good teacher and developing the active learner. The nine-step process, when viewed from the perspective of the advisor as teacher, offers practical application in a wide range of advising settings. In preparing a lesson, good teachers, and therefore good advisors, should keep the following goals in mind:

- clear objectives. What should students be able to do, understand, and value or appreciate as a result of teaching and advising?

- the standards of performance expected from students and the level of accountability they must have for learning specified material. Teachers and advisors need to state explicitly the standards and the procedures to meet those standards as well as the knowledge and skills students should be able to demonstrate as a result of teaching or advising. Advisors may find that an advising syllabus best articulates these standards of performance.

- a hook to grab students' initial attention. Called an "anticipatory set," the hook may be a teacher's action or statement that relates students' experiences to the objectives of the lesson and thus helps students translate abstract ideas into common, understandable terms. and lives. An advisor's well-placed inquiries (who, what, why, where, when) could well draw students more effectively into an advising conversation. The best approach will, of course, be guided by the particular situation and the advisor's ability to read it.

○ the input or information vehicles, such as lecture, film, or video, needed for students to learn. Advisors can use a broad assortment such as orientation and preregistration materials, course and resource guides, career information, and the advising syllabus.

After presenting the material, the good teacher, and thus the good advisor, will

○ use it to lead students to think critically through summarizing, problem solving, comparing, and so on. In the Hunter method, this step is called *modeling*.

○ check for understanding by asking questions that inspire students to a higher level of understanding than mere recall. According to the Hunter method, the instructor orders these questions according to the six levels of cognition in Bloom's (1956) taxonomy of educational objectives: moving from knowledge, comprehension, application, analysis, and synthesis, to evaluation.

○ provide an activity, exercise, or guided practice designed for students to codify the lesson and to demonstrate their mastery of the subject. This step along with the following two are particularly effective when advising at-risk students or other special populations.

○ guide the lesson to appropriate closure by reviewing and clarifying its key elements to help students make sense of the lesson and to plant key elements firmly in the students' conceptual network.

○ provide for independent practice so that students remember the information. The good teacher finds opportunities to incorporate learning into different situations as a way of reinforcing, applying, and integrating it into that conceptual network.

Four years after Hunter developed her method, educational theorists Rosenshine and Stevens (1986) studied the most the effective classroom instructional procedures, including Hunter's method, and concluded that the most effective teachers commonly use certain instructional strategies to encourage greater gains in student learning. These practices find easy translation to a host of advising settings:

○ Begin a lesson with a short review of previous learning.

○ Begin a lesson with a short statement of goals.

○ Present new material in small steps, providing for student practice after each step.

○ Give clear and detailed instructions and explanations.

○ Provide a high level of active practice for all students.

○ Ask many questions, check for student understanding, and obtain responses from all students.

- Guide students during initial practice.
- Provide systematic feedback and corrections.
- Provide explicit instruction and practice for seatwork exercises and monitor students during this time. (p. 377)

That is how it is done, step-by-step. These instructional strategies illustrate a full, rounded view of an effective teacher-advisor. Knowledge about teaching and learning theories and instructional pedagogies do not, by themselves, guarantee good teachers and advisors.

In 1971, Rosenshine and Furst published a detailed analysis of teacher behaviors that scholars still turn to as a source of solid, time-tested research on the characteristics of good teachers in classes of students who made the greatest measured gains in achievement. They reported 11 characteristics of a good teacher and showed that 5 behaviors were consistently found in good teachers:

- clarity—explain concepts clearly and plan for and demonstrate knowledge of the subject matter.
- variability—use a variety of strategies to deliver the message, instructional materials, and types of evaluation that determine student comprehension and learning.
- enthusiasm—show genuine care and concern for students, use movement, gestures, voice inflection, and smile, as well as demonstrate excitement or passion toward the subject matter.
- task-oriented, business-like behaviors—clearly state expectations for student performance verbally and in a syllabus, effectively use class time, and know how to encourage students to complete tasks at hand.
- opportunity to learn—identify the learning outcomes prior to instruction, provide all students with the opportunity to learn, and teach toward students' successful achievement of these learning outcomes.

In the years that followed Rosenshine and Furst's research on teacher performance criteria, many other studies corroborated and reflected their conclusions. One particularly practical, accessible piece that provides an overarching view is Rich's (n.d.) "7 Habits of Good Teachers Today." In it, Rich observed from her own extensive experience that effective teaching is first and foremost about relationships between people and the discovery and cultivation of their "hopes and dreams, and about a future we can't even envision" (para. 13). Teachers, like advisors, cannot automatically assume that students come into the classroom like blank slates or that they are willing and eager participants in the learning process. Good teachers and advisors must make the subject matter relevant to students' lives as well as take a holistic view of the learning process, which relies on the involvement of the students, other teachers, and family members of students. Rich suggested that advisors

- market the subject. A good teacher needs to be a good salesperson by demonstrating enthusiasm for the subject matter and showing its relevance to students' lives. In much the same way and on a variety of issues faced every day in their offices, advisors know that they simply cannot expect all students to buy into an idea, requirement, or course of study.

- know the subject. Knowledge of—and commitment to—the subject matter is, of course, key. It is the foundation upon which all else is built, but, as Rich wisely pointed out, knowledge is not enough to ensure learning; a teacher must communicate content effectively to a diverse student body.

- use a variety of teaching styles. One size does not fit all. Sensitivity to differences in student learning styles and ability to read signals students express verbally and nonverbally help teachers and advisors reach students and connect them with the material.

- build on family and out-of-school experiences. Students experience pressures and issues outside the classroom or advising setting that influence learning. Home and community comprise critical components of the educational and developmental process in promoting student learning. It is important, therefore, to enlist families as partners in the learning process (see Jennifer Varney's discussion on proactive advising—chapter 9).

- involve students as learning partners. If students are expected to change ideas, attitudes, and behaviors, instructors must engage them in their own learning. Rich suggested that students develop their own learning goals for a course (or advising session). If students cannot articulate any goals, they should work together with the teacher/advisor to develop them.

- collaborate with other adults. Teaching, as with advising, is not a solitary effort. Practitioners need to talk and learn from each other in more ways than offering moral support and sharing teaching strategies; they need to share professional development opportunities.

- ensure students are considered with care and affection. In determining student success in and out of the classroom, everyone in the institution needs to address students' deep human need to feel recognized. Advisors, in particular, play a powerful and central role in student success by providing the opportunity (sometimes the only one) for an ongoing, durable relationship with someone who cares about their academic goals and career aspirations (para. 16–38).

10 Strategies for Demonstrating Care and Concern for Students

What strategies might advisors and teachers employ to let students know they care about them? The following time-tested, practical strategies (Drake & King, 2010) help advisors both make the most of their time with advisees and communicate the importance and power of the advising relationship:

1. Over the centuries, many sages, philosophers, pundits, and divines have urged that one use people's names as a signal of true listening and caring. Among these proponents of name use, Dale Carnegie observed that "a man's name is to him the sweetest and most important sound in any language." Advisors should learn and use advisees' names.

2. William James stated that "the deepest principle in human nature is the craving to be appreciated." Teachers and advisors can affirm students by respecting their opinions. Even when disagreeing with the premises on which students base their ideas or wanting to direct students away from a particularly destructive position, advisors can, nevertheless, acknowledge students by saying out loud "I respect your opinion" and really mean it.

3. Advisors need to acknowledge that advisees are experts in areas about which advisors know little. Students bring to the classroom and advising sessions their unique perspectives, frames of reference on the world, culture, academic experiences, and so forth. Advisors can learn much about and from students and enrich contacts with them if they are willing to learn from them. Ralph Waldo Emerson echoed this advice: "Every man I meet is in some way my superior, and in that I can learn of him."

4. Advisors must listen carefully to learn students' unique frames of reference. One often hears a different message than intended by the speaker, so advisors and teachers need to pay careful attention to students' verbal and nonverbal communication. By listening and watching body language, advisors can ask the best questions and prompt students to reveal themselves, thus positioning themselves to work effectively with students.

5. By communicating enthusiasm, advisors signal attentiveness and concern to students. Enthusiasm and an upbeat approach impart a warmth and interest in students that have the power to transform. Enthusiasm is also contagious.

6. For each advising meeting, advisors must clarify the goals with students. Is today's goal to resolve a problem or to discuss an issue? Is it to review degree requirements or graduation plans? Identifying the issues or concerns at the beginning of an appointment makes for much more comfortable and productive sessions. Unfortunately, students sometimes leave advising meetings feeling like the subject of the following Stephen Leacock image: "He flung himself from the room, flung himself upon his horse and rode madly off in all directions."

7. Allowing for periods of silence in conversations with students, advisors should let unanswered questions hang in the air until the student addresses them. Some students just need time to deliberate or form a response. One is reminded that deliberating is not necessarily delaying.

8. Some measure of self-disclosure promotes trust and encourages self-disclosure in others. Advisors can use it to reassure students that they are not alone in

their situation, that their advisors have gone through the same or similar situations. Of course, advisors should not recite their whole life history, but should offer enough information to communicate some identification with their advisees' experiences with the intention of offering comfort and encouragement.

9. Advisors should admit when they do not know the answers to students' questions and try to find the correct answers or refer students to the appropriate office or resource. Advisors should never perpetuate an institution's reputation for giving students the runaround. Keeping handy a list of campus resources and contact people, along with their telephone numbers, e-mail addresses, and web sites, should help to stem the formation of a poor institutional reputation for wasting students' time and reinforce the feeling that advisors are looking out for students.

10. By documenting all advising contacts—whether they be in person, one-on-one, in a group setting; via phone, e-mail, text message, Facebook; or by any other form of communication—advisors keep records that may be useful both practically and legally. Whether these notes are stored in an individual folder or in an electronic database, the records should always provide students, as well as others with vetted access to the file, an accurate record of students' academic progress.

Student Perspectives of Good Teachers

Research studies on effective teachers, as well as strategies for enhancing teaching and learning processes, have been published from nearly every conceivable point of view, as the chapters in this book suggest. These studies provide approaches for improving instruction and interactions with students. Many scholars look at the causes of student behaviors (and misbehaviors) within and beyond the classroom and the interventions used to address them. However, the research literature on the professional development of teachers seldom addresses student perceptions of effective teaching practices or the causes of teacher behaviors (and misbehaviors) in and outside the classroom.

Brown and McIntyre (1993) took a different tack. Instead of focusing on student "non-compliance" and other types of student misbehaviors, they looked at teachers as sources of behaviors that negatively influence student satisfaction (i.e., from the students' perspectives) in the college classroom. Their study showed that students think good teachers create relaxed, enjoyable, and safe classroom atmospheres; retain control of the classroom; provide interesting and motivating work; make clear their expectations for students; help students who encounter difficulties; and have high expectations for their students.

Research on characteristics of effective teachers and teaching from the students' perspective has generally not been translated into the advising literature. These studies, however, have close relevance to effective advising practices. In a recent study, Delaney, Johnson, Johnson, and Treslan (2010) identified the characteristics that university students believe essential for effective teachers and teaching. Through an open-ended question instrument, they found nine predominant themes, nine characteristics, and nine sets of behaviors essential for effective teaching. In sum, students defined the best teachers as respectful, knowledgeable, approachable, engaging, communicative, organized, responsive, professional, and humorous, but they most highly valued respect, even over disciplinary knowledge or the ability to communicate effectively. Without any effort in translation, one can effectively overlay these characteristics of good teachers onto good advisors: The best advisors demonstrate precisely the same teacher behaviors deemed most important to students.

Kearney (1991) reported that students portrayed effective teachers as those with attributes like "love for the teaching profession, the ability to establish rapport with students, solid knowledge of the subject matter, a sincere concern for students, a high level of professionalism, self-confidence about teaching the course, an open and friendly nature, and the ability to create a challenging classroom environment" (p. 22). Conversely, students also voiced the sources of their dissatisfaction and resistance to teaching both within and outside the classroom by elaborating on college instructors' "misbehaviors" that impede their learning. They depicted some of their teachers as "unable to relate to students, uncaring, preoccupied with other work, uninformed about course content, fearful about initiating personal relationships with students, outdated, selfish and self-centered, and not being committed to the teaching profession" (p. 21). Of the 28 types of misbehavior reported in the Kearney study, three broad categories emerge as primary sources for student dissatisfaction and resistance. To use Kearney's precise terms, these categories are incompetence, offensiveness, and indolence.

Incompetence. Students reported that some teachers were either unwilling or unable to help students succeed. "The misbehaviors included in this factor suggest that incompetent teachers do not seem to care about either the course or the students themselves, do not know their students' names, will not review for exams and fail to allow for student input during class" (Kearney, 1991, p. 28). They provide students with incorrect information, give vague or disorganized lectures, and openly contradict themselves in class. In addition, students considered incompetent those teachers who demonstrated no enthusiasm for the course work, spoke in a monotone, failed to enunciate clearly, and talked either too loudly or softly.

Offensiveness. The misbehaviors that students associate with offensiveness suggest that teachers could be "mean, cruel and ugly" (p. 29). Some offensive teachers

"humiliate students in front of the class, insult and publicly embarrass them . . . use profanity, become angry or yell and scream in their effort to intimidate students. These same teachers are rude, self-centered, moody, and whiners; moreover, they condescend to students by acting superior and arrogant." They appear to be "rigid, inflexible and authoritarian." (Kearney, 1991, p. 29)

Indolence. Indolent teachers are characterized by the absent-minded professor stereotype. They either do not show up for class or show up late. They return student assignments late and change due dates for assignments and their syllabi without appropriate advance notice to the class. Students also report indolent teachers as being disorganized and often making their exams and classes too easy (Kearney, 1991, p. 30).

Kearney (1991) observed that such negative teacher (mis)behaviors often lead to poor attendance, classroom disruptions, and lower student achievement. Kearney ended the report as she began it, by urging teachers to "consider students' perceptions as well as our own in our decisions about what we do and say in the classroom" (p. 31). The positive and negative aspects of teacher behavior can be used to characterize the best and worst advisors.

Implications for Advisors

The teacher's and the advisor's central responsibility is to facilitate learning. In the same way teacher effectiveness depends upon a strong command of the subject, well-calculated instructional methods, honed pedagogical skills, and genuine care and concern for students, so too must the advisor as teacher act as a facilitator of learning, have knowledge of academic and cocurricular resources, and communicate to students in a way that both encourages their self-actualization and demonstrates sincere concern for them. Many research findings over the years, as well as various chapters in this book, offer divergent roads from which to view the advising-as-teaching paradigm. All of them circle back to the understanding that advising is, indeed, a teaching and learning process, and as such, places advisors at the nexus between students who enter the academy uninformed and undefined and those who leave with identities and life direction shaped by positive interactions with faculty members and professional advisors. In the end, the complexity and richness of the advising-as-teaching approach relies on the critical connections that advisors make with students.

Advising-as-Teaching Scenario

Scenario II

A second-year student, Ali, comes to Drew to discuss withdrawing from school: "I'm really not doing well this term. It's not the courses or the professors—I just don't feel like I fit in. A few of my friends left after last year, and I haven't really found any new ones. My new roommates are not really like me, so they kind of stick together by themselves. I'm not in any clubs or anything like that, although I do work off campus. Also, I feel my parents and I have spent lots of money, but I'm not sure it's worth spending more if I'm not that interested. Do you have any suggestions? What do you think I should do?"

DREW: It sounds like this year hasn't gone as well as you would have hoped.	**Clear Objectives** Determine what the student needs to understand and do as a result of advising.
ALI: That certainly is true.	
DREW: If you were granted one wish—to change the way things are right now—what would you wish for?	Ali wants to belong and have direction.
ALI: I'd wish it was last year again.	
DREW: Why is that?	
ALI: I would have friends and a goal.	
DREW: So, am I correct to assume that if we could change two issues for you the first would be having friends here and the second would be having an academic or career goal?	
ALI: Yeah, I guess so. I really want to feel like I belong and I want some sort of direction for my life.	
DREW: Let's deal with your first goal and talk about what it would take for you to feel like you belong. How will you know when you belong?	**Standards of Performance** Set the standards for what is expected of advising and of the student.
ALI: I guess it would be when I know there's a place where I can be with people who accept me for myself—where I can just be me.	Ali wants to have friends who enjoy the same activities and wants a career goal.
DREW: What would that look like?	
ALI: It will be a place where the people like to do the same things I do.	
DREW: Okay. You said your second goal is to find some kind of direction. What do you mean by that?	
ALI: I'd like to know what kind of job I'd be good at, what I would enjoy doing. I thought I wanted to be a doctor, but I found out this year that I'm no good at chemistry. Now I don't know what I'm going to do.	

DREW: Are you ready to take some steps to help you feel like you belong and have some direction? ALI: Yeah, I guess I am!	**Anticipatory Set** Create an advisor action or statement meant to focus student attention on the objectives. Ali provided the anticipatory set by bringing the problem to Drew, who garners student interest by tackling the problems Ali describes.
DREW: Let's talk about finding your niche here. What kind of things do you enjoy doing? ALI: Well, I like playing video games while I listen to music. I do that to relax. DREW: Are there any things you've always wanted to do? ALI: I always thought it would be cool to skydive. DREW: That's interesting. Did you know there is a skydiving club in town? There are several students from the college who belong to that group. ALI: That might be okay. DREW: What kind of job can you picture yourself doing in 5 years? ALI: I don't really know but I know I don't want to work in an office. I'd rather be doing something, maybe even outside. DREW: That's a start. How about if we get you to our Career Services Office? They have lots of resources to explore careers where you wouldn't be tied to a desk.	**Input** Provide the information needed for students to gain the knowledge or skill needed to meet the objective(s). Drew discusses possible options with Ali.

DREW: Let's look at some of the resources available to you. Where would you like to start?	**Modeling**
ALI: I'd like to see the skydiving club.	Drew shows Ali an end product of their work, taking Ali to the application level: problem solving, comparison, summarizing, and so forth.
[Drew shows Ali the club's web site]	
ALI: That's cool! Is there anything for gamers?	Drew shows Ali web sites of the various options, and they discuss some career assessment tools.
DREW [looking at web]: Here's a campus gaming group. What do you think about those activities?	
ALI: They might be worth checking into.	
DREW: How about we look at the Career Center site?	
ALI: Sure.	
DREW: Look, here are some tools for discovering what you like to do that you can complete from any computer.	
ALI: That looks kind of interesting.	
DREW: You can make an appointment with the Career Center staff and then take the findings from these tools with you. Would you like to do that?	
ALI: Yeah, that would be okay.	
DREW: Tell me, which of these things will you do first?	**Check for Understanding**
ALI: First I think I'll see if I can hook up with the gaming group, then maybe the skydivers.	Use questioning strategies that probe for the high levels of understanding needed to ensure transfer. Questions progress from the lowest to the highest of the six levels of the cognitive domain of the Bloom's Taxonomy of Educational Objectives: knowledge, comprehension, application, analysis, synthesis, and evaluation.
DREW: That's a good first step to finding better connections here. What's next?	
ALI: Well, I could play with those assessments you showed me on the career site.	
DREW: Be sure to print off the results of the assessments. You will find them handy.	
	Ali tells Drew which actions will be taken first.

DREW: How about making an appointment now with the Career Services staff? ALI: Okay. How do I do that? DREW [pointing to the mouse]: You take the mouse. See the "contact" icon in the right corner? [Ali nods.] Click on that. ALI: It says I can make an appointment from here. How about next Friday? Would that work? DREW: I think that would be a great idea. Why don't we make an appointment to talk again the following week? We can chat about what you have accomplished toward belonging and find a career direction.	**Guided Practice** Allow the student to demonstrate a grasp of new learning by working through an activity or exercise under direct supervision. Ali uses the advisor's computer to book an appointment with career services.
ALI: I have our next meeting in my phone notes. DREW: So, two weeks from today we'll meet again. We'll discuss what you have done to reach your two goals, to feel like you belong and find a career direction. I will be interested to hear how you feel about what's happened. ALI: It will be good to do something besides sit around and worry.	**Closure** Help the student make sense out of what has just been taught in the process of forming a coherent picture, consolidating the facts, and eliminating confusion and frustration. Ali makes an appointment with the advisor for two weeks from today to discuss what happens.
DREW: I'm excited for you and will be interested to see who you meet between now and then. Be sure to bring copies of anything from your career exploration that you'd like me to see. ALI: I'll do that. See you then.	**Independent Practice** Provide an opportunity for independent practice and reinforcement. Ali will bring materials from the career appointment to the follow-up advising session.
Note: Scenario discussion by Marsha Miller based upon Hunter (n.d.) lesson plan.	

References

Appleby, D. C. (2008). Advising as teaching and learning. In V. N. Gordon, W. R. Habley, & T. J. Grites (Eds.), *Academic advising: A comprehensive handbook* (2nd ed.) (pp. 85–102). San Francisco, CA: Jossey-Bass.

Bloom, B. S. (1956). *Taxonomy of educational objectives. Handbook 1: Cognitive domain.* New York, NY: Longman.

Brown, S., & McIntyre, D. (1993). *Making sense of teaching*. Buckingham, UK: Open University.

Carnegie, D. (n.d.). *Dale Carnegie quote*. Retrieved from http://www.1-famous-quotes.com/quote/131549

Chickering, A. (n.d.). *The seven vectors: An overview*. Retrieved from http://www.cabrini.edu/communications/ProfDev/cardevChickering.html

Clifton, D. O., & Anderson, E. C. (2002). *StrengthsQuest: Discover and develop your strengths in academics, career, and beyond*. Washington, DC: The Gallup Organization.

Creamer, D. G. (2000). Use of theory in academic advising. In V. N. Gordon & W. R. Habley (Eds.), *Academic advising: A comprehensive handbook* (pp. 18–34). San Francisco, CA: Jossey-Bass.

Crookston, B. (2009). A developmental view of academic advising as teaching. *NACADA Journal, 29*(1), 78–82. (Reprinted from *Journal of College Student Personnel, 13*, 1972, pp. 12–17; *NACADA Journal, 14*[2], 1994, pp. 5–9)

Cuseo, J. (2012). *Academic advisement and student retention: Empirical connections & systemic interventions*. Retrieved from http://www.uwc.edu/sites/default/files/imce-uploads/employees/academic-resources/esfy/_files/academic_advisement_and_student_retention.pdf

Delaney, J. G., Johnson, A. N., Johnson, T. D., & Treslan, D. L. (2010). *Students' perceptions of effective teaching in higher education*. St. Johns, Newfoundland, Canada: Distance Education and Learning Technologies.

Drake, J., Hemwall, M., & Stockwell, K. (2009). *A faculty guide to academic advising* (Pocket Guide Series, PG08). Manhattan, KS: National Academic Advising Association.

Drake, J., & King, N. (2010). *Advising as a teaching and learning process*. (Building the Framework CD Series, Rec001CD). Manhattan, KS: National Academic Advising Association.

Emerson, R. W. (n.d.). *Ralph Waldo Emerson quotes*. Retrieved from http://www.brainyquote.com/quotes/quotes/r/ralphwaldo125377.html

Erikson, E. H. (1959). *Identity and the life cycle*. New York, NY: International Universities.

Folsom, P. (Ed.). (2007). *The new advisor guidebook: Mastering the art of advising through the first year and beyond* (NACADA Monograph, No. 16). Manhattan, KS: National Academic Advising Association.

Hagen, P., & Jordan, P. (2008). Theoretical foundations of academic advising. In V. N. Gordon, W. R. Habley, & T. J. Grites (Eds.), *Academic advising: A comprehensive handbook* (2nd ed.) (pp. 17–35). San Francisco, CA: Jossey-Bass.

Hemwall, M. K., & Trachte, K. (1999). Learning at the core: Toward a new understanding of academic advising. *NACADA Journal, 19*(1), 5–11.

Hunter, M. (n.d.). *Madeline Hunter's lesson plan*. Retrieved from http://template.aea267.iowapages.org/lessonplan/

Hunter, M. (1982). *Mastery of teaching*. El Segundo, CA: TIP.

James, W. (n.d.). *William James quotes*. Retrieved from www.brainyquote.com/quotes/quotes/w/williamjam125466.html

Kearney, P. (1991). *What students don't like about what teachers say and do*. Retrieved from ERIC database. (ED343191)

Kohlberg, L. (1969). Stage and sequence: The cognitive-developmental approach to socialization. In D. A. Goslin (Ed.), *Handbook of socialization: Theory in research* (pp. 347–480). Boston, MA: Houghton-Mifflin.

Leacock, S. (n.d.). *Steven Leacock quotes.* Retrieved from http://www.brainyquote.com/quotes/quotes/s/stephenlea125495.html

Lowenstein, M. (2005). If advising is teaching, what do advisors teach? *NACADA Journal, 25*(2), 65–73.

McGillin, V. A. (2000). Current issues in advising research. In V. N. Gordon & W. R. Habley (Eds.), *Academic advising: A comprehensive handbook* (pp. 365–380). San Francisco, CA: Jossey-Bass.

Nutt, C., & Campbell, S. (2010). *The role of academic advising in student retention and persistence* (Pocket Guide Series, PG07). Manhattan, KS: National Academic Advising Association.

O'Banion, T. (2009). 1994 (1972): An academic advising model. *NACADA Journal, 29*(1), 83–89. (Reprinted from *Junior College Journal, 42,* 1972, pp. 62, 63, 66–69; *NACADA Journal,* 1994, *14*[2], pp. 10–16)

Perry, W. G., Jr. (1970). *Forms of intellectual and ethical development in the college years: A scheme.* New York, NY: Holt, Rinehart & Winston.

Piaget, J. (1952). *The origins of intelligence in children.* New York, NY: International University.

Reynolds, M. M. (2010). *An advisor's half dozen: Principles for incorporating learning theory into our advising practices.* Retrieved from http://www.nacada.ksu.edu/Resources/Clearinghouse/View-Articles/Learning-theory-in-academic-advising.aspx

Rich, D. (2007). *7 habits of good teachers today.* Retrieved from http://www.scribd.com/doc/47020541/7-Habits-of-Good-Teachers-Today

Rosenshine, B., & Furst, N. (1971). Research on teacher performance criteria. In B. O. Smith (Ed.), *Research in teacher education* (pp. 27–72). Englewood Cliffs, NJ: Prentice Hall.

Rosenshine, B., & Stevens, R. (1986). Teaching functions. In M. C. Witrock (Ed.), *Handbook of research on teaching* (3rd ed.) (pp. 376–391). New York, NY: Macmillan.

Ryan, C. C. (1992). Advising as teaching. *NACADA Journal, 12*(1), 4–8.

Vygotsky, L. S. (1978). *Mind in society: The development of higher psychological processes.* Cambridge, MA: Harvard University Press.

Williams, S. (2007). From theory to practice: The application of theories of development to academic advising philosophy and practice. Retrieved from http://www.nacada.ksu.edu/Resources/Clearinghouse/View-Articles/Applying-Theory-to-Advising-Practice.aspx

3

LEARNING-CENTERED ADVISING

Maura M. Reynolds

I say moreover that you make a great, a very great mistake, if you think that psychology, being the science of the mind's laws, is something from which you can deduce definite programs and schemes and methods of instruction for immediate schoolroom use. Psychology is a science, and teaching is an art; and sciences never generate arts directly out of themselves. An intermediary inventive mind must make the application, by using its originality.

—William James, 1899

When Wilbert McKeachie's *Teaching Tips* was published in 1950, it was the only book of its kind on the market (Nilson, 2010). The 13th edition, released in 2010, joined an ever-growing number of books, journals, and web sites focused on improving college teaching and learning. In the intervening years, researchers in neuroscience, cognitive psychology, and higher education have shared well-researched, comprehensive descriptions of strategies and principles for enhancing student learning. Although most of these findings have been focused on improving learning in a classroom setting, they offer exciting possibilities for infusing learning-centered principles coherently and intentionally into academic advising. Currently, practitioners can find much information about techniques and tools to improve advising, often presented as isolated ideas or tips, such that they cannot see how or why the tools promote student learning.

Other contributors to this book discuss the many approaches advisors can use in their advising practice. In this chapter, I explore principles that undergird learning-centered advising, regardless of the approaches advisors use, and suggest a coherent and integrated approach to learning-centered advising.

7 Principles for Good Practice

Perhaps the best known description of teaching practices that promote learning was published by Chickering and Gamson (1987), who consolidated and published ideas generated at a meeting attended by other scholars of higher education. The response to their concise article was enthusiastic: Within 10 years, more than 150,000 copies of these seven principles were ordered from the Johnson Foundation (Chickering & Gamson, 2000).

Chickering and Gamson (1987) wrote that good practice in undergraduate education

- ○ encourages contact between students and faculty members,
- ○ develops reciprocity and cooperation among students,
- ○ advances active learning,
- ○ allows for prompt feedback,
- ○ supports an emphasis of time on task,
- ○ communicates high expectations, and
- ○ induces a respect for diverse talents and ways of learning (p. 3).

They focused on translating research into accessible, understandable, practical, and widely applicable material. Although they directed their work toward the faculty, they hoped to reach other audiences as well, including administrators, those in state and national agencies, and policy makers (Chickering & Gamson, 2000). They succeeded admirably. At the end of their article, they challenged stakeholders to create an environment favorable to these good practices. They included, among other descriptors of a positive climate for learning, this tantalizing sentence: "Advising is [would be] considered important" (Chickering & Gamson, 1987, p. 5). They did not elaborate, however, on how advising might create an environment for learning or why advising should be considered important.

14 General, Research-Based Principles for Improving Higher Learning

In 1993, Angelo expanded Chickering and Gamson's (1987) seven-point list by delineating a "teacher's dozen" research-based, practical, and easily understood principles:

1. Active learning is more effective than passive learning.
2. Learning requires focused attention and awareness of the importance of what is to be learned.
3. Learning is more effective and efficient when learners have explicit, reasonable, positive goals, and when their goals fit well with the teacher's goals.
4. To be remembered, new information must be meaningfully connected to prior knowledge, and it must first be remembered in order to be learned.
5. Unlearning what is already known is often more difficult than learning new information.
6. Information that is organized in personally meaningful ways is more likely to be remembered, learned, and used.

7. Learners need feedback on their learning, early and often, to learn well; to become independent learners, they need to become self-assessing and self-correcting.

8. The ways learners are assessed and evaluated powerfully affect the ways they study and learn.

9. Mastering a skill or body of knowledge takes great amounts of time and effort.

10. Learning to transfer, to apply previous knowledge and skills to new contexts, requires a great deal of directed practice.

11. High expectations encourage high achievement.

12. To be most effective, teachers need to balance levels of intellectual challenge and instructional support.

13. Motivation to learn is alterable; it can be positively or negatively affected by the task, the environment, the teacher, and the learner.

14. Interaction between teachers and learners is one of the most powerful factors in promoting learning; interaction among learners is another. (pp. 5–7)

As is clear from his title, Angelo directs his principles to the teaching faculty, and he hopes that the impact of these principles will be actualized in the classroom.

Angelo's and Chickering and Gamson's principles continue to be influential. In 1998, the American Association for Higher Education, the American College Personnel Association, and the National Association of Student Personnel Administrators published a list of 10 learning principles (*Powerful Partnerships*) that emphasize collaborations between academic and student affairs personnel and organizations; the similarities to the earlier principles are striking.

Chickering and Gamson's (1987) principles were cited by The Ohio Learning Network, a consortium of colleges and universities that used technology to enhance distance learning, because they provide the foundation of high-quality distance-delivery methods (Watwood, Nugent, & Deihl, 2009). Virginia Commonwealth University's Center for Teaching Excellence made the case that these 1987 principles are essential in an online environment and provided vignettes to suggest ways they can be adapted to online teaching and can support meaningful learning in online classes (Watwood et al., 2009).

Connecting Learning Principles to Advising

Although the learning principles delineated here come from research about classroom teaching, they promote student learning, a goal shared by academic advising. Some teachers and advisors may assume that student learning is automatic, the result of good teaching or good academic advising. However, students learn for and by themselves; it is a process, a change, a response to experiences. Advising and teaching techniques and tools matter, not as ends in themselves, but as means of fostering and supporting student learning. When teaching and advising are learning centered, the focus rests on students (not teachers or advisors): What are students learning? How are they learning? Can they apply their learning? Will their learning support and encourage further learning? While some principles from the 7- and updated 14-point lists are better suited for the classroom, some give promise for strengthening learning in the advising setting.

Clear, Reasonable, and Positive Goals

Learning is more effective when students have clear, reasonable, and positive goals. Few new-to-college students understand the process or content of academic advising. Many assume that an advisor helps primarily with scheduling and registering for classes and, with the advent of online registration and degree evaluations, meetings with an academic advisor may no longer be mandatory. As Jayne Drake pointed out in her chapter, outstanding teachers, like outstanding advisors, must set clear objectives about what students should be able to do, understand, and value as a result of teaching or advising.

Research indicates that students fail to learn and retain new material when they do not understand the structure or the context of it (Svinicki, 2004). Without seeing the overall framework and goals for academic advising or apprehending the reasoning behind the general education and degree requirements, students may think they are learning small, discrete items, rather than realize that they are experiencing a sequenced and logical progression toward specific goals and learning outcomes.

For example, students may believe that general education requirements are arbitrarily created, disconnected, and listed to form obstacles to negotiate before taking classes in their majors. They may think that they should accumulate course credits rather than build real-world skills and capabilities. Despite their helpfulness, degree audits and evaluations can foster these misconceptions. Because advisors have continuing contact with students, they may be more able to help students see the *logic of the curriculum* (Lowenstein, 1999) than faculty members who may teach students in one class. Advisors can help students see the connections among their classes, in their majors and minors, as well as in general education requisites, and can encourage them to consider and articulate the transferable skills they are developing through their experiences in and out of the classroom. This learning principle reminds advisors that when students understand the structure—the big picture—they can learn more effectively and efficiently. The Task Group on General Education made a point in 1988 that remains true today: "Perhaps the most urgent reform on most campuses in improving general education involves academic advising. To have programs and courses become coherent and significant to students requires adequate advising" (p. 43).

Communicating goals or learning objectives for academic advising is equally important (Martin, 2007), which some advisors accomplish by creating an advising syllabus (Trabant, 2006) while others employ less formal means. No matter the vehicle, for students to understand the structure and purposes of advising, they need to know the expectations for their learning through advising. Learning goals for students change as they progress through their programs, and the objectives should be reasonable in number and function; for example, a first- or second-year student might need to learn how and why to meet with faculty members, to understand how to undertake and read a degree evaluation, to set accurate expectations for the amount of time and effort needed to be successful in classes, or to grasp the purposes of the curriculum. For more advanced students, learning objectives might involve articulating ways their education has helped them develop the skills they will need after college, evaluating the courses and out-of-class experiences that will prepare them for the work they hope to undertake, or investigating internships or off-campus study experiences.

Such clear and reasonable learning goals help students realize that academic advising involves more than scheduling and registration. When advisors remind students of these learning goals throughout their college careers, rather than assume that students will remember them from an advising syllabus or early meeting, students may understand that academic advising offers a carefully sequenced series of learning opportunities.

To promote learning effectively, advisors should state goals as positive and appealing objectives. Rather than list responsibilities of advisees, advisors might include the benefits of advising for students or a list of circumstances in which a student might want to consult an advisor (for issues not related to registration). This broad scope of advising, which shows issues other than just scheduling and registering, shows advising as an attractive and inviting learning-centered activity for both advisors and students.

Learning Requires Active Involvement

The passive human brain, with listening as the sole learning modality, cannot focus for long (Svinicki, 2004). For active learning, students must get involved; that is, they need to think about the content of their learning not just passively receive information. Advocates for active learning focus on the process rather than on the outcome. Advisors can involve students actively, as well as send a message that advising involves more than registering for classes, by asking first-time students to respond in writing to questions such as "What are your goals for your first year in college?" "What were your favorite classes in high school?" "What are your greatest strengths?" By raising these questions when students are preparing to select classes for their first college semester and keeping responses in an advising folder or electronic portfolio, advisors can revisit the questions as students progress by adding specifics to root questions such as "How are you managing your time?" "Have you met with your professors?" "What has been your most demanding challenge this term and how have you dealt with it?"

Advisors could ask the following questions of experienced students: "How are you the same as when you began in college? How have you changed?" "What do you intend to do and to be when you complete your program? What resources can you use right now to help you reach this vision?" Advisors might ask students on academic probation "What resources do you plan to use this term?" or "What do you intend to do differently this term? How will these changes help you?" By writing their responses, students actively engage in learning-centered advising, provide rich material that advisors can use in future meetings, and offer information on areas for growth that advisors can help students monitor.

Referring students to other offices and people on and off campus, asking them to develop a term-by-term plan for finishing their program, expecting them to complete a task before they come to an advising appointment encourage their active learning. In addition to fostering active involvement, these activities potentially help students understand the learning goals of advising and to value the learning process.

Motivated Students Learn More Effectively

Motivation is not fixed; it can be changed. In the context of academic advising, *motivating* means stimulating students' desire to learn. When advisors explain the goals of advising and the benefits they can accrue by being active participants, students may become intrinsically motivated to take advantage of the opportunities for learning that advising offers and may appreciate the relevance and applicability of learning to their lives in and after college. Students may also be extrinsically motivated to be involved in advising if they recognize that advisors can help them complete their programs in a timely fashion or provide letters of recommendation that will help them get a job. Students are intrinsically motivated when they value advisors and advising for their importance and relevance; they are extrinsically motivated when they see advisors and advising as a means to an end.

Research on the connections among extrinsic motivation, intrinsic motivation, and student learning leads to no clear conclusions about the relative effectiveness of extrinsic or intrinsic motivation in fostering learning (Nilson, 2010). However, several scholars have asked students about the activities and situations that motivate them to learn in the classroom. The critical influences respondents cited included the professor's enthusiasm for the material and the teaching of it, the relevance and applicability of the material, clear organization, an appropriate level of difficulty, active learning approaches, and professor's rapport with students (Sass, 1989). In her chapter on advising as teaching, Drake explores these influences in greater detail. Sass's results offer good news for academic advisors, who without power over students' levels of motivation to learn, can control their own attitudes, behaviors, and the methods they use to present and organize information.

At every meeting, advisors can enhance students' skills of reflection, self-assessment, goal setting, and decision making, which they will need throughout their time in college and in the real world. By reminding students of the skills they are developing, advisors may help them understand the relevance and applicability of advising and increase their motivation to take full advantage of it. When advisors introduce inexperienced college students to opportunities that may await them in a few years (e.g., internships, off-campus study, or independent research), students may remain focused when they face difficulties or boredom.

High Expectations Encourage High Achievement

Like all teaching, learning-centered advising offers developmental opportunities to students, and advisors who employ this strategy must tailor expectations to individuals and their needs. A one-size-fits-all approach is not appropriate. Advisors should expect much from their students as well as support and encourage them to meet high levels of achievement. However, advisor discussions with first-year students and their expectations of them should differ from the material and outcomes discussed with juniors and seniors. Expectations for a military veteran returning to complete a 2-year program while working full-time and parents of young children will not mirror those for full-time, traditional-aged students at a residential liberal-arts college. If advisors believe in the power of learning-centered advising, they should expect students to take as much advantage of it as is reasonable.

Advisors can also encourage students to set high expectations for their own learning. Students should embellish initial goals for grades earned or credits completed with plans for taking advantage of cocurricular experiences, finding avenues for leadership, exploring research opportunities, and stretching themselves by taking demanding classes. When setting high expectations, discussing them with advisors, and monitoring their progress to achieving their objectives, students make the most of their time in college. Advisors can be important resources in such endeavors.

Studied in a classroom setting, high expectations exerted a significant positive impact on first-year students' attitudes toward learning. Furthermore, researchers learned that high expectations, combined with other learning principles and practices, factored into successful outcomes for underprepared college students (Cruce, Wolniak, Seifert, & Pascarella, 2006).

Students Need Feedback

To learn well, students need feedback. To become independent learners, they must learn to give themselves feedback. If they keep a file or electronic archive of students' written responses to reflection and self-assessment questions, advisors will discover rich opportunities to provide feedback and encourage students to reflect on their experiences. When advisors ask students at the end of a term to look at the goals they had set, advisors provide an opportunity for self-reflection and self-assessment. Furthermore, when advisors ask students to assess how their recent successes will affect the goals they set for the upcoming term, students can reflect on the past as well as plan for the future. Learning-centered advising demands reflection and self-assessment, skills that demand work and can induce pain, especially if hoped-for futures prove impossible or unrealistic. Baxter Magolda and King (2008) provided a sequenced series of questions that promote students' self-assessment and self-authorship: For example, "What new perspectives have you encountered?" and "How have these experiences affected the ways you see things?" can guide students to explore their experiences, the reasons they are meaningful to them, and how they interpreted them. These practices create the building blocks of self-assessment and self-authorship.

According to Pizzolato (2006), Baxter Magolda's learning partnerships model (LPM) can help advisors promote students' self-authorship. When advisors encourage students to identify and assess academic options ("What are your thoughts about the choices for class enrollment next semester?" or "What majors are you considering?"), they help students develop confidence and belief that their ideas matter and that they are capable of effectively weighing decisions rather than relying on the opinions of others. Challenging students to explain the processes they used to make academic decisions, suggesting a variety of options to them, and brainstorming possible responses to difficult academic situations give students practice in self-assessment. (See chapter 8 by Janet Schulenberg.)

Interactions Promote Learning

Interactions between students and advisors can promote learning; interactions among students are equally important. Reporting on the results of the National Survey of Student Engagement, Kuh (2008) reiterated the impact of academic advising: Students at 4-year colleges who met with advisors at least twice during the academic year tended to participate in the five benchmark activities important to student success and engagement. In addition, he found that contact with an advisor is related to self-reported gains in personal and social development and in more frequent use of deep approaches to learning. Advisors can have a powerful effect on students and their learning.

Peers also play an important role in fostering learning. Panels of experienced students who talk with newer students about major selection, study abroad, internships, job search, extracurricular activities, or service learning can enrich the learning environment and can give the seasoned students an opportunity to enhance their self-assessment skills in a public context. Group advising sessions also permit students to hear questions and comments of others, perhaps prompting them to consider new areas or concerns. A group advising session in a living unit may encourage further informal conversations about advising issues long after the session has ended. Listening to other students, sharing their own ideas, and responding to others' thoughts and opinions sharpen thinking and deepen understanding.

A Caveat

Despite the importance of employing enhanced learning principles, advisors must remember that they are not teaching skills, approaches, or values; they are teaching students. The characteristics of each student—academic preparation, hopes and dreams, experiences, cognitive development, background, and eagerness to learn, among other descriptors—should affect advisors' decisions about how, what, when, and why they teach as well as the ways and content that students learn. When working with such wonderfully diverse student cohorts, advisors face challenges when meeting students' learning needs and helping them make the most of their time in college. Fortunately, advisors are bright, committed, and hard-working professionals prepared to answer this call.

Implications

While each learning principle individually helps create a culture that fosters student learning, research suggests that when applied in total, the magnitude of their impact on student learning is multiplied (Cruce et al., 2006). The combined principles challenge advisors to treat learning in an intentional and integrated way rather than focus on a particular technique, tool, or axiom.

> There is no universal best teaching [or advising] practice. If, instead, the point of departure is a core set of learning principles, then the selection of teaching [or advising] strategies . . . can be purposeful. The many possibilities then become a rich set of opportunities from which a teacher [or an advisor] constructs an instructional program, rather than a chaos of competing alternatives. (Donovan, Bransford, & Pellegrino, 1999, p. 19)

Such principles generate implications beyond enhancing students' learning; they serve as guidelines for enhancing advisors' learning as well. In the midst of ever-increasing responsibilities and limited time, do advisors reflect on their own learning? Do they set high expectations for themselves as advisors? Do they find ways to increase their motivation? Do they discuss advising with peers and learn from others? Have they set clear, reasonable, and positive goals for themselves?

The words of William James with which this chapter begins remind advisors of the need to adapt the principles to their particular situations and students. Advising is a complex human activity; learning principles that work at one college or with one student may not be as successful for another. Inventive and original minds must apply learning principles. As they discover diverse ways to implement these principles, advisors will focus on learning as the primary goal of academic advising. When advisors ignore the knowledge about new ways humans learn, they risk using advising sessions in inefficient, ineffective, and perhaps even counterproductive ways. Advisors' time and energy are too valuable to spend carelessly; the learning students can gain from advising is too vital to their success for advisors to fail in offering various active-learning opportunities.

Learning principles also offer rich areas for contemplation and discussion among advisors as they work intentionally and coherently to infuse learning into the advising arena. Angelo (1993) called his principles "pump-primers" (p. 4) and listed three goals (adapted here for academic advising). To meet the first goal, advisors think, talk, and read about the connections between known research on learning and advising practice. Whether the learning principles add up to 7, 14, or some other number, their importance lies in way they are applied to practice. Using Angelo's suggestions, advisors could compile a list of learning principles that guide their own advising practices and compare their lists with those of other advisors. What a discussion-rich and stimulating topic for a brown bag lunch, department meeting, or advising workshop!

Adapting Angelo's (1993) second goal, advisors could use the list of their own principles for learning as criteria for assessing their current advising practices. When advisors consider the principles most important to them, they can better evaluate the success of the advising practices that embody them. If they use an advising syllabus, for example, is it focused on learning-centered principles or rules? Adapting Angelo's third goal, advisors could identify the implications of learning principles and develop practical applications for encouraging active advisee learning.

While this chapter has included some ways to apply learning principles, individuals must generate and validate them if they are to move from research to practice, from espoused theories to theories in practice. Advisors need to ask, "What would I do differently if I focused on learning?" and "How can I ensure that every advising experience is learning centered?"

Angelo (1993, p. 4) made the claim that applying his principles will promote higher learning:

> I define higher learning as an active, interactive process that results in meaningful, long-lasting changes in knowledge, understanding, behavior, dispositions, appreciation, belief, and the like. The key terms in this definition are *meaningful, long-lasting*, and *changes*. Higher learning is *meaningful*, if the learner understands and appreciates what is learned; that means that something learned by rote but not understood would not qualify. By *long-lasting*, I mean learning that will endure in accessible memory at least beyond the end of the term. And *changes* here means not simply the addition of knowledge but also the transformation of ways of understanding and organizing the knowledge learned. This is a demanding definition of higher learning . . . but having an explicit definition does help me make difficult decisions about what and how to teach.

Higher learning is surely a lofty goal for academic advising. It is a goal, however, that practitioners can achieve when they fulfill the promise and potential of advising.

References

American Association for Higher Education, American College Personnel Association, & National Association of Student Personnel Administrators. (1998). *Powerful partnerships: A shared responsibility for learning: A joint report*. Retrieved from http://www.myacpa.org/pub/documents/taskforce.pdf

Angelo, T. (1993). "A teacher's dozen": Fourteen general, research-based principles for improving higher learning in our classrooms. *AAHE Bulletin, 45*(8), 3–7, 13.

Baxter Magolda, M., & King, P. (2008). Toward reflective conversations: An advising approach that promotes self-authorship. *Peer Review, 10*(1), 8–11.

Chickering, A. W., & Gamson, A. F. (1987). Seven principles for good practice in undergraduate education. *AAHE Bulletin, 39*(7), 3–7.

Chickering, A. W., & Gamson, A. F. (2000). Development and adaptations of the seven principles for good practice in undergraduate education. In M. Svinicki (Ed.), *Teaching and learning on the edge of the millennium: Building on what we have learned* (pp. 75–81). San Francisco, CA: Jossey-Bass.

Cruce, T., Wolniak, G., Seifert, T., & Pascarella, E. (2006). Impacts of good practices on cognitive development, learning orientations, and graduate degree plans during the first year of college. *Journal of College Student Development, 9*(4), 365–383.

Donovan, M. S., Bransford, J. D., & Pellegrino, J. W. (Eds.). (1999). *How people learn: Bridging research and practice.* Washington, DC: National Academy Press.

James, W. (1899). *Talks to teachers on psychology: And to students on some of life's ideals.* New York, NY: Henry Holt and Company.

Kuh, G. (2008). Advising for student success. In V. N. Gordon, W. R. Habley, & T. J. Grites (Eds.), *Academic advising: A comprehensive handbook* (2nd ed.) (pp. 68–84). San Francisco, CA: Jossey-Bass.

Lowenstein, M. (1999). Academic advising and the logic of the curriculum. *The Mentor: An Academic Advising Journal, 2*(2). Retrieved from http://www.psu.edu/dus/mentor/000414ml.htm

Martin, H. (2007). *Constructing learning objectives for academic advising.* Retrieved from http://www.nacada.ksu.edu/Resources/Clearinghouse/View-Articles/Constructing-student-learning-outcomes.aspx

Nilson, L. (2010). *Teaching at its best: A research-based resource for college instructors* (3rd ed.). San Francisco, CA: Jossey-Bass.

Pizzolato, J. (2006). Complex partnerships: Self-authorship and provocative academic advising practices. *NACADA Journal, 26*(1), 32–45.

Sass, E. (1989). Motivation in the college classroom: What students tell us. *Teaching of Psychology, 16*(2), 86–88.

Svinicki, M. (2004). *Learning and motivation in the postsecondary classroom.* Bolton, MA: Anker.

Task Group on General Education. (1988). *A new vitality in general education: Planning, teaching, and supporting effective liberal learning.* Washington, DC: Association of American Colleges.

Trabant, T. D. (2006). *Advising syllabus 101.* Retrieved from http://www.nacada.ksu.edu/Resources/Clearinghouse/View-Articles/Creating-an-Advising-Syllabus.aspx

Watwood, B., Nugent, J., & Deihl, W. (2009) *Building from content to community: [Re]Thinking the transition to online teaching and learning.* Retrieved from http://www.vcu.edu/cte/pdfs/OnlineTeachingWhitePaper.pdf

4

DEVELOPMENTAL ACADEMIC ADVISING

Thomas J. Grites

Developmental academic advising continues to be the most fundamental and comprehensive approach to advising practice. It enables the academic advisor to take a holistic view of each student to maximize that student's educational experiences in an effort to foster his or her current academic, personal, and career goals toward future success. Properly practiced, it encourages academic advisors to use their own skills to identify each student's skills, abilities, and expectations; to know the resources and opportunities available to the student; and to support maximum growth (development) in academic, personal, and career goals. Simply stated, developmental academic advising allows the practitioner to accept the student on a three-dimensional continuum and facilitate growth in each one through the coordination of a variety of experiences. These efforts result in the most successful and rewarding college experience possible.

Historical Contributions

Although the specific term *developmental academic advising* did not become the widely adopted standard for the advising process until 1984, the concept was certainly on the minds of several authors prior to that time. The term, as it is known today, took shape in a number of significant early publications.

Pre-1982: The Student Development Influence

1970. Melvene D. Hardee provided the earliest comprehensive set of observations about the importance of student–faculty interactions to be facilitated through the academic advising process. She provided these descriptions from the student personnel point of view as reflected from her experience as a student affairs administrator and professor of Higher Education and Specialist in Student Personnel Administration at Florida State University. In her monograph *Faculty Advising in Colleges and Universities* (1970), she addressed the demand of students to become more involved in institutional governance—a primary characteristic that pervaded American higher education in the 1960s. In her preface she asserted,

> In the institution's program of faculty advising, the teacher and the student confront each other and discuss the reciprocal responsibility of institution and student for improving education. This powerful personal medium has not yet been used as it could be.
>
> The faculty adviser and the student analyze and judge educational and vocational goals and opportunities, learning skills and teaching methods, curricular choice and limitations, and student and teacher performance. This authentic partnership can produce the renewal of the educational process and a merited restructuring of the system. (p. v)

Amazingly, even prophetically, her observations and suggestions—even the language she chose—remain essential components of the academic advising framework today, decades after inspiring much of the initial thinking that resulted in the concept of developmental academic advising.

Hardee described both students and faculty members as "ingredient[s] in the learning environment" who were facing opposite cultures. Students (in the 1960s) engaged in new liberal social values and behaviors related to sex, drugs, and rock-and-roll while demanding alternative academic curricula to that historically offered. Although some faculty members advocated for these new student agendas, most expressed loyalty to their traditions of research, publication, consultation, and community involvement. To Hardee, academic advising seemed the likely vehicle for bringing the new student expectations and old faculty practices together.

However, Hardee also realized the stereotypic (yet realistic at the time) advising roles of faculty advisors. She described these roles as the "automat" (strictly provides information), the provider of the "thousand-mile checkup" (verifies degree requirements), the one to "patch-after-crash" (advocates when the student confronts social or academic penalties), or the "malevolent benevolent" (overprotects the student like a mother hen). These descriptions characterize the *prescriptive* advising approach later described by Crookston (1972/1994/2009). She also proposed remedies that included more administrative support, in-service professional training, and rewards as well as selective criteria, a clear articulation of responsibilities, and evaluation for faculty advisors.

She further suggested that the content of the academic advising experience includes the philosophy of contemporary higher education by providing relevance for the general curriculum (against which students were rebelling), the nature of the college experience, the environment of the campus as a community, and the role of the college campus with society at large. This content very much resembled that which Crookston later called "developmental" advising. She even advocated for more computer-assisted advising such as that offered between her home institution and the local community college.

Most importantly, Hardee reiterated differentiation between

> (a) *faculty advising,* an activity dispatched by members of the teaching faculty and directed toward assisting students in their educational, vocational, and personal

concerns at a defined level of competence, and (b) *counseling*, which enlists the efforts of persons who are specifically trained and experienced in the areas of educational, psychological, or clinical counseling procedures. (p. 9)

This statement alone provided a fundamental basis for the developmental academic-advising concept ultimately proffered in 1984.

Specifically, Hardee introduced the following important terms: the *teacher-learner environment* and the *student's educational, vocational, and personal concerns*. A wonderful description of Hardee's life and her influence on higher education is available to American College Personnel Association members in the Spring 2012 issue of *ACPA Developments*.

1972. Two articles from 1972 are frequently cited in the academic advising literature and now receive acknowledgment as classics, as noted in a special edition of the *NACADA Journal* in 1994. Burns Crookston (1972/1994/2009), professor of higher education at the University of Connecticut, and Terry O'Banion (1972/1994/2009), writing from the community college perspective, described two approaches slightly different from that of Hardee, but both advocated for a student development approach in an environment of faculty-based academic advising. Both contributed significantly to the concept of developmental academic advising; Crookston provided a conceptual framework, while O'Banion offered a pragmatic structure.

Crookston provided three important elements to the basic concept of developmental academic advising: a) a *developmental view* that implied growth as an outcome; b) *academic advising as teaching* that articulated the learning process in which students and advisors became engaged; and c) *prescriptive* advising that established a dichotomy and continuum along which the advising process could be viewed. These terms and concepts laid the foundation for developmental academic advising still advocated today.

Perhaps the most important, and often misunderstood, of these concepts is the first. Crookston's developmental approach focused on change—the kind that is inevitable in society, that occurs within students as they progress through the higher education milieu and experience, and that must occur within academic advisors as they attempt to assist students in their progression. It did not mean remediation, however, as it was sometimes interpreted in later years when used to make the remedial efforts in higher education more acceptable. Crookston also emphasized the importance of the *negotiated agreement* between students and advisors in which learning, that is, growth, change, or development, is the outcome.

Crookston emphasized the commonality of functions of advising with those of the classroom teacher, as both were concerned with "facilitating the student's rational processes, environmental and interpersonal interactions, behavioral awareness, and problem-solving, decision-making, and evaluation skills" (1972, p. 12). Engaging students in intellectual discourse about the curriculum and cocurriculum and assisting them in recognizing their strengths, limitations, and potentialities provided a process for (mostly faculty) academic advisors to use their teaching strategies to achieve the same kinds of change sought in the classroom. The National Academic Advising Association (NACADA) advising-as-teaching mantra and concept statement (National Academic Advising Association, 2006) are rooted in this description.

Perhaps the most pragmatic and most frequently applied aspect of Crookston's classic article, the contrast between his developmental view and the prescriptive model, seems the most readily understood. Crookston described the differences along 10 dimensions and concluded that a "key developmental concept is the university viewed as an intellectual learning community within which individuals and social systems interact in and out of the classroom and utilize developmental tasks within and outside the university for personal growth" (1972, pp. 16–17).

In describing "An Academic Advising Model," almost simultaneously with Crookston, O'Banion (1972) asserted that "the purpose of academic advising is to help the student choose a program of study which will serve him in the development of his total potential" (p. 62). His first two steps in a five-step process include aspects of life outside the college experience and into vocational (career) goals that young people need to explore to make the academic advising process meaningful. O'Banion recognized that this exploration process most frequently began at the third step—program choice (the major)—and usually remained the focus of the last two steps: course selection and scheduling. In a way, O'Banion also described Crookston's developmental–prescriptive continuum. By suggesting that his model formed "a logical sequence for individual decision-making and for institutional programming" (1972, p. 66), he provided another perspective that resulted in the developmental advising approach.

O'Banion was also quite explicit in identifying the skills, knowledge, and attitudes necessary to perform each step in his model. Because he wrote from the community college perspective, he viewed counselors as the group who could best perform these tasks, although he recognized that many of them, as trained therapists, would not want to undertake advising. Similarly, he recognized the value of faculty members in the process, but also acknowledged that some would be wed to their disciplines and perhaps unwilling and untrained to perform some of the tasks he described in his model. Thus he advocated a team approach that used the respective skills of counselors and teaching faculty members "so that the student will have the greatest possible opportunity to discover his potential through the college experience" (1972, p. 69).

1982–1984: The Concept Established

In "Developmental Approaches to Academic Advising" (1982), editors Roger Winston, Steven Ender, and Theodore Miller, student development educators and administrators, first articulated the concept and term *developmental academic advising*. In their opening chapter, they reiterated the movement to educate the whole student, but they took "strong exception to the dualistic approach to educating the whole person and believe that the integration of personality and intellectual development is an essential goal of higher education" (p. 4). In other words, the responsibility for this holistic approach could not be separated by academic affairs and student affairs organizational and administrative lines. They further asserted that "such an integrated approach not only is possible, but that its touchstone is the academic advising process" (p. 4).

These influential contributors to the field observed that the growing emphasis to educate the whole student, the more diverse college student population (first generation through returning adults), the increasing institutional focus on student retention, the emerging research on student satisfaction, and students' need for caring and supportive role models on campus combined to provide a strong rationale for developmental academic advising. They also recognized that the perception of academic advising at that time was focused mostly on course selection and recordkeeping, so they offered a more comprehensive operational definition:

> Developmental advising both stimulates and supports students in their quest for an enriched quality of life; it is a systematic process based on a close student-advisor relationship intended to aid students in achieving educational and personal goals through the utilization of the full range of institutional and community resources. (Winston, Ender, & Miller, 1982, p. 8)

While this 1982 seminal work began to illustrate the importance of academic advising as a much more meaningful, complex, and collaborative process to be acknowledged in the higher education community, the need and thirst for more such explication became evident. The results included five national conferences on academic advising; NACADA chartered and growing as a national professional association; a professional, refereed journal exclusively about academic advising; and flourishing regional conferences. Academic advising grew into a prominent fixture on the higher education landscape.

In 1984, Roger Winston, Theodore Miller, Steven Ender, and Thomas Grites edited and published the hallmark text that established the concept of *developmental academic advising* as a favored term among advising professionals and in the advising literature. Contributors to the book provided a comprehensive review of the growing body of literature related to academic advising, a set of theoretical perspectives that created the foundation for the concept, and a wide range of practical examples, guidelines, and applications for its implementation. The editors refined and expanded the first operational definition as follows:

> *Developmental academic advising* is defined as a systematic process based on a close student-advisor relationship intended to aid students in achieving educational, career, and personal goals through the utilization of the full range of institutional and community resources. It both stimulates and supports students in their quest for an enriched quality of life. Developmental advising relationships focus on

identifying and accomplishing life goals, acquiring skills and attitudes that promote intellectual and personal growth, and sharing concerns for each other and for the academic community. Developmental academic advising reflects the institution's mission of total student development and is most likely to be realized when the academic affairs and student affairs divisions collaborate in its implementation. (Winston, Miller, Ender, & Grites, 1984, p. 19)

This definition reflects the previous work described above, but its essence lies in the specification of the interrelated areas that affect students as they live the college experience—*educational, career,* and *personal* goals. Clearly, the educational goals describe anticipated intellectual growth, ultimately important for application in meaningful and productive career settings over one's work life and demonstrable personal qualities and behaviors such as responsibility, self-direction, and shared decision making. The advisor needs to recognize the interrelationships and effects of goals on each other and assist the student in doing the same as they work together to maximize the accomplishment of all of them. Further, the advisor must recognize that the level of goal achievement varies by individual student and over time, often coming to fruition long after the campus experience is over.

To explain the application of developmental process, Winston et al. (1984) devoted several chapters to a wide range of developmental theories. Three such theories relate most directly to the three key areas of developmental academic advising: education, career, and personal goals.

Student Educational Goals. William Perry's (1970) scheme of intellectual and ethical development provided the framework for the cognitive, intellectual aspect of developmental academic advising. Perry's four broad categories provide a hierarchy that academic advisors can use to gauge the level of simple-to-complex thinking at which students function as they confront challenges such as course and major selection, strive to succeed intellectually in a new educational environment, and define their future roles in society.

Perry's hierarchy includes the *dualistic* level of thinking in which the student seeks a perfectly correct solution to challenges, dwells on the informational aspect of advising, and expects others to provide answers to problems. The next level of Perry's hierarchy, *multiplicity,* characterizes student realizations that a number of choices (e.g., majors) might be appropriate, but a particularly right one exists and the advisor will assist in determining the best one for the student.

In Perry's *relativistic* stage, students recognize their interests, skills, abilities, limitations, values, and relationships such that they are better able to make their own decisions about majors, careers, activities, and resources that will enhance their educational lives. Within the relativistic stage, students show various levels of *commitment* to ideas. Specifically, they internalize their values, abilities, and other attributes to make their own decisions about majors, lifestyles, career aspirations, and even about politics, religion, and other dimensions of life after college.

Student Career Goals. The career goal component of developmental academic advising is based on Donald Super's life span and career maturity theory of career development (Super, 1976, 1980, 1983). Super grounded his approach in one's self-concept, which changes (develops) over time as the individual experiences new work and other personal environments. His life-career rainbow (1976) includes four segments (home, community, school, workplace) in which individuals play interrelated and changing roles as they progress (mature or develop) through five stages of their career lives.

In terms of advising, the most significant stage in Super's life-career rainbow is that of exploration, which describes the quest of young people (ages 15–24 years) who experiment with potential or simulated career alternatives through a variety of courses, work experiences, hobbies, internships, and the like to make (tentative) career choices. They mature as they clarify their interests, abilities, and values as they ultimately complete a degree program.

Student Personal Goals. Although Russell Thomas and Arthur Chickering's chapter in the Winston et al. (1984) book did not include a reiteration of the latter's widely cited work from 1969, Chickering's theory of student development provided the impetus for his authorship in the later work. In the chapter entitled Foundations of Academic Advising (pp. 89–118), Thomas and Chickering examined a number of other developmental theorists whose work complemented Chickering's own contributions. However, Chickering's original article provided the fundamental principles to support the personal aspect of the developmental academic-advising concept.

Chickering's (1969) seven vectors of student development for young adults demonstrate the influences that affect the development of college students' identities. He argued that the vectors had both direction and magnitude, and though more prominent at different points in a student's life, they mostly characterize the stage of people between 17 and 25 years of age. The following brief descriptions summarize Chickering's vectors:

- developing competence—maturing in intellectual, physical, social, and interpersonal areas;

- managing emotions—gaining self-control (especially aggression and sexual impulses) as well as balancing positive and negative emotions;

- developing autonomy—separating from parental authority, becoming self-sufficient, yet learning to be interdependent and collaborative;

- establishing identity—(the core of the theory) honing self-awareness and acceptance as well as clarifying values;

- freeing interpersonal relationships—developing mature relationships and tolerating diversity;

- developing purpose—clarifying educational, vocational, and lifestyle plans;

- developing integrity—adopting a personal set of core values and beliefs, behaving according to them, and tolerating ambiguity.

With these theoretical perspectives in place, Winston et al. (1984) selected a variety of authors to elaborate on both the conceptual and practical applications of developmental academic advising. The contributors described the conceptual relationships between and among the planning aspects of academic advising, namely educational, career, and life planning; the various approaches to generic decision making by students; and a strategic intervention model for academic advising.

In their epilogue, the editors suggested that "academic advising can be conceived as the institution's quality control mechanism" (Winston et al., 1984, p. 539) analogous to that in industry; academic advisors "are the most appropriate ones to assume the responsibility of educational quality control and can thereby enhance the quality of the educational experience of *every* student" (p. 541); and academic advisors "are in the best position to assure that rigorous academic standards are maintained and at the same time that students are able to use the resources available on the campus to accomplish their goals and to personalize their educational experience" (p. 541). The developmental academic-advising approach was proffered as the means to achieve such quality.

Developmental Academic Advising Today

With a relatively long history, a few challenges, and a recent flurry of different approaches described and advocated, the concept of developmental academic advising remains the fundamental approach in the field. To recognize this assertion one must fully understand the essence of the approach, which I provide based on my work as one of the original editors of *Developmental Academic Advising* (Winston et al., 1984). A few points of clarification and elaboration of the following principles provide this understanding:

1. *Developmental academic advising is not a theory.* It is based on developmental theories and perspectives, but the practice is an advising strategy, a method, a technique, an approach, a way of doing advising, but with a conceptual framework.

2. *Developmental academic advising is holistic.* The approach includes the education and the development of the whole student (educational, career, and personal) and acknowledges that these dimensions cannot be treated independently because situations influencing one dimension will often affect the other dimensions.

3. *Developmental academic advising is based on student growth (success).* Through the developmental approach, advisors attempt to take students from their point of entry, along each dimension, and facilitate growth. Whether underprepared or in an honors program (educational dimension), undecided or 100% committed to a major (career dimension), first-generation or Ivy League

legacy student (personal dimension), the advisor uses the developmental approach to assist them in moving positively along the continuum of each dimension.

4. *Developmental academic advising is a shared activity.* Both students and advisors contribute to this effort. Students must learn to be honest and forthcoming; advisors need to be tolerant and provocative; both must be trustworthy.

The developmental academic advisor gathers information to recognize the student's position along the educational, career, and personal dimensions, discusses where the student plans to be, and assists the student in getting to that point as readily as possible. One can get to the specifics of the approach by asking some of the following questions: "What can the student (and advisor) learn from the advising experience?" "How and what can the advisor teach the student through the experience?" The developmental academic advisor always sees the advising experience and relationship as an opportunity to teach—something—within the context of one or more of the dimensions. This simple approach should be at the core of every theoretical and practical approach to academic advising.

Developmental Academic Advising Strategies

Following the principles of developmental academic advising described above, what practices characterize the concept? What does a developmental academic advisor look like? What does he or she need to know? How does one plan an advising session? How does she or he respond to varying conditions, situations, students? In the broadest sense and in a word, the way to get answers to all these questions is *assessment*.

Aspects. The academic advisor using the developmental academic-advising approach must first understand the different aspects of the academic advising process—informational, relational, and conceptual. Then, the developmental academic advisor must undertake a self-assessment to distinguish these aspects and recognize how the advising interaction is influencing a student. The developmental academic advisor must be knowledgeable (to accommodate the informational role); compassionate, caring, concerned, and friendly (to exude the relational role); and skilled (to enable the conceptual role). The latter aspect is perhaps the most frequently underused.

Students typically seek advising, at least initially, to seek information, as recognized by O'Banion (1972/1994/2009). Most advisors appear friendly and knowledgeable, especially in an initial advising encounter, and they consistently fulfill their responsibilities in disseminating information and maintaining relational roles. However, with large advising loads, frequent time constraints, and a typical schedule of intermittent advising sessions with the same student, they can easily overlook the conceptual aspect of advising; therefore, they must constantly assess whether they adequately practice all three aspects adequately in their work.

Dimensions. In practicing the developmental approach, the practitioner must also reflect upon (assess) the interrelated educational, career, and personal dimensions of the student's life to help determine the goals, paths, opportunities, obstacles, and resources that will affect the outcomes of the advising process. These dimensions create the basis for the developmental academic advising concept as described by Chickering (1969), Perry (1970), and Super (1980).

Developmental academic advisors do not necessarily administer formal assessment instruments to each advisee, but rather always remain cognizant of the interactions among the three dimensions. In doing so, they gauge the level at which the student can use the information available in the educational dimension (Perry, 1970), determine the extent to which the student has examined the elements of career exploration and choice (Super, 1980), and discern a student's ability to function independently in assuming responsibility, making decisions, and formulating future plans (Chickering, 1969).

In practical terms these dimensions can be illustrated with examples. To measure the advisee's ability to use information, the developmental academic advisor might ask the student about the reasons behind the courses under consideration. Responses could indicate that employment or other personal obligations reflect the student's sense of urgency, or they could illustrate a lack of motivation, irregular sleeping habits, substantial commuting distances, or excessive social activities. Other responses might indicate an unwillingness to take risks with unfamiliar course content, fear of one's skill deficiencies in oral or written communication, or instructor preference based solely upon peer comments. Such responses provide opportunities for the developmental academic advisor to explore the reasons used in the simple function of course planning and to engage the student in discussions that foster educational, career, and personal growth.

Might an alternative course selection result in better opportunities to explore an entirely new area of knowledge, to improve one's research skills, or to experience a new teaching technology? Is the student aware of the ways the course selections might be relevant to a chosen career field or job within or related to it? Has he or she determined the magnitude of the balance required to work a certain number of hours, engage in a modicum of social life, meet personal obligations, and fulfill the expectations and demands of each course? The developmental academic advisor might ask these types of questions to initiate student exploration that does not encourage the creation of a schedule based on the need to fit five courses, back-to-back, on Tuesday and Thursday.

Similarly, the advisor may use the inquiry on course selection to determine the student's expectations for an anticipated career, whether other available course options might enhance the opportunity to enter that career field, and plan for alternative careers if needed. Topics of discussion might include the market competitiveness in the field, the need for postgraduate licensure or an advanced degree, the plan for an internship, or exploration of other opportunities that might enhance the student's success in achieving the expressed career aspirations. Such enhancements as a minor, an internship, international study, volunteer opportunities, independent study, or research projects might help students create a comprehensive plan for the future.

Process. How does the developmental academic advisor steer the conversation in ways that enable an adequate assessment of student situations? The simple answer? Ask questions. The most effective developmental academic advisor probably asks many more questions than gives answers, even while practicing the informational aspect of the job. For example, the student might ask a question that does not relate to the issue she or he is trying to clarify. Sensing the confusion, the advisor might ask a counterquestion to shed light on the cause of the student's concern. More importantly, the queries can help the advisor acquire more information, determine the rationale for the student's question, or stimulate more or new student thinking about the topic.

For example, perhaps one of the most difficult and frequent questions asked of advisors is "Why do I have to take ____? I'm a ____major." The developmental academic advisor might provide the standard "well-rounded person" explanation, but most students see such a response as trite. To maximize the educational component of the developmental academic advising approach, the practitioner might prepare specific responses for different majors, but should also be able to use the case at hand to show direct relevance of requirements to the student's major and career intentions, to describe additional value about the course(s) under discussion, and identify alternatives to the requirement. Most important, the student needs to come away with a better understanding of the curriculum and its rationale; that is the goal of the developmental academic advisor in this situation.

The developmental academic advisor should always be prepared to show the relevance of the curriculum when answering student questions:

> A good [enter any job title] will likely be required to write reports, proposals, or at least professional correspondence; prepare presentations and deliver them to diverse audiences; work in a team environment; do research to obtain the most current and valid information about a topic; interpret quantitative data; and participate in online and self-paced learning environments.

The developmental academic advisor must find such relevance for every course in the student's curriculum, especially the elective portion.

The importance of this relevance and need for scrutiny of course selections rests with the realization that the baccalaureate degree is earned by students who have sampled a very minute portion of the total array of courses offered by an institution. To illustrate this little-known fact, one can simply calculate the percentage of courses needed to earn a degree as that part of the total number of courses offered by the institution, for example, 40 courses to earn the degree out of hundreds (even thousands) available at the institution. The percentage will range from well below 1% to 10% at best. This means that for every course selected, dozens to hundreds of courses will never be taken by the undergraduate. Therefore, every course selected is enormously important and valuable for both educational growth and career enhancement.

Another common question asked of advisors illustrates another opportunity to enhance student development: "What can I do with a major in ____?" The developmental academic advisor recognizes that a response of "What interests you?" will not yield as useful information as "What do you like to study, read about, hear lectures about, write about, talk about, think about?" The developmental academic advisor realizes that interest does not necessarily translate to a desire to study the subject as a major. The developmental academic advisor understands that the student is operating at Perry's (1970) dualistic or multiplistic stage of intellectual development and views each major as leading to a job directly related to that field.

However, one's interest in the popular CSI television series does not mean that he or she will enjoy studying chemistry, biology, and psychology. One "interested in computers" may not be at all interested in undertaking the demands of learning calculus, various programming languages, and symbolic logic to complete a computer science major. Conversely, if students enjoy the material they study most in their major, then the quest for learning is much more exciting, motivational, and meaningful.

Summary

The developmental academic advisor assists students in constructing degree plans and curricular enhancements that foster the abilities applicable to a variety of fields and jobs such that the student utilizes the skills developed in college. When the strategy works, the advising outcome is, as illustrated in the examples, a planned, strategic, intentional use of the curriculum and cocurriculum to maximize the opportunities and value of the undergraduate experience.

This review, analysis, and application of the developmental academic advising approach illustrates the essence of advisor roles; that is, it shows that advisors assist students in achieving their educational, career, and personal goals in an integrated or holistic way. The approach was certainly practiced by some academic advisors before the 1970s and 1980s, but until those watershed decades, the concept and approach had not been identified, named, and recognized as the fundamental approach to the academic advising practice of today.

The developmental academic-advising approach established the principles upon which other approaches have evolved as they, too, are used to support students in their quest for success in the higher education learning environment. As long as academic advisors continue to strive for such student success, the developmental academic-advising approach will continue to guide them in their practice.

Developmental Advising Scenarios

As the process continues with an individual advisee, a reassessment occurs for each session—probably not with a complete overt review of each aspect or dimension—but as the advisor's purposeful reflection about the student's previous learning. Scenarios I and II illustrate the developmental academic-advising approach.

Scenario I

A first-generation college sophomore, Riley, says to an advisor, Skylar, "I'm having trouble in two of my classes. I don't understand what the professor is talking about in one of them, but it's a required course in my major. The other is only a gen ed course, but I keep getting low grades on the writing assignments. I was always good in writing in high school. If I do poorly, this will lower my GPA, and I just got off academic probation last term. I want to stay in my major, but I don't know if I can pass this one course and that would really disappoint my family. What do you suggest I do?"

o o o

Skylar recognizes that Riley has introduced elements of all three dimensions of concern—informational, relational, and conceptual—best addressed by developmental advising. The educational dimension seems to be the most critical because Riley expresses academic difficulty overall (just off probation) and explains different kinds of problems (comprehension and writing) in two current courses. Skylar might query Riley about the courses in which understanding is a problem: Were prerequisites necessary? Is the course required this term? Is the instructor new to the institution? Is extra help available, such as through the Writing Center? Is Riley mindful of the course withdrawal policy and deadline? Also, Skylar wants to know the reasons that Riley was placed on academic probation and Riley's choice of major. Skylar asks whether Riley is working, possesses study habits and skills compatible with the academic expectations of the courses, and lives on or off campus. Skylar should remind Riley that gen ed courses are no less valuable than those in the major and point out that, therefore, they should not be less demanding than any other course in the curriculum.

Next, Skylar may want to broach a discussion of careers. If the remaining course work in the current major will present future academic issues, what alternative majors might be available for Riley to pursue in route to a specific career?

Finally, Riley's concern about a family reaction raises the personal dimension. Does Riley face financial pressure or student debt that concerns the parents? As a first-generation student, Riley's pride may be at stake.

After gathering all this information, Skylar might strategically offer alternatives that Riley could consider. Unless an impending deadline forces an immediate decision, Skylar might suggest that Riley reflect on some of their discussions and return for an appointment to reassess the status of each dimension.

Scenario II

A second-year student, Ali, comes to Drew to discuss withdrawing from school: "I'm really not doing well this term. It's not the courses or the professors—I just don't feel like I fit in. A few of my friends left after last year, and I haven't really found any new ones. My new roommates are not really like me, so they kind of stick together by themselves. I'm not in any clubs or anything like that, although I do work off campus. Also, I feel my parents and I have spent lots of money, but I'm not sure it's worth spending more if I'm not that interested. Do you have any suggestions? What do you think I should do?"

o o o

Ali is experiencing problems in the academic dimension that are precipitated from the personal one. Drew must carefully ascertain why Ali does not "fit in" and is not involved in any groups that might provide the support needed to succeed at the institution. Ali also may face financial challenges, so determining the true cause of dissatisfaction may be difficult. Strategic questions are required, such as "What were your friends like who left after last year?" "Do you need to talk with someone in the Financial Aid office to see what options you have?" "Are you considering transferring or simply leaving school altogether?" "Are you able to recover from not doing well this term if other factors are improved?" Because the academic dimension does not seem to be the cause of Ali's dissatisfaction, Drew should also determine Ali's particular career plans, if any, as clues that suggest that a different educational environment altogether may benefit Ali. After discussing careers, Drew and Ali can plan according to life goals.

Also, once a plan is established, Drew can determine the resources available on campus to assist Ali, such as student groups, faculty mentors with whom Ali might find a sense of connectedness and belonging, residence hall personnel who could help Ali acquire single-room housing or move in with different roommates, if possible, or a transfer advisor who can facilitate a move to a more appropriate institution.

Drew also must consider whether Ali is trying to hide or mask an academic problem that is at the heart of the problem. In fact, Ali may be experiencing issues with which Drew is not well versed, and Drew must be ready to contact the necessary referral sources on Ali's behalf.

In both cases, the practitioners used a developmental advising approach. The advisors recognized the interrelationship of the educational, career, and personal dimensions, acknowledged that the students are functioning at different places on the continuum of each dimension, and made them more aware of their status on each (their position on the continuum). Both Skylar and Drew asked strategic questions that enabled Riley and Ali to become partners in the resolution of their own problems.

Of course not all students will heed the advice given, but the developmental academic advisor can feel assured that the best effort has been afforded all students to foster growth (development) in their educational, career, and personal lives. In doing so, the developmental academic advisor has demonstrated commitment to NACADA's professional expectations and standards—the Concept of Academic Advising (2006) and the Core Values of Academic Advising (2005)—as well as integration of the teaching and learning institutional mission by engaging students in a review and assessment of their individual characteristics, values, and motivations as means of promoting success. Similarly, the advisor has shown responsibility for all entities involved in the advising process: the student, the institution and its overall community, and the profession. They have completed a job well done.

References

Chickering, A. W. (1969). *Education and identity*. San Francisco, CA: Jossey-Bass.

Crookston, B. B. (2009). A developmental view of academic advising as teaching. *NACADA Journal, 29*(1), 78–82. (Reprinted from *Journal of College Student Personnel, 13*, 1972, pp. 12–17; *NACADA Journal*, 14[2], 1994, pp. 5–9)

Hardee, M. D. (1970). Faculty advising in colleges and universities. In the *American College Personnel Association student personnel series, No. 9*. Washington, DC: American Personnel and Guidance Association.

National Academic Advising Association. (2005). *NACADA statement of core values of academic advising*. Retrieved from http://www.nacada.ksu.edu/Resources/ Clearinghouse/View-Articles/Core-values-of-academic-advising.aspx

National Academic Advising Association. (2006). *NACADA concept of academic advising*. Retrieved from http://www.nacada.ksu.edu/Resources/Clearinghouse/View-Articles/ Concept-of-Academic-Advising-a598.aspx

O'Banion, T. (2009). 1994 (1972): An academic advising model. *NACADA Journal, 29*(1), 83–89. (Reprinted from *Junior College Journal, 42*, 1972, pp. 62, 63, 66–69; *NACADA Journal*, 1994, 14[2], pp. 10–16)

Perry, W., Jr. (1970). *Intellectual and ethical development in the college years*. New York, NY: Holt, Rinehart, and Winston.

Super, D. E. (1976). *Career education and the meanings of work*. Washington, DC: U.S. Government Printing Office.

Super, D. E. (1980). A life-span, life-space approach to career development. *Journal of Vocational Behavior, 16*, 282–298.

Super, D. E. (1983). Assessment in career guidance: Toward truly developmental counseling. *Personnel and Guidance Journal, 62*, 555–562.

Winston, R. B., Jr., Ender, S. C., & Miller, T. K. (Eds.). (1982). Developmental approaches to academic advising. *New Directions for Student Services, 17*, 3–18. doi: 10.1002/ ss.3711982170

Winston, R. B., Jr., Miller, T. K., Ender, S. C., & Grites, T. J. (Eds.). (1984). *Developmental academic advising*. San Francisco, CA: Jossey-Bass.

VOICES FROM THE FIELD

SO, I'VE BEEN THINKING . . . O'BANION IN REVERSE

Patrick Cate

"So I have been thinking. . . ." Whenever I start a morning meeting with my staff and say those words, I can almost feel their worry. However, undeterred, I want to share a recent blog I created about thoughts that may interest the larger advising community, including my staff.

Lately, I have been thinking that I have missed something that has been staring me in the face. I use an advising method called the "targeted advising model" with undeclared students and have experienced wonderful successes with it—both in terms of the quantitative results and positive student stories; it is based on a metaconceptual framework that includes O'Banion's (1972/1994/2009) model of developmental advising (see King, 2005, for a summary of developmental advising). I have been presenting this model at a number of conferences and at individual institutions to help improve teaching and learning for undeclared students outside my institution.

But I wonder: What if O'Banion had it backwards: the right steps, but backwards?

Much discussion centers on O'Banion's theory and the recent modifications to it, but in most—if not all—of the iterations, O'Banion's directional concept stays intact. In general, proponents suggest that students follow O'Banion's stages in order, and while some stages overlap or a student may to skip a step, the advisor and advisee will start the session talking about life goals and end with selecting courses. Time and time again, when I present this model, advisors tell me that this theory is difficult to apply in practice. Students get stuck and frustrated at Step 1, lose interest in the process, and seek the immediate answer for "What class do I take?"

In the targeted advising model, motivational interviewing (MI) is important for success, and one of the key concepts of MI is rolling with resistance. When talking with a student, advisors do not challenge students to overcome perceived barriers but encourage them to explore obstacles. In the common case of math phobia, for example, instead of saying, "Oh, you will be fine; I have faith in you," the advisor using MI would ask, "What tells you that you may not be able to do this course?" The student may give good reasons for knowing they will struggle in math but the issue is explored, well thought out, and advising can be applied more appropriately. (Honestly, in this case, oftentimes a student is not facing a competency issue, but fears the unknown. I find this particularly true with students who only need the foundational math required of all students.)

Maybe advisors need to roll with student resistance to developing life goals. What if advisors started where students are on the career development pathway? To answer the question, for the last year or so, I have been moving advising in the exact opposite direction that O'Banion recommends. Some students struggle with career exploration discourse. They run into high barriers and seemingly lack the in-depth vision to find the personally important aspects of career choices. With these students, I look at the courses that offer subject matter that they want to learn; they can relate easier to this course of action.

Once we have looked at the interesting course work, the advisee and I can begin to see commonalities in his or her interests. Patterns emerge such as a desire to learn about how groups of people interact, the genetic basis of cancer, or the education of young people. Those choices can be translated into majors and minors. Once we get the major in place, we talk about the way people have used those degrees (see Carnevale, Strohl, & Melton, 2009) and the possibilities that may exist for the particular student. We then can talk about the lifestyle that comes with this choice and how it fits the advisee's perception of the future.

Students who have experienced this process with me tell me it was very empowering. In terms of outcome measures, my college has seen people improve their GPAs, stay in their chosen majors, and take opportunities that they may not have otherwise, such as study abroad or internships. The numbers are few at this point, but at the very least, these students are engaged in their learning.

This strategy, of course, does not affect all students. Many students come into the office with a rough idea (at least) of their life and career goals, and those students generally like working through the O'Banion model step-by-step in the intended direction and achieve a passion for their learning that they may not have had before. However, I will say that I see these students much less frequently than those who perform better in the reverse O'Banion model.

The concept of using O'Banion backwards relies on the existence of synergy in career exploration not inattention or blindness to career and educational opportunity. That is, unless tuned into it, individuals will miss the overtly obvious. A great example of this is when purchasing a new car: While on the lot, one may think, "Wow, I don't think I have seen very many of these, and in this color!" While driving home and the weeks that follow, the new car owner soon realizes that a lot more of those cars are on the road than she or he originally thought. The cars were on the highway the entire time, but the person just did not notice them.

O'Banion's model offers one concept that seems to be true whether addressed backward or forward. The order is logical and important. Skipping steps in either direction causes a disconnect in thinking for the student. In fact, I often find myself keeping the student on track. I have observed that students who jump to a step for which they may not be ready get the "Yeah, but . . ." disease: "I would like to take

Early American History . . ., yeah but I can't because I don't know what a history degree does for a job." The positions of the steps seem to be very important.

So I have been thinking that O'Banion's model might work as well or better in reverse. What do you think?

References

Carnevale, A. P., Strohl, J., & Melton, M. (2009). *What's it worth? The economic value of college majors*. Retrieved from http://cew.georgetown.edu/whatsitworth/

King, M. C. (2005). *Developmental academic advising*. Retrieved from http://www.nacada.ksu.edu/Resources/Clearinghouse/View-Articles/Developmental-Academic-Advising.aspx

O'Banion, T. (2009). 1994 (1972): An academic advising model. *NACADA Journal*, *29*(1), 83–89. (Reprinted from *Junior College Journal*, 42, 1972, pp. 62, 63, 66–69; *NACADA Journal*, 1994, 14[2], pp. 10–16)

A NEW LIGHT: VIEWING THE PRACTICE OF ACADEMIC ADVISING FROM DIFFERENT PERSPECTIVES

As the advising field matured, scholar-practitioners began looking at advising practice in new ways. Based upon the social sciences that have traditionally informed the field, the chapters included in part two illustrate ways to approach advising from different perspectives. When advisors change their viewpoint, they challenge themselves and students to grow and learn in new and different ways.

5

MOTIVATIONAL INTERVIEWING

HELPING ADVISORS INITIATE CHANGE IN STUDENT BEHAVIORS

Judy Hughey and Robert Pettay

Academic advisors work with students in the decision-making process regarding majors, courses, and careers as well as personal issues about behaviors that influence students' ability to achieve success in college. Decisions related to study habits, health behaviors (including alcohol and drug use), and relationships affect the likelihood of success or failure in the students' academic career. Motivational interviewing (MI) is an appropriate approach for addressing these decisions and other student issues. The advisor can utilize MI to assist students in developing motivation to make a choice or to change a behavior. Required for student development, change may result naturally as a consequence of growth and time, influenced by brief interventions with a professional or other person or facilitated by the faith and hope of the individual (Miller & Rollnick, 2002).

MI is a collaborative, person-centered partnership of guidance to elicit and strengthen motivation for change based on the four general principles of a) expressing empathy, b) developing discrepancy, c) rolling with resistance, and d) supporting self-efficacy (Martino & Hopfer, 2009). Motivation is fundamental to change and requires readiness, willingness, and belief in the ability to change. Intrinsic motivation for change arises in an accepting, empathetic, and empowering interaction that provides a safe zone for the individual to take risks and explore values and needs (Miller & Rollnick, 2002). This safe zone for a student often forms in the presence of an academic advisor through discussions of a possible change and an analysis of the student's level of motivation to adjust. Therefore, advisors need not ask, "Why isn't this student motivated more?" but instead question, "For what is the student motivated?" Advisors need to help students determine their willingness and confidence levels to improve their academic experience. Using MI, advisors assist students in identifying issues affecting their academic progress or personal growth and provide support to overcome ambivalence about change.

Based on collaboration, evocation, and autonomy (Miller & Rollnick, 2010a), MI allows the advisor and student to work in partnership as the student articulates aspirations and reaches goals. As an autonomous agent, the student has the right and capacity for self-direction and the ability to make an informed choice. We present MI as an appropriate approach for academic advisors to use to help students with a variety issues, including choosing or changing a major, a career, or academic or personal behavior. We recommend that academic advisors implement MI strategies with students needing to make behavioral changes for the purpose of personal or academic success. The MI approach shares common principles and can be implemented collaboratively with other approaches including appreciative advising (Bloom, Hutson, & He, 2008).

The origins of MI lie in Carl Rogers's person-centered psychotherapy (Markland, Ryan, Tobin, & Rollnick, 2005) with constructs of Rogers's humanistic theory consistent with the MI characteristics of empathy, warmth, genuineness, and immediacy. Student centered and intrinsically oriented, Rogers's theory requires "necessary and sufficient interpersonal conditions for fostering change" (Miller & Rose, 2009, p. 2). MI places the responsibility for motivating students to change with the advisor and the impetus to make and sustain the change with the advisee. MI is built on the Rogerian humanistic principles of unconditional positive regard, respect for the advisee, and support of self-esteem as the advisee examines the need for change and the motivation to engage in the change process.

Four Processes in the Use of the Motivational Interview

Miller and Rollnick (2010b) identified four MI processes: engaging, guiding, evoking, and planning. Engaging, the relational foundation, involves listening to the student's dilemma to determine if MI is the appropriate approach. Guiding involves the directional focus of MI including identifying a change goal, setting the agenda, and if necessary, giving information and advice—but only with student permission and in a way that honors the student's autonomy. When providing suggestions, advisors should try to offer several options to the student. Evoking, the crux to MI, requires the advisor to recognize and elicit change talk, a critical component to which advisors must be attuned, from the student (Miller & Rollnick, 2010b). Planning involves negotiating change goals and plans, strengthening commitment, and implementing and adjusting behavior change. The specific change plan is negotiated when the student is ready and involves setting goals, considering change options, arriving at a plan, and eliciting commitment.

Motivational Interview Outcomes

Other than validating the research base and effectiveness of MI, the outcomes of research often seem abstract to practitioners. However, they provide data related to implementation. Amrhein, Miller, Yahne, Palmer, and Fulcher (2003) provided skill-based techniques that advisors can use when implementing MI with advisees. Their data indicate the need to measure the strength (not frequency) of the advisee's change talk. They discussed the need to evaluate the pattern of the language including the degree of commitment the student expresses throughout the session and the words used to close the session. An increase in commitment language articulating the need, want, ability, and dedication to change positively predicts sustained change.

Moyers, Miller, and Hendrickson (2005) found that, when implemented in a student-centered setting and by a facilitator using well-developed interpersonal relations skills, MI correlates with behavior change. Important interpersonal relations skills used in MI include advanced reflection, strength finding, identification of discrepancies, appropriate confrontation, and motivation for the change process. The advisor's ability to engage the advisee empathically in a supportive environment and the advisee's verbalization intentions for positive change, in the context of an action plan for implementing change, significantly increase the probability for behavior change (Gollwitzer, 1999).

General Principles of the Motivational Interview

Four general principles underlie MI: expressing empathy, developing discrepancy, rolling with resistance, and supporting self-efficacy (Martino & Hopfer, 2009). The advisor employs empathetic listening, characterized by an attitude of acceptance, throughout the MI process (Martino & Hopfer, 2009). The critical components of empathetic listening, as well as acceptance of the individual, relate to rolling with resistance. Empathetic advisors see the student's behaviors and perspectives as understandable, comprehensible, and valid; they do not consider the student's ambivalence to change as abnormal.

Mottarella, Fritzsche, and Cerabino (2004) stated, "An advisor needs to give specific care to establish a relationship with the advisee and convey warmth and support in the relationship" (p. 57). Mahoney (2009) suggested that rapport skills of appreciating the individual, presence, and compassion are integral to developing a strong, facilitative relationship with the student.

The acceptance of the student's unique experiences will nurture the relationship; however, the advisor uses MI to encourage a change of behavior by helping the student resolve ambivalence about change. By showing discrepancies between the student's current state and his or her desired state, the advisor helps an advisee see the importance of change; however, the advisor needs to allow the student to voice concerns and must give reasons for change, not pressure or coerce it. Through open-ended questions, the advisor helps a student clarify goals and values that conflict with current behavior. In addition, the advisor can present possible consequences of continuing the behavior.

Rolling with resistance refers to the way an advisor responds to students reluctant to change. First, the advisor should not argue with the advisee regarding the change, because by defending the status quo, the student can be further entrenched into a behavior that even the student wants to change. The advisor can provide information and offer different perspectives on a situation, but the final decision on goals and change is under the ownership of the student.

A student may desire and believe in the importance of a change but lack confidence in the ability to make the transition. Bandura (1994) described self-efficacy as an individual's belief about her or his capability to perform in ways that influence life events; it is a key component of motivation to change. The advisor can support self-efficacy through open questions related to belief in ability to change and past successful experiences; for example, "What helped you earn a 3.0 GPA last semester?"

Motivational Interview Strategies

Miller and Rollnick (2010b) provided several strategies to build momentum to change. The student needs to establish the importance of change and determine his or her level of confidence to create desired change as measured by a confidence ruler scaled from 0 to 10. To use the confidence ruler, an advisor might ask a student on academic probation the following question: "On a scale of 0 to 10, with *0* being not important at all and *10* being extremely important, how important is it for you to get off of academic probation?" The following question relates to the confidence in the student's ability to work toward academic success: "On the scale of 0 to 10, with *0* being not confident to *10* being extremely confident, how certain are you that, if you decided to get off of academic probation, you could do it?"

Asking Open Questions, Affirming, Reflecting, and Summarizing

The importance and confidence rulers allow the advisor to establish where the student currently stands regarding the behavior or issue being discussed. The advisor can then utilize different strategies, such as those offered by Miller and Rollnick (2010b), to implement MI for the desired change. For example, a technique of asking open questions, affirming, reflecting, and summarizing (OARS) supports the student in the resolution of the ambivalence he or she currently holds toward the desired change.

By asking open questions, advisors encourage students to talk and help establish accepting and trusting relationships. By avoiding the question-answer trap, in which the advisor asks questions that restrict the student to a *yes* or *no* response, advisors can better understand the issue and also gauge a student's level of determination to change. Miller and Rollnick (2010b) provided the following example of an open question: "Hello. Are there things that you would like to discuss with me today?"

By providing affirmation, advisors offer support to, build rapport with, and encourage self-efficacy in the student. Direct affirmations demonstrate positive regard and can make the student feel valued as well as boost the positive aspects of the relationship: "You seem committed to making things better and it has been enjoyable visiting with you today."

Reflective listening is one of the most important skills required for MI (Miller & Rollnick, 2010a) because, to pursue change talk and goals, the student must be allowed to examine aloud the current situation and determine a reasonable strategy for change. Failure to listen reflectively may result in negative expressions, such as ordering, warning, giving advice, persuading with logic, and disagreeing (Gordon, 1970), which distract the student from the desired focus.

Summarization, the final component of OARS, allows the advisor to connect ideas presented and reinforce concepts discussed in the session such that the student's change talk yields a clearer understanding of the situation. Summarizing also demonstrates to the student that the advisor has been actively listening and is engaged in the process. The advisor can use summaries to make transitions from one focus area to another, which can serve as a synopsis for the session (Miller & Rollnick, 2002). The collaborative tone of the summary allows the student to add or delete information and can be utilized at the beginning of the next meeting to build on progress.

Evoking Change Talk

Miller and Rollnick (2010b) provided four different categories of change-talk questions including those that elicit recognition of the disadvantages of the status quo and the advantages of change as well as inspire optimism for and intention to change. Explaining disadvantages of the status quo, the advisor may ask the following questions:

○ What do you think will happen if you do not decide on a career?

○ What worries you about being on academic probation?

○ If you do not change, what do you think will eventually happen to you?

To show advantages of change, the advisor might adopt the following courses of inquiry:

○ What would be the benefits of choosing a major?

○ If you were off academic probation, how would your life be different?

○ What would be the positive outcomes of deciding on a career?

To elicit optimism about change, the advisor may prompt the advisee with the following queries:

○ What makes you believe this change is possible?

○ Tell me about a situation in which you have overcome similar challenges successfully?

○ Who is available to provide you support in making this change?

Advisors can gauge the intention to change by asking the following:

○ How are you feeling about your academic situation at this time?

○ What changes are you willing to try?

○ What do you intend to do now?

Through active listening and open questions, the advisor has the opportunity to determine the student's commitment and confidence to change. Preparatory change talk involves the recognition of the issue and focuses on DARN (Miller and Rollnick, 2010b):

- D—Desire to change: "How much does this behavior concern you?"
- A—Ability to change: "How could you make this change?"
- R—Reason to change: "What is a good reason for making this change?"
- N—Need to change: "How important is it to you to make this change?"

The student's expression of a desire to change current behaviors points the advisor to the issues the student is experiencing. In some cases, such as when a student faces academic probation, one direction for change is clearly preferable. However, for other concerns, such as career choice, the advisor needs to help the advisee resolve ambivalence and move forward with life. In any case, because change requires action, the advisor needs to inspire the student to move from discussion to action and can use either a directive or nondirective MI approach, depending on the situation.

Implementing change talk involves eliciting a commitment to change, a call to action, articulation of steps in the change process, and elaboration of goals that motivate the student to continue exploration in a single direction. By responding with interest and encouragement, the advisor supports the student's pursuit of a line of thought; she or he can prompt the advisee with directed questions such as, "In what ways will the change affect your situation?" or "What other concerns do you have about making this change?"

Reflecting change talk can also encourage exploration of circumstantial content. By summarizing change talk, advisors collect the different change statements made by the student to enhance motivation. By selectively referring to resistance in the past tense and change talk in the present tense, the advisor helps push the student toward the desired outcome.

In a nondirective situation, the advisor can provide support as the student attempts to resolve ambivalence and make a decision about change itself. In this situation the advisor can help the student select goals by exploring both sides of an issue and clarify values by helping the student identify areas he or she deems most important.

Tackling Resistance

Resistance early in the process is often related to withdrawing and decreased likelihood of behavior change (Martino & Hopfer, 2009). Resistance can be manifested through arguing, challenging, discounting, expressing hostility, interrupting, and ignoring (Miller & Rollnick, 2010b).

Strategies for responding to resistance include, among others, reflective listening statements. Miller and Rollnick (2002) discussed simple, amplified, and double-sided reflections as well as the processes of shifting focus, reframing, agreeing with a twist, emphasizing personal choice and control, and coming alongside as possible methods to deal with resistance.

Through simple reflection, advisors respond to resistance with nonresistance. Acknowledgment of the student's feelings can remove defensiveness and allow the student to further explore emotions related to the issue. In this scenario, a student may say, "I'm trying; I just wish the teacher would leave me alone," to which the advisor replies, "You are working at doing better."

In an amplified reflection, the advisor responds to resistance in an exaggerated form. While done with empathy, it makes students back off and explore their ambivalence from a different perspective. For example, a student may express frustration in the following way: "I can't give up going out at night. What would my friends think?" The advisor, using an exaggerated response may challenge the advisee: "You couldn't handle how your friends would react."

A double-sided reflection captures both sides of the ambivalence from the student's perspective. A student says, "I know that you are trying to help me, I am just not going to change." The advisor responds, "On one hand, you feel that there are some issues to address that I am trying to help you with, and on the other hand, my suggestions are not acceptable."

To shift attention away from a seemingly big barrier to change, the advisor, in general, defuses the initial concern of the student to change, then directs the conversation toward a more workable solution. Through reframing, the advisor reinterprets the student's concerns to provide a new meaning or interpretation of the situation (Miller & Rollnick, 2002). To agree with a twist, an advisor offers initial agreement as well as a slight change of direction or a reflection followed by a reframe. In all strategies, by emphasizing personal choice and control, the advisor acknowledges to the student that the final decision rests upon her or him.

Creating Readiness

MI involves building intrinsic motivation and a commitment to change. Therefore, advisors need to look for signs of readiness for change, including decreased resistance or discussion about the problem, resolve, change talk, and questions about change as well as indications of envisioning and experimenting. To start the process with change talk, an advisor can use the following question as offered by Miller and Rollnick (2010b): "What changes, if any, are you thinking about making to help your academic situation?"

As the process continues, the expertise of the advisor becomes more applicable because the student may be ready for information, including that regarding resources. In the interaction, the advisor should only seek to enhance the motivation of the student to change by encouraging setting goals, considering change options, arriving at a strategy, and eliciting commitment (Miller & Rollnick, 2010b). An advisor might ask the following question to start a discussion on goals: "How would you like things to be different?"

To keep the student thinking about solutions, the advisor can introduce brainstorming, an effective approach when considering change options and implementation plans. Brainstorming used to initiate the planning process often begins when an advisor utilizes an open question such as, "What do you think is the first step?"

Planning

The relational factors of safety and acceptance created in the advising environment begin to promote positive change (Miller, 1983). By providing validation and optimism, the advisor thus increases motivation to make the needed changes. The following question creates student optimism: "What makes you think you will be successful in making this change?"

In the safe environment they have created, advisors must appropriately confront advisees about the consequences of leaving issues unaddressed. Advisors may be hesitant to challenge students for fear of the implications if the dialogue does not go as planned. However, advisors must call attention to discrepancies and inconsistencies between words and behaviors, or behaviors, values, and goals demonstrated by the advisee. Advisors should confront in a concise, strong, and nonjudgmental tone of voice about the words and behaviors of the advisee:

> You say your academics are a priority for you. However, we are 6 weeks into the semester and I have reports from your instructors stating that you have missed at least one class every week and failed to complete all of the assignments. The good news is we are only 6 weeks into the semester. What ideas do you have for addressing these issues?

While presenting discrepancies, information, and concern, advisors must recognize that the choice of the advisee should never be questioned. Once the student has determined what to change, the advisor takes the next steps: eliciting commitment, initiating the plan, and encouraging the student to implement the change. At the conclusion of the advising session, the advisor can reiterate the main points discussed, reminding students of the given strength value for the change issue, issuing a brief description of the advisor's beliefs about the advisee's strongest strength, and offering affirming words that encourage the advisee to higher levels of self-efficacy.

Prochaska and DiClemente Stages of Change

The transtheoretical model (TTM), introduced by Prochaska and DiClemente (1984), provides a format for demonstrating individual progression, and sometimes regression, on a continuum of behavioral change along five stages. While Miller and Roll-nick (2009) stated that MI is not based on it, the TTM evolved in the same time frame, and characteristics of the models show a logical connection. The TTM provides a conceptualization of the manner and reasons change occurs over time through six stages: precontemplation, contemplation, preparation, action, maintenance, and termination (Prochaska & Velicer, 1997).

During the precontemplation stage, people are not intending to take action in the foreseeable future (usually measured as 6 months). Students in the precontemplation stage may be unaware of the ways their current behaviors or decisions exert negative effects on their academic or personal development, or they may have attempted change in the past without success. In the contemplation stage, an individual intends to change in the next 6 months. A student in the contemplation stage may be aware of the pros of change, but also is cognizant of the cons associated with it. Preparation involves the intent to take action in the immediate future, typically within the next month. Students in the preparation stage develop a plan of action to elicit change. In the action stage, the student has made changes in behavior within the past 6 months. Maintenance involves working to prevent relapse and is estimated to last from 6 months to 5 years (Prochaska & Velicer, 1997). An advisor who knows the student's stage of change can determine appropriate MI strategies (see Table 5.1).

Table 5.1. Stages of change and motivational interview strategies

Stage of Change	Motivational Interview Strategies
Precontemplation The student is unwilling, unable, or uncommitted to change.	○ Establish rapport ○ Elicit student's perception of problem ○ Explore pros and cons of behavior ○ Express concern, keeping door open
Contemplation The student acknowledges concerns and considers change.	○ Discuss ambivalence ○ Examine student's values in relationship to change ○ Emphasize student's free choice
Preparation The student is committed to making change in the near future.	○ Clarify goals and strategies for change ○ Offer menu of options for change ○ Enlist social support
Action The student is actively taking steps to change, but is not at the maintenance level.	○ Encourage student to maintain behavior ○ Help identify high-risk situations ○ Assist in finding support for change

Source: Center for Substance Abuse Treatment (1999).

Best Practices

Academic advisors must be knowledgeable and skilled in the theoretical frameworks and best practices with impact on the academic and career needs of their students. Academic advisors select student development theories, strategies, and interventions to implement in their advising programs based on a number of factors: advisor's strengths, skills, and knowledge base in pedagogical content as well as the needs and developmental levels of the advisee. They accept the challenge to implement an approach that will help them to fulfill their important responsibility of "supporting and facilitating students' career and academic planning and development" (Hughey & Hughey, 2009, p. 1).

MI offers an effective approach and provides a framework to inspire and promote success. Flexibility, creativity, and ability to think strategically are critical to success in the workforce of the future. Casner-Lotto and Barrington (2006) emphasized the following knowledge and skills that research has shown to be most important to future career success: a) critical thinking and problem solving, b) information technology application, c) proficiency in teamwork and collaboration, d) creativity and innovation, and e) appreciation for diversity. Furthermore, Feller and O'Bruba (2009) stated, "Commitment to maximizing advisees' strengths, articulating concrete goals, and building action plans captures how advisors add value" (pp. 39–40). The MI approach offers appropriate strategies for skill building and value added.

Motivational Interview Response

Because the workplace and economy call for those who appreciate the lifelong learning and change processes, students should be prepared when they leave an educational institution to transition throughout their personal lives and professional careers, and advising plans, created through thoughtful insight and evolving as an advisee matures, should incorporate goals for change behaviors. Based on collaboration between advisor and advisee, the advising plan requires advisees to articulate specific long- and short-term goals, consider the barriers to achieving maximum success, and list specific solutions to overcome obstacles (Figler & Bolles, 2007). The plans should include discussions of the advisee's network and support systems necessary for success in change behaviors. Feller and O'Bruba (2009) recommended that advisors provide homework assignments that reinforce learning as a lifelong process and keep students engaged in the steps necessary to meet long-term goals.

Motivational Interview Scenarios

Scenario I

A first-generation college sophomore, Riley, says to an advisor, Skylar, "I'm having trouble in two of my classes. I don't understand what the professor is talking about in one of them, but it's a required course in my major. The other is only a gen ed course, but I keep getting low grades on the writing assignments. I was always good in writing in high school. If I do poorly, this will lower my GPA, and I just got off academic probation last term. I want to stay in my major, but I don't know if I can pass this one course and that would really disappoint my family. What do you suggest I do?"

∘ ∘ ∘

In this scenario, Skylar creates rapport with Riley based on mutual collaboration and respect. Using a nonjudgmental tone of voice and demonstrating genuine interest, Skylar engages Riley in a discussion of goals, issues, values, behaviors, as well as the need and motivation to change. First, Skylar could begin the session, using one of the following suggestions, with the goal of setting the agenda and clarifying the presenting issues for Riley:

○ Tell me about your ultimate career goal. What do you see as your strengths? Describe your passions.

○ I commend you for meeting with me to discuss these important academic issues. It takes courage to be honest about difficult topics.

○ What are your academic goals? Specifically, what is your goal for a grade in each of the courses?

Skylar could specifically start with the rating: "On a scale of 0 to 10, with *0* being not at all important and *10* being very important, how important do you think it is for you to improve your academics and earn a B in each course?" If Riley responds by saying "a 9," Skylar follows up by prompting, "What keeps it from being a 10?" and "What would it take for you to get to 10?" A response of "10" means that Riley probably has a good understanding of the need for the change and is open to continue the discussion toward implementing it. Operationalizing the plan for Riley includes changing the behaviors that create barriers to academic success, making a commitment to engage in the new behaviors, which might include involving others, following through with the commitment by writing an action plan, and ultimately completing the action. The change talk could proceed as follows:

SKYLAR: "What are two critical behaviors you believe you would need to change to improve your academic standing? How do your current behaviors fit with your career goals?"

RILEY: "I probably need to stop partying on Wednesday and Thursday nights and missing classes the following mornings. I also tend to get sidetracked when I try to study."

SKYLAR: "Tell me your version of what is going on the nights you decide to go out with your friends and party. What is your interpretation of the benefits of those nights?"

During the discussion with Riley on behavior modification, Skylar promotes greater awareness of the ways partying affects Riley's academic goals. With the intent of increasing Riley's motivation and commitment to change, Skylar makes evocative statements such as the following examples illustrate:

○ I hear you saying that all of your friends party. Partying helps you to relax, not to think about the troubles you are having in your courses, the stress of school, and the disappointment you feel about your grades. You enjoy drinking with your friends because it is more fun than sitting in your room studying for courses you do not enjoy. It sounds like you might be afraid of being lonely if you stay home studying while others are out drinking.

○ In the past, the positives about partying with your friends during the week outweighed the negatives. Going out helped you feel good about your social life and helped you to cope with not having the grades you need and want. However, now it seems partying during the week only seems to be making your grades worse and perhaps making you feel more anxious about your courses and the reality of being forced to leave school for academic reasons.

Skylar could further assist Riley in reflecting ambivalence to change by using a double-sided reflection: "On one hand, I hear you saying you realize if your grades do not improve you will likely have to leave school. On the other hand, you enjoy partying with your friends during the week. And, you believe there is a direct correlation between partying during the week with your friends and your grades."

Continually encouraging an advisee to consider the future helps him or her to stay focused on long- and short-term goals. With the following questions, Skylar directs Riley toward seeing two extreme outcomes:

○ What is the worst thing that would happen if you stopped partying on weeknights?

○ What is the best thing that could happen if you stopped partying on weeknights?

○ Close your eyes and consider for a minute what your life would look like if you changed these behaviors exactly as you want.

This thread encourages the advisee to see and feel differences created by changing behaviors. Acknowledgments about the need to change and expressions of a desire to do so sometimes fail to coincide with an intention to change. An advisor needs to measure the strength of commitment to change by evaluating the language of the student. Verbs indicating a high commitment to change include *will, intend, plan, guarantee, resolve, swear,* and *promise.*

Change is difficult. Sometimes afraid of failure, students choose to maintain ineffective, familiar behaviors rather than risk adopting new behaviors with unknown consequences. The advisor can help by expressing optimism in the student's ability to be successful in the change process.

Specifically, Skylar should validate any willingness of Riley to reject peer pressure and acknowledge the courage and hard work necessary to make changes to achieve significant goals. Skylar might consider using some of the following inquiries with Riley:

○ What difficult goals have you achieved in the past? What strategies did you use to be successful with those goals? Could you tell me more about that?

○ What strategies worked for you last semester?

○ What would you like to see changed this semester?

Advisors need to affirm the good decisions the student has made in previous semesters. When they do not achieve the expected academic success, students sometime feel embarrassed and appreciate affirming statements from an advisor.

Students are more likely to engage and sustain change if they have strong self-efficacy. Advisors can reinforce self-efficacy by prompting students to articulate their own successes:

○ You have made good decisions and good grades in the past. I'm sure you can make good decisions and good grades again.

○ What has been your greatest academic success in school?

○ What worked best for you in the past when you experienced academic difficulties?

Specifically, Skylar may employ thought-provoking inducements with the goal of bolstering Riley's self-efficacy for change:

○ There are pros and cons to making behavior changes in your life. To achieve your goals, it seems that you might need to change your behaviors that are not working for you.

○ What are the not-so-good things about change?

○ What won't you like?

○ How will this affect you?

○ What are the good things about change?

○ How will it affect you?

○ I hear you saying that if you choose not to party and to stay home and implement different study tools, you could have more energy to devote to the study process, have more time to meet with a tutor, and have a greater opportunity to enhance your learning and academic performance. However, making this change would mean finding new strategies to deal with the stress in your life and other times to spend time with your friends in social settings.

An advisee may offer discrepant statements without being cognitively aware of the conflict. In a concerned yet nonjudgmental or angry tone of voice, a skilled advisor will make the student aware of the disparities in the thoughts, feelings, behaviors, or goals based on previous statements or actions. By presenting contradictions, Skylar helps Riley discover and address unrevealed issues. Through heightened awareness of behaviors inconsistent with goals and values, students may experience the growth that leads to change. Therefore, Skylar may point out to Riley, "I am concerned because, on one hand, you say you want to improve your grades and make B's in your courses. On the other hand, you just shared with me that you went drinking with your friends Wednesday and Thursday nights and missed Thursday and Friday morning classes."

Skylar would then seek to engage Riley in change talk and strengthen the desire and direction of the discussion by asking for elaborations on the needed adjustments, past experiences, and the important positives that could result in reduced weeknight partying. The discussion could include the following advisor statements and questions:

○ There is usually more than one possible course of action.

○ I can tell you about what's worked for other people.

○ You are the best judge of what works for you.

○ Let's think about several ideas and strategies; what might be a few of the barriers that would keep these ideas from being successful?

○ I have some ideas about how you could improve your academic habits, study skills, and grades. However, I am interested in your ideas. What can you suggest?

○ What do you think best suits your learning preferences, strengths, passions, and interests?

○ What do you think you can or could do?

○ Which solution makes the most sense to you?

○ What happened the last time you tried to make a change in your behavior?

○ How will it be different this time?

○ Let's be specific with strategies for when the barriers block the way of success again.

An advisor can increase an advisee's commitment to change by placing goals on paper and asking the student to sign the document. Such documentation also makes the goals seem more concrete. Skylar may implement the following strategy with Riley:

"Riley, please write down three statements about changes that you are going to make within the next week, the next month, and the next six months."

After Riley responds, Skylar could continue:

You might not be aware of the tutoring services scheduled this semester in the University Learning Center. I have a copy of the schedule to share with you. In addition, I am giving you a handbook of study skills and time management strategies. I encourage you to spend Wednesday and Thursday evenings with the tutor in the University Learning Center. Because I have seen your transcript and know you have been academically successful in the previous years, and I have heard you say that you know your education is critical to your career goals, I am confident that you can earn B's in these courses. You indicated a desire of 9 and maybe a 10 on a scale of desire to change behaviors. Your desire and willingness are present. Of course, the decisions to make the changes are *your* decisions to make. I am here to help and support you. However, *you* will be the person who must live with the consequences of your decisions for a lifetime.

Summary

Fried (2006) stated one of the foremost goals of higher education is to transform a student mentally, physically, and emotionally and elevate each aspect to a higher level. Academic advisors possess the ability to empower advisees academically, personally, and socially to result in enhanced career and professional opportunities. MI offers an approach for academic advisors to implement to help in this transformation process.

References

Amrhein, P. C., Miller, W. R., Yahne, C. E., Palmer, M., & Fulcher, L. (2003). Client commitment language during motivational interviewing predicts drug use outcomes. *Journal of Consulting and Clinical Psychology, 71*, 862–878. Bandura, A. (1994). Self-efficacy. In V. S. Ramachaudran (Ed.), *Encyclopedia of human behavior* (Vol. 4, pp. 71–81). New York, NY: Academic Press.

Bloom, J. L., Hutson, B. L., & He, Y. (2008). *The appreciative advising revolution.* Champaign, IL: Stipes.

Casner-Lotto, J., & Barrington, L. (2006). *Are they ready to work? Employers' perspectives on the basic knowledge and applied skills of new entrants to the 21st century U.S.*

workforce (Final Report). Washington, DC: The Conference Board, Corporate Voices for Working Families.

Center for Substance Abuse Treatment. (1999). *Enhancing motivation for change in substance abuse treatment* (Treatment Improvement Protocol [TIP] Series, No. 35). Rockville, MD: Substance Abuse and Mental Health Services Administration. Retrieved from http://www.ncbi.nlm.nih.gov/books/NBK64967/

Feller, R., & O'Bruba, B. (2009). In K. F. Hughey, D. Burton-Nelson, J. K. Damminger, & B. McCalla-Wriggins (Eds.), *The handbook of career advising* (pp. 19–47). San Francisco, CA: Jossey-Bass.

Figler, H., & Bolles, R. (2007). *The career counselor's handbook*. Berkeley, CA: Ten Speed Press.

Fried, J. (2006). Rethinking learning. In R. P. Keeling (Ed.), *Learning reconsidered 2: A practical guide to implementing a campus-wide focus on the student experience* (pp. 3–9). Washington, DC: ACPA, ACUHO-I, ACUI, NACA, NACADA, NASPA, NIRSA.

Gollwitzer, P. M. (1999). Implementation intentions: Simple effects of simple plans. *American Psychologist, 54*, 493–503.

Gordon, T. (1970). *Parent effectiveness training*. New York, NY: Wyden.

Hughey, K. F., & Hughey, J. K. (2009). Foundations of career advising. In K. F. Hughey, D. Burton-Nelson, J. K. Damminger, & B. McCalla-Wriggins (Eds.), *The handbook of career advising* (pp. 1–18). San Francisco, CA: Jossey-Bass.

Mahoney, E. (2009). Career advising competencies. In K. F. Hughey, D. Burton-Nelson, J. K. Damminger, & B. McCalla-Wriggins (Eds.), *The handbook of career advising* (pp. 48–67). San Francisco, CA: Jossey-Bass.

Markland, D., Ryan, R. M., Tobin, V. J., & Rollnick, S. (2005). Motivational interviewing and self-determination theory. *Journal of Social and Clinical Psychology, 24*, 811–831.

Martino, S., & Hopfer, C. (2009). *An introduction to motivational interviewing: Blending clinical practice and research*. NIDA Clinical Trials. Retrieved from http://www.newbegin.net/resources/Documents/MI%20presentation%20martino.pdf

Miller, W. R. (1983). Motivational interviewing with problem drinkers. *Behavioural Psychotherapy, 11*, 147–172.

Miller, W. R., & Rollnick, S. (2002). *Motivational interviewing: Preparing people for change*. New York, NY: Guilford Press.

Miller, W. R., & Rollnick, S. (2009). Ten things that motivational interviewing is not. *Behavioural and Cognitive Psychotherapy, 37*, 129–140.

Miller, W. R., & Rollnick, S. (2010a, June). *What makes it motivational interviewing?* Presentation at the International Conference on Motivational Interviewing (ICMI). Stockholm, Sweden.

Miller, W. R., & Rollnick, S. (2010b, June). *What's new since MI-2?* Presentation at the International Conference on Motivational Interviewing (ICMI). Stockholm, Sweden.

Miller, W. R., & Rose, G. S. (2009). Toward a theory of motivational interviewing. *American Psychologist, 64*, 527–537.

Mottarella, K. E., Fritzsche, B. A., & Cerabino, K. C. (2004). What do students want in advising? A policy capturing study. *NACADA Journal, 24*(1&2), 48–61.

Moyers, T. B., Miller, W. R., & Hendrickson, S.M.L. (2005). How does motivational interviewing work? Therapist interpersonal skill as a predictor of client involvement within motivational interviewing sessions. *Journal of Consulting and Clinical Psychology, 73*(4), 590–598.

Prochaska, J. O., & DiClemente, C. C. (1984). *The transtheoretical approach: Crossing traditional boundaries of therapy*. Homewood, IL: Dow/Jones Irwin.

Prochaska, J. O., & Velicer, W. F. (1997). The transtheoretical model of health behavior change. *American Journal of Health Promotion, 12*, 38–48.

6

APPRECIATIVE ADVISING

Jennifer L. Bloom, Bryant L. Hutson, and Ye He

With the increasing student diversity in higher education settings and the demand to prepare the 21st-century workforce for a more globalized society, postsecondary administrators, faculty members, and staff face the task of best meeting the needs of their students, future employers, and communities. In addition to addressing the consistent gap between enrollment and retention (Habley, Valiga, McClanahan, & Burkum, 2010), institutions are charged with enhancing the academic success of college students so that they not only complete degree requirements to graduate, but also embark on their postgraduation plans with excellent communication, collaboration, critical thinking, and creativity skills (Partnership for 21st Century Skills, 2011, para. 1). As integral players in ensuring that these student retention and success objectives are met (Kuh, Kinzie, Schuh, & Whitt, 2005; Tinto, 1993), academic advisors are challenged to do more than just offer good advice about courses. To offer great advising support, they need to take the initiative in "engaging students in reflective conversation about educational goals," addressing "the nature of higher education, academic decisions, and the significance of those decisions," and "encouraging student change toward greater levels of self-awareness and responsibility" (Schulenberg & Lindhorst, 2010, p. 27).

Appreciative Advising (AA) is a framework for guiding advisors wishing to move from providing good service to providing great service to students (Collins, 2001). It entails the intentional and collaborative practice of asking positive, open-ended questions that help students optimize their educational experiences and achieve their dreams, goals, and potentials (Bloom, Hutson, & He, 2008). AA involves a six-phase model highlighting the appreciative mind-set that empowers advisors and students to a) build trust and rapport with each other (disarm); b) uncover their strengths and assets (discover); c) be inspired by each other's hopes and dreams (dream); d) co-construct plans to make their goals a reality (design); e) provide mutual support and accountability throughout the process (deliver); and f) challenge each other to set higher expectations for their educational experiences (don't settle) (Bloom et al., 2008).

Appreciative Advising Matters

AA is a social constructivist advising framework and approach rooted in appreciative inquiry (AI), an organizational change theory focused on the cooperative search for the positive in every living system and leveraging this positive energy to mobilize change (Cooperrider & Whitney, 2005). The promotion of unconditional positive questioning, the engagement of people at both the individual and organizational levels, and the systematic approach to action research offer significant implications to the field of academic advising (Amundsen & Hutson, 2005; Bloom & Martin, 2002; Kamphoff, Hutson, Amundsen, & Atwood, 2007).

As one of the few research-based advising models, AA has demonstrated impact and effectiveness on student academic performance, academic success, and retention in various advising settings (Bloom et al., 2008; Bloom et al., 2009; He, Hutson, & Bloom, 2010; Hutson & He, 2010). At the University of North Carolina at Greensboro (UNCG), for example, AA was first introduced and used at the program level with students on academic probation. After the thoughtful integration of the AA model into academic retention programming at UNCG, the retention rate of students on academic probation improved 18% with a statistically significant grade-point average (GPA) gain of .73 ($p = .03$) (Kamphoff et al., 2007). Later, the AA model was expanded at UNCG and applied to first-year experience programming as well (Hutson, 2010a). The findings of an outcomes-based evaluation of the first-year experience program indicated that students participating in the AA-enhanced first-year experience program obtained higher GPAs (2.72 compared to 2.49) and higher retention rates (77.5% compared to 75.5%) than nonparticipants. More importantly, the evaluation results demonstrated students' enhanced perception of self-knowledge, academic preparedness, interdependence, social behavior, and confidence. Similar positive outcomes were uncovered with students enrolled in sophomore experience courses (Hutson, He, Davis, & Ross, 2009), those returning from dismissal and engaged in learning contracts (Clark & Hutson, 2007; Hutson, 2010b), and advisees needing to identify new programs of study (Hutson & Clark, 2007).

Similarly, at the University of South Carolina (USC), the AA framework has been adapted and used through the Academic Success Coaching in the Academic Center for Excellence (ACE) program, through which advisors and students focused on their strengths and engaged all students in applying academic strategies for success (Robinson & Bloom, 2011). Since its implementation in 2007, the ACE program experienced more than 10-fold growth in student visits. A significant increase was also observed with academic probation students' term GPA (1.93 postprogram compared to 0.91 preprogram). The survey results also revealed the strong relationships and rapport students built with their ACE coaches at USC.

In addition to academic advising programming, the AA framework has been expanded to a broader appreciative education model that can be used in a variety of student affairs areas other than academic advising: adult/transfer student support, financial aid, admissions, career services, orientation, tutoring, parent programming, and other student success services (Bailey-Taylor, 2009; Bloom et al., 2009; Fippinger, 2009; Grogan, 2010; Hutson & He, 2010; Traynor & Bloom, 2012). At their core, all of these appreciative education variations feature the six phases of AA and demonstrate the potential of the campus-wide adaptation of a broader appreciative education model in promoting college student success.

The Six Phases of Appreciative Advising

Six phases guide academic advisors in implementing the AA framework: disarm, discover, dream, design, deliver, and don't settle (Bloom et al., 2008). The middle four phases are based on the 4-D cycle of the organizational development theory of AI; however, Bloom et al. (2008) supplemented the AI phases by addition of the disarm and don't settle phases. Advisors do not necessarily go through all six phases in each advising session nor necessarily employ them sequentially.

Disarm

The disarm phase is focused on helping advisors make a positive first impression with students and allaying any fear or suspicion that students might have about meeting with their advisor (Bloom et al., 2008). The disarm phase is a crucial component of successful appointments, especially first meetings, because many students have unclear ideas about the expectations of them, remember bad experiences they have had with high school or college institutional officials, or anticipate being unprepared for the appointments and fear being perceived as stupid. Thus, advisors need to make students feel welcomed and assured that the advisor wants to help advance, not impede, their academic progress.

The disarm phase begins before students arrive for their appointments. For example, the communications sent out to students inviting them to attend advising appointments should be positively worded and welcoming. Similarly, advising office staff should analyze their web sites to ensure that they are user-friendly and that they include pictures of advisors as well as some basic information about them. Advisors should design their office space as well as the office waiting area to make them safe and welcoming environments (Strain, 2009).

When students arrive for their appointments, advisors disarm them by walking to the waiting area and enthusiastically greeting them, shaking hands, and welcoming them to the office. This introduction gives advisors the opportunity to engage in some small talk with students on the walk back to their office, helping to put the students at ease. Nonverbal and verbal immediacy behaviors (Rocca, 2007) that advisors employ can make a positive first impression. Nonverbal behaviors include smiling, head nodding, maintaining appropriate eye contact, removing distractions (such as cell phones and computers), and displaying appropriate, welcoming gestures. Examples of verbal immediacy behaviors include calling students by the correct name, giving feedback to them, and using inclusive pronouns (Rocca, 2007). Advisors can utilize basic questions, such as the following, to break the ice with students:

- What has been the highlight of your day so far?
- Did you watch the game last night? What did you think of the outcome?
- What do you think of this weather we have been experiencing lately?

Discover

In the discover phase advisors continue to build rapport with students and learn about their strengths, skills, and abilities (Bloom et al., 2008). Advisors use positive, open-ended questions to learn about students and their stories. Because students arrive at college with an amazing breadth of experiences, the discover phase allows advisors to get a glimpse into their accomplishments and achievements to this point. This emphasis on understanding students' stories is congruent with the hermeneutics approach to advising as discussed by Sarah Champlin-Scharff and Peter Hagen in chapter 13. The discover phase is important because through AA one can build on students' feats to accomplish new objectives during their collegiate careers. To begin building their relationships and learn more about student accomplishments, advisors can employ the following examples of discover-phase discussion points:

- Describe a goal that was important to you and how you accomplished it.
- Who is the most important role model in your life right now? What do you admire about that person?
- If you were able to take a class for free and grades were not issued for it, what class would you take? Why?

Dream

In the dream phase, advisors elicit students' hopes and dreams for their futures (Bloom et al., 2008). "A dream is an inspiring picture of the future that energizes your mind, will, and emotions, empowering you to do everything you can to achieve it" (Maxwell, 2009, p. xiii), clearly helpful to students embarking on the college, and for many, the adult journey. Again, the key to learning about students' dreams lies in the power of the discussions academic advisors initiate with them. For example, advisors might ask advisees to

- draw a picture of your ideal life 20 years from now, including both your career and personal life. Tell me about what you have drawn in this picture.
- describe one career you have always wanted to pursue but did not think you could.
- imagine that you are on the cover or a magazine 15 years from now. What magazine is it and why are you on the cover?

Design

Helping students identify their life and career goals proves a vital step toward devising an effective plan for making their dreams a reality (Bloom et al., 2008). In the design phase, advisors partner with students to create plans for accomplishing the visions shared in the dream phase. Students must participate in the creation of their plans to take ownership of them (Bandura, 1997). This cocreation echoes one of the hallmarks of the self-authorship and learning partnership model discussed by Janet Schulenberg in chapter 8. The plan needs to include not only the classes students should take, but also the experiences they should intentionally seek outside the classroom to meet their life and career goals. Such extracurricular activities include those associated with joining appropriate campus clubs, pursuing leadership positions on campus and in the community, and seeking out campus resources (such as tutoring and supplemental instruction) that can help them succeed academically.

Academic advisors can employ the following directives in the design phase:

○ Brainstorm on the steps you will need to take to accomplish your dreams (goals).

○ Identify people in your life who can help you reach your goals.

○ Discover the campus resources you can utilize to help make your dreams a reality.

Deliver

In the deliver phase, students take responsibility for executing their plans created in the design phase while advisors express confidence in students' ability to follow through with the plans (Bloom et al., 2008). Devising a good plan is important, but it means little if students do not accomplish the tasks outlined in it. Advisors play a key role by reviewing the priorities in the plan, inviting students to return to them when they run into roadblocks, and reiterating their confidence in the students' ability to complete the objectives. Tichy (2002) stated, "Simply put, a leader's job is to energize others. Notice that I don't say it's part of their job; it is their job. There is no 'time off' when a leader isn't responsible for energizing others" (p. 297). Halvorson (2011) suggested writing the plan down on paper, thinking ahead about obstacles the students will likely encounter, and then anticipating strategies to work around those barriers. Either the student or the advisor can write down the specifics, including the obstacles and the work-arounds to circumvent them. Examples of deliver questions that advisors can ask students to motivate them to complete their plans include the following:

○ In your opinion, what is the most important item on the to-do list we created together?

○ What obstacles do you expect to face in executing this plan we developed together?

○ What are some strategies you can use when you encounter roadblocks?

○ When your motivation starts to run low, what specific steps can you take to reenergize yourself?

Don't Settle

During the don't settle phase advisors do not rest on their laurels but strive continually to encourage improved student performances (Bloom et al., 2008). Kuh et al. (2005) captured the essence of the don't settle phase through the term *positive restlessness*. They coined the term to refer to institutions in the DEEP Study, which retained students at a rate better than the entering-student demographics had predicted. In the context of AA, the term reminds and encourages students and advisors alike to strive for self-improvement. Advisors need to help students learn how to set increasingly higher expectations for themselves. By continuing to read, refining their skills, and demonstrating an unquenchable thirst for new knowledge, advisors serve as important role models, demonstrating a spirit for continually seeking to better themselves. In addition, depending on the students' situation, advisors and students may decide to update their initial plan during the design phase based on circumstantial changes experienced since the last appointment. Advisors can bring up these questions in follow-up conversations in the don't settle phase:

○ What have you done well since our last meeting? What is one thing you could have done even better?

○ When was the last time you thought you could not accomplish a goal but then completed it anyway?

○ If I challenged you to become the best person you could possibly become, what would you need to do differently?

Features of Appreciative Advising

AA provides a true theory-to-practice package for academic advisors. Not only is AA derived from research-based theories such as AI, it also provides concrete suggestions advisors can use to enhance the quality of advising services. With a focus on specific verbal and nonverbal behaviors in advising, AA emphasizes the process of communication, which is often the main means through which advisors deliver their services. In addition, action research efforts have been intentionally and systematically integrated into the development of the AA framework to make it more applicable in various advising settings (Bloom et al., 2009). The factors leading toward student success and retention through the AA framework demonstrate that advisors and students engaged in AA extend their cognitive understanding beyond that determined by educational settings and experiences.

In addition to the cognitive dimension, AA emphasizes student development of metacognitive and affective skills and strategies as well. The metacognitive dimension of AA encourages advisors and students to monitor their cognitive development through thoughtful reflection, and the affective dimension addresses motivational factors that guide the applications of learned skills and strategies. Figure 6.1 shows the metacognitive, cognitive, and affective dimensions of the AA framework.

Figure 6.1. Appreciative advising role in developing the metacognitive, cognitive, and affective skills that affect academic success

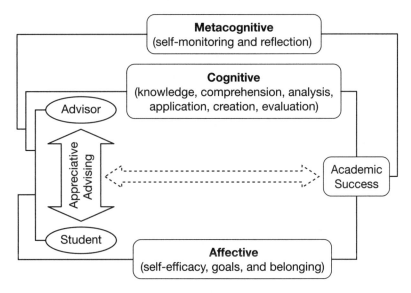

Similar to most advising approaches described in this book, AA emphasizes students' cognitive development through advising. While students' knowledge and comprehension of higher education processes and procedures are critical to their success, AA extends the students' abilities for analysis, application, creation, and evaluation (Bloom, 1956). Particularly in the design and delivery phases, students engage with advisors to co-construct academic plans, analyze campus resources, and seek alternative pathways to achieve academic goals. Different from traditional one-way knowledge delivery models of advising, the AA framework features two-way interactions through which the "curse of knowledge" (Heath & Heath, 2007) can be avoided and the academic decision-making process modeled.

In addition to the cognitive dimension, metacognitive skills are deliberately included in the AA framework that advisors scaffold and model to advisees. *Metacognition* refers to individuals' awareness and capability toward reflecting, monitoring, and intentionally developing their cognitive processes. In other words, in addition to using cognitive skills, such as note taking, to maximize comprehension and communication, students with strong metacognitive skills reflect on the best way to take notes in different contexts. In the AA discover phase, the advisor encourages student self-reflection by asking questions such as "What are your best learning experiences?" "When do you feel the most empowered in college?" and "When have you felt the most successful as a college student?" Such reflections are then paraphrased and summarized to connect to students' current academic environment and lead to intentional monitoring of best strategies as discerned based on learner background and prior experiences rather than on advisors' knowledge.

Finally, the AA framework explicitly addresses the affective aspect in learning, which some may neglect in their work with students. However, advisors should recognize that students typically come to advising sessions with a problem of some kind, even if it only involves issues related to course registration. Depending on the nature of the concern, students may be armed with anxiety, frustration, and sometimes fear. Regardless of the extent of their cognitive and metacognitive skills developed through advising, if they are not disarmed of those negative affections, they may not be as motivated, willing, or intentional in applying the skills of learning, and therefore, the outcome of the advising session may be unsuccessful. In that sense, the affective aspect is probably the most important feature of AA that advisors need to consider. The affective factors that the AA framework explicitly addresses are highly connected to student motivation and influence students' self-efficacy, goals, and sense of belonging (Alderman, 2004).

Self-efficacy is typically defined as one's beliefs in the capabilities to achieve in certain domains (Bandura, 1997). People with a strong sense of self-efficacy express a positive outlook when facing challenges, remain resilient even when experiencing failures, and feel more confident in their abilities to acquire additional knowledge to overcome challenges. Bandura (1997) identified four main sources of self-efficacy: physiological state, mastery experiences, vicarious experiences, and verbal persuasion. In the AA framework, these sources are intentionally integrated through the disarm, discover, and don't settle phases. During the disarm phase, the advisors attend to the physical environment and their own assumptions to create a safe and welcoming environment that eases students' physiological state. Through discover, advisors ask students to revisit their mastery and vicarious experiences to set models for future achievement. During all phases and especially in don't settle, advisors use verbal persuasion (e.g., "I believe you can accomplish your goals") to challenge students to set higher expectations and continue challenging themselves.

A *goal* defines an individual's aspirations for achievement (Locke & Latham, 1990). The best goals are those "that spell out exactly what needs to be accomplished and that set the bar for achievement high," which "result in far superior performance than goals that are vague or that set the bar too low" (Halvorson, 2011, p. 5). Through dream and don't settle in the AA framework, advisors solicit students' dreams and goals to trigger their intrinsic motivation for success and to encourage them to set challenging, desirable, yet feasible goals.

A *sense of belonging* is an important aspect of one's basic social needs (Maslow, 1954). It entails one's fundamental need to feel connected and related to others. College students experience higher levels of self-efficacy and are more likely to be academically successful when they feel that they belong (Astin, 1993; Bean, 1980; Tinto, 1993). Freeman, Anderman, and Jensen (2007), for example, examined college students' sense of belonging as it related to their academic motivation and found that instructors' warmth and openness, enthusiasm, organization, and encouragement for student participation directly influence students' sense of belonging. The AA framework offers a unique interactive process in which advisors and students engage in learning from each other through disarm, discover, dream, design, deliver, and don't settle. The advisor–student relationship developed from such a process shifts the traditional dynamic in which advisors hold the authority in providing help to students. Instead, this relationship empowers students because they quickly see the attributes they bring to the institution and ways to align their hopes and dreams to meet institutional expectations and values.

The impact of the AA framework is not only evident in students' development; it is seen in advisors' professional growth as well. Through the co-construction of the academic plan (design) and systematic follow-up (deliver), advisors enhance their cognitive abilities in analyzing and evaluating resources to facilitate students' academic development. As an important aspect of the AA framework, advisors also focus on their reflection of their own professional beliefs and visions, and uncover their strengths (discover) to further their metacognitive understanding of the profession (Hutson, Bloom, & He, 2009). From an affective perspective, advisors examine their assumptions (disarm), become reenergized through students' hopes and dreams (dream), and challenge—and are challenged by—the needs and expectations of new generations of students (don't settle). In addition, in her qualitative study, Howell (2010) found that participants felt more effective as advisors and better able to utilize their own strengths and skills after adopting the AA approach; they also acknowledged enjoying better relationships with their students as well as with friends and family members outside of the advising setting. In essence, the AA framework not only provides a list of steps that guide the advising process, but more important, it inspires advisor thinking that leads to thoughtful, reflective, and intentional verbal and nonverbal communication behaviors.

Appreciative Advising Scenario

To illustrate how the AA framework can be used in daily advising with students, AA interactions are applied to Scenario I. The phases of AA and their impact on students' cognitive, metacognitive, and affective development are discussed.

Scenario I

A first-generation college sophomore, Riley, says to an advisor, Skylar, "I'm having trouble in two of my classes. I don't understand what the professor is talking about in one of them, but it's a required course in my major. The other is only a gen ed course, but I keep getting low grades on the writing assignments. I was always good in writing in high school. If I do poorly, this will lower my GPA, and I just got off academic probation last term. I want to stay in my major, but I don't know if I can pass this one course and that would really disappoint my family. What do you suggest I do?"

Advisor–Advisee Interactions	**AA Phase** and *Related Skills*
SKYLAR: Hi Riley! How are you doing? Thank you for stopping by today. How can I help you?	**Disarm** Welcome students and make them feel comfortable. Ask open-ended questions to draw stories from students. *Affective* Foster relationship and belonging.
RILEY: I am doing all right, but I'm having trouble in two of my classes. That's why I am here to see you today.	
SKYLAR: Here, have a seat. Why don't you tell me more about it?	
RILEY: Well, I don't understand what the professor is talking about in one of them, but it's a required course in my major. The other is only a gen ed course, but I keep getting low grades on the writing assignments. I was always good in writing in high school. If I don't do well, this will lower my GPA, and I just got off academic probation last term. I want to stay in my major, but I don't know if I can pass this one course and that would really disappoint my family. What do you suggest I do?	
SKYLAR: It sounds like this has got you worried. First, let's back up for a minute before we start brainstorming about your options together. Could you please remind me how many courses you are taking this semester?	**Disarm** Shift away from problem-focused conversation. **Discover** Refocus the conversation from problem-solution to discovering and highlighting student strengths, assets, and prior/other successes. *Affective* Ease student anxiety and frustration.
RILEY: Oh, I am taking five courses. I like the other three. It's just the two courses I am having trouble with.	
SKYLAR: Why don't we talk a little more about the courses you like first? What are they? Why do you like them?	
RILEY: Well, two of those are gen ed courses and the other one is in my major, education. The two gen ed courses are great. I love the discussions going on in class. I feel like I know what's going on and I always have something to share in class too.	
SKYLAR: How about the course in your major?	
RILEY: That class is different. There is a field experience component to it. So you are not only reading the stuff, but also seeing how it is in action in the classrooms and putting it to use. We have a lot of writing assignments in that class too, but I am pretty good with that type of writing. It's different.	

SKYLAR: I see. It sounds like you really enjoyed the courses where you can participate in the discussion and liked the field experience component to get more hands-on experiences.	**Discover** Summarize and paraphrase. *Cognitive*
RILEY: Yes, exactly.	Demonstrate ways to articulate strengths.
SKYLAR: You mentioned that you are an education major; are you planning on teaching in schools here after graduation?	**Dream** Solicit students' goals, hopes, and dreams.
RILEY: Yeah, I want to teach in an elementary school after I graduate. My mom is an elementary teacher, and I always wanted to be an elementary teacher just like her.	Remind students their purpose of learning. *Affective* Encourage motivation and goal setting.
SKYLAR: That's great. I had some really good elementary teachers too. Looking back, they really taught me a lot.	**Disarm** Self-disclosure to relate to students' experiences to build connections.
RILEY: I know! It's really rewarding in elementary classrooms this semester to see how the kids learn. I really enjoyed that.	*Affective* Promote sense of belonging.
SKYLAR: But you are a little concerned about the two courses you are taking this semester. One is in the major and the other is a gen ed course with a heavy writing emphasis?	**Discover** Recast students' concerns. *Cognitive*
RILEY: Yes. The one in my major is actually a math class. I have never been really good at math since elementary school. I don't think we worked that much on those probability problems, you know. I have no idea what the professor is asking us to do, and I am afraid that I may do really poorly in that one.	Invite students to summarize.

SKYLAR: I see. The math that is being taught in elementary schools is becoming more and more challenging. I think fifth grade students are learning about probability now. If you really want to be an elementary school teacher, it is probably an area worth investing more effort in.	**Design** <u></u> Connect back to dream. Identify potential resources.
RILEY: You are right. My mom is actually team teaching with another teacher this semester and she is teaching fifth grade math and science.	*Affective* Encourage goal setting and motivation.
SKYLAR: That's a great resource you have! Your mom can probably give you some tips!	
RILEY: I have not thought about that, but I guess you are right.	
SKYLAR: Have you talked with anyone about it? The professor or maybe some classmates or friends?	**Design** Co-construct a plan with students to identify academic resources and support.
RILEY: Some of my classmates feel the same way. They probably do better on those quizzes, but they said they didn't understand that professor either. We sometimes get together and study for those quizzes, you know.	*Cognitive* Analyze and evaluate learning strategies.
SKYLAR: That's a really good strategy. It would be very helpful to join a study group and you can share your notes and get ready for the midterm. How about tutors? Have you thought about getting some tutoring help?	*Metacognitive* Demonstrate ways to seek alternative paths (e.g., discussing with professors teaching other courses).
RILEY: You mean having a private tutor?	
SKYLAR: You could do that, or there is also a tutoring service on campus. You can be paired with a tutor to work one hour every week to help you prepare for this course.	
RILEY: Really? I didn't know that.	
SKYLAR: Yes, the University Tutoring Center offers that service. Here's their web site [showing the brochure with the web URL listed]. You can also check with the Math Department. They also offer walk-in tutoring services for students.	

RILEY: I see. I will check those out.	
SKYLAR: You said that you haven't talked directly with the professor yet, right?	
RILEY: Well, I don't know if I should do that. I mean, I don't really have a question, you know. I just feel like I don't know the content well enough.	
SKYLAR: How about the professors teaching those other three classes you like, especially the one in your major? Maybe you can find a time to chat with them and see if they have any tips for you.	
RILEY: Oh, yeah, I can do that. I really like Dr. Smith. She teaches the other course in my major. She would be good to talk to.	
SKYLAR: So for this class, we said that you will continue with your study group, find out more about the tutoring services, and get some tips and suggestions from Dr. Smith and maybe your mom. That would probably be a good starting point to get some support for that course.	**Design** Present summary of plan. **Deliver** Create follow-up plans. **Don't Settle** Challenge students to reach their potential. *Cognitive* Demonstrate summarizing. *Affective* Encourage students to develop self-efficacy.
RILEY: Yeah, I think that might help. But what if it still doesn't work?	
SKYLAR: I really think these strategies will help a lot. You will see the results once you try them out. Also, you know that you do have the option to drop this course before the deadline and register for it again next semester. Maybe you can try the tutoring out for two weeks and then decide. We can touch base in two weeks and see how it goes.	
RILEY: Okay, that sounds good. So how about that other course?	
SKYLAR: Well, what ideas do you have?	**Design** Encourage students to participate in the co-construction of the plan. *Metacognitive* Guide students to follow similar cognitive process in analyzing and summarizing learning strategies.
RILEY: I guess I can work with my study group and get someone to read my writing too. Is there a tutoring service for writing on campus too?	
SKYLAR: Yes, there's actually a writing center on campus. You can definitely get some support there. They recently launched an online chat function and they also can give you feedback through e-mail.	
RILEY: Oh, that's great.	

SKYLAR: You also mentioned that you have always been good at writing and are doing well with the writing assignments in other classes. I wonder what makes this class different.	**Discover** Connect to students' strengths and assets. *Metacognitive* Encourage students' reflection.
RILEY: I don't know. I guess it's the style of writing. That professor wanted all theories and citations, and he said I cannot use "I" in my writing. How am I supposed to write what I think then?	
SKYLAR: I see. So it's really not that you are not good at writing, it's the specific genre of writing that is challenging.	**Discover** Recast and model appreciative, rather than deficit-based, thinking. *Affective* Build students' self-efficacy.
RILEY: I guess so.	
SKYLAR: You know, the library offers some workshops on searching for academic journals and using correct citation styles. In fact, there are some workshops scheduled for next week. Will that be something you might be interested in?	**Design** Identify campus resources. *Cognitive* Analyze and apply campus resources. *Affective* Articulate concrete steps toward goals.
RILEY: Sure.	
SKYLAR: Great. So we said that you will find someone to give you feedback on your writing, check out the Writing Center, and register for some workshops offered by the library. I think this will really help you to see how you can write in that particular style. You could probably get some feedback from your professor too.	
RILEY: Yeah, I can definitely try those things. Thank you so much for the suggestions.	
SKYLAR: You are welcome. I am glad I can help. Here is my contact information. In two weeks, could you send me a quick e-mail just to update me on your progress? I will also call or send an e-mail to the Writing Center and see if they have any other recommendations for working on academic writing skills. I will let you know if I find out any new information that might be helpful.	**Deliver and Don't Settle** Set expectations for following up. *Affective* Enhance belonging through collaboration in steps toward students' goals (e.g., advisors take on tasks rather than leaving all the responsibilities to the students to carry out the plan).
RILEY: That would be great. Thank you.	

While the scenario presented in this chapter may be oversimplified compared to the complex nature of advising, it illustrates how advisors might use the AA framework in their daily interactions with students and intentionally facilitate students' cognitive, metacognitive, and affective development. As is demonstrated in the scenario, AA phases do not project a list of sequential steps. Instead, the phases reflect the adaptable applications of the AA mind-set.

Summary

The AA framework provides a theory-to-practice approach to enhance the success of both advisors and students. As an action research-driven advising framework, AA not only offers specific techniques and questions through the six phases (disarm, discover, dream, design, deliver, and don't settle), but also highlights the connections among advisors' professional development, the advising process, and student success from cognitive, metacognitive, and affective perspectives. Many advisors may find that they are already implementing the strategies that the AA framework promotes. Rather than a new way of advising, AA is a reflective, systematic, and adaptive framework that enhances advisors' intentional facilitation through all advising sessions. It calls for advisors to not only know what to do in advising but also to reflect on why and how to provide better services for all students through advising.

References

Alderman, M. K. (2004). *Motivation for achievement: Possibilities for teaching and learning* (2nd ed.). Mahwah, NJ: Lawrence Erlbaum.

Amundsen, S. A., & Hutson, B. L. (2005, October). *Appreciative advising: A new paradigm in advising at-risk students*. Presentation at the Annual Conference of the National Academic Advising Association, Las Vegas, NV.

Astin, A. W. (1993). *What matters most in college: Four critical years revisited*. San Francisco, CA: Jossey-Bass.

Bailey-Taylor, A. (2009). Revolutionizing your counseling techniques with appreciative advising. *Student Aid Transcript, 20*(1), 12–15.

Bandura, A. (1997). *Self-efficacy: The exercise of control*. New York, NY: Freeman.

Bean, J. (1980). Dropouts and turnover: The synthesis and test of a casual model of student attrition. *Research in Higher Education, 12*, 155–187.

Bloom, B. S. (1956). *Taxonomy of educational objectives*. Boston, MA: Allyn and Bacon.

Bloom, J. L., Hutson, B. L., & He, Y. (2008). *The appreciative advising revolution*. Champaign, IL: Stipes.

Bloom, J. L., Hutson, B. L., He, Y., Amundsen, S., Buyarski, C., Christman, P. D., . . . Kucharczyk, L. M. (2009). How eight institutions have incorporated appreciative advising. *The Mentor: An Academic Advising Journal, 11*(2). Retrieved from http://www.psu.edu/dus/mentor/090422jb.htm

Bloom, J. L., & Martin, N. A. (2002). Incorporating appreciative inquiry into academic advising. *The Mentor: An Academic Advising Journal, 4*(3). Retrieved from http://dus.psu.edu/mentor/020829jb.htm

Clark, J. A., & Hutson, B. L. (2007, October). *Reaching out to those who have been dismissed: An application of appreciative advising.* Presentation made at the Annual Conference of the National Academic Advising Association, Baltimore, MD.

Collins, J. (2001). *Good to great.* New York, NY: Harper Collins.

Cooperrider, D. L., & Whitney, D. (2005). Appreciative inquiry: A positive revolution in change. In P. Holman & T. Devane (Eds.), *The change handbook* (pp. 245–263). San Francisco, CA: Berrett-Koehler.

Fippinger, A. (2009). An appreciative approach to training undergraduate admissions student workers. *College and University: Educating the Modern Higher Education Administration Professional, 85*(1), 53–56.

Freeman, T. M., Anderman, L., & Jensen, J. M. (2007). Sense of belonging in college freshmen at the classroom and campus levels. *The Journal of Experimental Education, 75*(3), 203–220.

Grogan, J. L. (2011). The appreciative tutor. *Journal of College Reading and Learning, 42*(1), 80–88.

Habley, W. R., Valiga, M., McClanahan, R., & Burkum, K. (2010). *What works in student retention?* Iowa City, IA: ACT.

Halvorson, H. G. (2011). *Succeed: How we can reach our goals.* New York, NY: Penguin Group.

He, Y., Hutson, B. L., & Bloom, J. L. (2010). Appreciative team building in learning organizations. In P. Hagan & T. Kuhn (Eds.), *Scholarly inquiry in academic advising* (Monograph No. 20) (pp. 133–141). Manhattan, KS: National Academic Advising Association.

Heath, C., & Heath, D. (2007). *Made to stick: Why some ideas survive and others die.* New York, NY: Random House.

Howell, N. (2010). *Appreciative advising from the academic advisor's viewpoint: A qualitative study* (Unpublished doctoral dissertation). University of Nebraska, Lincoln.

Hutson, B. L. (2010a). The impact of an appreciative advising–based university studies course on college student first-year experience. *Journal of Applied Research in Higher Education, 2*(1) 3–13.

Hutson, B. L. (2010b, April). *Uncovering assets of at-risk college students through learning contracts: An application of appreciative advising.* Paper presented at the Annual Meeting of the American Educational Research Association, Denver, CO.

Hutson, B. L., Bloom, J. L., & He, Y. (2009). Reflection in advising. *Academic Advising Today, 32*(4), 12.

Hutson, B. L., & Clark, J. A. (2007, October). *Using appreciative advising with at-risk nursing students: A strengths-based approach to internal transfer.* Presentation made at the Annual Conference of the National Academic Advising Association, Baltimore, MD.

Hutson, B. L., & He, Y. (2010). Appreciative Advising Inventory: Identifying college student assets for successful transition. *The Journal of College Orientation and Transition, 19*(1), 23–36.

Hutson, B. L., He, Y., Davis, B. A., & Ross, R. A. (2009). The impact of an appreciative advising–based sophomore university studies course on college student academic achievement: Patterns and effects. *Proceedings of the 2009 Hawaii International Conference on Education, 7,* 260–276.

Kamphoff, C. S., Hutson, B. L., Amundsen, S. A., & Atwood, J. A. (2007). A motivational/empowerment model applied to students on academic probation. *Journal of College Student Retention: Research, Theory, and Practice, 8*(4), 397–412.

Kuh, G. D., Kinzie, J., Schuh, J. H., & Whitt. E. J. (Eds.). (2005). *Student success in college: Creating conditions that matter.* San Francisco, CA: Jossey-Bass.

Locke, E. A., & Latham, G. P. (1990). *A theory of goal setting and task performance.* Englewood Cliffs, NJ: Prentice Hall.

Maslow, A. (1954). *Motivation and personality.* New York, NY: Harper.

Maxwell, J. C. (2009). *Put your dreams to the test.* Nashville, TN: Thomas Nelson.

Partnership for 21st-Century Skills. (2011). [Home page]. Retrieved from http://www.p21.org/

Robinson, C. R., & Bloom, J. L. (2011, April 13). Empowering at-risk probationary students using appreciative advising inside and outside the classroom [Webinar]. Innovative Educators.

Rocca, K. A. (2007, February). *Immediacy in the classroom: Research and practical implications.* Presentation at the Student Motivations and Attitudes: The Role of the Affective Domain in Geoscience Learning Conference, Northfield, MN.

Schulenberg, J., & Lindhorst, M. (2010). The historical foundations and scholarly future of academic advising. In P. Hagen, T. Kuhn, & G. Padak (Eds.), *Scholarly inquiry in academic advising* (Monograph No. 20) (pp. 17–28). Manhattan, KS: National Academic Advising Association.

Strain, A. L. (2009, October 7). What message is your office space conveying to students? *The Mentor: An Academic Advising Journal, 11*(4). Retrieved from http://dus.psu.edu/mentor/091007as.htm

Tichy, N. M. (2002). *The leadership engine.* New York, NY: Harper Collins.

Tinto, V. (1993). *Leaving college: Rethinking the causes and cures of student attrition* (2nd ed.). Chicago, IL: The University of Chicago Press.

Traynor, D. S., & Bloom, J. L. (2012). *Reframing career services appointments using appreciative advising.* Manuscript submitted for publication.

VOICES FROM THE FIELD

APPLYING APPRECIATIVE ADVISING

Joseph Murray

The appreciative advising (AA) framework of asking positive, open-ended questions to help students identify and achieve their dreams, goals, and potentials (Bloom, Hutson, & He, 2008) offers a powerful tool for practitioners. For example, the first three stages (disarm, discovery, and dream) specifically apply to the admission process. As they seek to build rapport with the students they recruit, admissions counselors can employ disarm techniques, which also help create a positive first, and perhaps only, impression with prospective students and family members. After establishing rapport and effectively targeted messages, admissions counselors use the discover phase to learn about a student's educational goals, intended majors, campus life expectations, extracurricular activities, and career directions. Then, they delve into the student's past accomplishments and transition into the dream phase to learn about a student's hopes for the future. This information enables admissions counselors to share the opportunities both inside and outside the classroom at the institution they represent.

At Miami University (of Ohio) Hamilton Campus (MUH) the admissions staff uses the disarm, discover, and dream AA phases during their open houses and campus visits with prospective students and families. In fact, explanations of the AA philosophy serve as a recruitment tool because prospective students know from the very beginning that they will be treated as unique, valuable individuals. This level of student attention and respect sets MUH apart from competitors. Sharing the AA structure with incoming students also makes clear that the partnership between students and advisors is critical to helping students achieve their educational goals. The AA process works best when students are willing and engaged in participating in the process; it is undertaken *with* students, not *to* students, to achieve the desired outcomes.

MUH students engage the AA process in their first academic-advising appointment. The Advising Office, with the help of the faculty, developed an AA syllabus that all first-time and new transfer students receive as part of the registration packet. The syllabus outlines five AA phases introduced at orientation (omitting disarm), which advisors stress as important for students to know (even if they do not read it in advance).

In addition to spelling out the AA framework, advisors explain the learning outcomes for each advising appointment planned over the student's entire academic career, in part, because most MUH students do not follow a typical 4-year plan. However, institutions with a traditional student body develop learning outcomes for the advising appointments by year. In either case, at each session, students should receive information about topics covered and taught in each meeting and clear expectations for their role in the advising process. At MUH, the learning outcomes for advising relate to the four components built into every foundation class taught as part of the general education requirement:

- thinking critically,
- understanding contexts,
- engaging with other learners, and
- reflecting and acting.

This document helps advisors hold students accountable throughout the advising process. It empowers the advisor to say to a junior, "No, I am not going to pick and schedule classes for you, which is now your job. At this point, we need to be talking about career aspirations, graduate school, adding a minor, résumés, and cover letters." This document provides a great way to talk with first-generation students about the college classroom, the purpose of a syllabus and how to use it, and the expectations of the faculty.

At MUH, students on academic probation and those returning from suspension or dismissal experience AA to a greater extent than their peers. Like at many other institutions, MUH students who fit into these at-risk categories create a learning contract called the *academic recovery program* (ARP). The signed agreement outlines certain conditions placed on students, such as a registration hold mandating that the student see an advisor to sign up for classes, limitations on the number of credit hours allowed per semester (e.g., 14), the use of tutoring and other support resources, a study skills class, and frequent check-in meetings. The advisor initiates the first ARP appointment by asking students to fill out an *Appreciative Advising Inventory* (n.d.), which gives them an opportunity to ask students about their experiences in seven categories:

- commitment to learning,
- positive values,
- social competencies,
- positive identity,
- support and connectedness,
- empowerment, and
- boundaries and expectations.

The advisors use student responses to items in these seven areas to help target and guide conversations, referrals, and resources. For example, the advisor looks at a student response to an item such as "I know at least three people who work at my university that I can go to for advice and support" to determine if the student experiences tangible connectedness to MUH. If the answer indicates that the student does not know many professionals at the university, the advisor develops an action plan that might include asking the student to visit the office hours of at least one faculty member or encourage a meeting with an appropriate administrator on campus. The *Appreciative Advising Inventory* (n.d.) allows the advisor to focus the conversation and generate a precise intervention during limited appointment times.

MUH adopted the AA framework in 2007. Since then, staff have observed a remarkable improvement in the quality and quantity of advising interactions as well as a constantly improving retention rate. Without imposing mandatory advising, practitioners now average more than 9,000 appointments per year in the advising office (MUH enrolls approximately 4,500 students). Clearly, MUH students value the conversations and seek out advising.

The advising office is fairly small: Four full-time advisors, including the director, three half-time, and two less-than-half-time employees offer advising and support. The advisor staff–student ratio is nearly 900:1, not an ideal percentage, which translates into 45-minute appointments once a semester. However, even with these staff and time limitations, MUH advisors effectively use the AA model, proving that long meetings at multiple times per semester are not a prerequisite for AA to have a meaningful impact on students.

References

Appreciative Advising. (n.d.). *The Appreciative Advising Inventory*. Retrieved from http://www.appreciativeadvising.net/aa-inventory.html

Bloom, J. L., Hutson, B. L., & He, Y. (2008). *The appreciative advising revolution*. Champaign, IL: Stipes.

7

STRENGTHS-BASED ADVISING

Laurie A. Schreiner

Two paradigms have dominated higher education since its inception almost a millennia ago. Until the 1960s, the dominant paradigm reflected a *survival of the fittest* mentality, in which only the brightest students were admitted and educators were charged with weeding out those incapable of stellar achievement. As increased access into colleges and universities within the United States became the norm in the early 1970s, the paradigm shifted toward one of *deficit remediation*. Under this later model, a wider variety of students were admitted and educators identified areas in which students were deficient and created an academic plan for remedial course work. Those advocating the deficit remediation approach believed that students are more likely to succeed if they spend most of their first year addressing areas of weakness (Schreiner, 2010).

Both modes of operations exist in the current higher education environment, but both fail to address a crucial element of student success: motivation. In this chapter, I present a new paradigm—strengths development—as a way of addressing the fundamental challenge of higher education: how to engage students in the learning process and motivate them to fulfill their potential.

Strengths-based advising represents a paradigm shift for higher education from failure prevention and a survival mentality to success promotion and a perspective of thriving. Rather than assessing the areas in which the student is deficient and in need of remediation, advisors using a strengths-based approach assess the talents and personal assets that students bring into the college environment and work with them to develop those competencies into strengths through gained knowledge and skills. Instead of focusing primarily on the problems students may be experiencing, advisors help students envision future possibilities and learn to leverage talents to address obstacles that may emerge in the future (Schreiner & Anderson, 2005). In addition to a goal of completing college, strengths-based advisors help students make the most of the college experience.

In this chapter, I provide an overview of strengths-based advising and its theoretical foundations along with evidence of its effectiveness. I outline steps in the advising process along with questions advisors can ask and tools they can use during each step. Throughout the chapter, the practical applications of this advising approach are emphasized.

Foundations of Strengths-Based Advising

The foundation for a strengths-based approach to advising contains interdisciplinary components. A strengths perspective has been evident within the field of social work for several decades. It is based on the assumption that clients possess the ability to overcome adversity, grow, and succeed (Saleebey, 1996, 2006; Weick, Rapp, Sullivan, & Kisthardt, 1989). Accounts of strengths-based development in business (Buckingham, 2007; Clifton & Harter, 2003; Hodges & Clifton, 2004; Rath & Conchie, 2008) illustrate another pillar of this approach. The business model utilizes feedback and awareness of talents in motivating people toward engagement and excellence, thus enabling companies to be more productive. Positive organizational scholarship, in the field of organizational development (Cameron, Dutton, & Quinn, 2003), contributes an important perspective on thriving, vitality, and meaning.

The current emphasis on the psychology of human strengths evidenced in the positive psychology movement (Aspinwall & Staudinger, 2003; Peterson & Seligman, 2004; Seligman & Csikszentmihalyi, 2000; Shushok & Hulme, 2006) also provides a theoretical foundation for the strengths-based approach to advising. Positive psychology emphasizes optimal human functioning and features connections to intrinsic motivation (Ryan & Deci, 2000), self-efficacy (Bandura, 1997), well-being (Diener & Biswas-Diener, 2008), and hope (Snyder, Rand, & Sigmon, 2002).

Finally, the talent development approach used in higher education (Kuh, Kinzie, Schuh, & Whitt, 2005) also forms part of the interdisciplinary foundation for strengths-based advising. It emphasizes that every student can learn under the proper conditions of appropriate challenge and support. An institutional commitment to talent development thus "arranges resources and learning conditions to maximize student potential so that students leave college different in desired ways from how they started" (p. 77). This commitment is also reflected in the theory and practice of appreciative advising as described by Bloom, Hutson, and He (2008) (see also chapter 6 by these authors).

The Strengths Development Philosophy

The bedrock under each interdisciplinary foundation of strengths-based advising rests on the premise that capitalizing on one's areas of greatest talent likely leads to greater success than investing comparable time and effort to remediate areas of weakness (Clifton & Harter, 2003). Fredrickson (2009) expanded on this point by emphasizing that "people who have the opportunity every day to do what they do best—to act on their strengths—are far more likely to flourish" (p. 189).

Advisors taking a strengths-based approach use students' talents, defined as "naturally recurring patterns of thought, feeling, or behavior that can be productively applied" (Clifton & Harter, 2003, p. 111), as the bases for educational planning (Schreiner & Anderson, 2005). These competencies include ways of processing information, interacting with people, perceiving the world, and navigating the environment. When multiplied by the knowledge and skills acquired in the learning process, these talents can be developed into strengths: "the ability to provide consistent, near-perfect performance in a given activity" (Clifton, Anderson, & Schreiner, 2006, p. 4). Buckingham (2007) and others (Linley, Willars, & Biswas-Diener, 2010) further suggested that strengths are not evidenced solely in performance, but also in energy: Strengths are those activities at which a person excels and that energize the person.

By emphasizing the talents students bring into the college environment, advisors can directly address the issue of student engagement in the learning process. As Ryan and Deci (2000) have established through their research, a sense of competence, involvement in supportive relationships, and freedom to choose activities contribute to intrinsic motivation. By identifying and nurturing students' strengths as well as highlighting areas of existing competence, advisors in supportive relationships with students motivate them to become engaged in the learning process. They foster intrinsic motivation by helping students identify the many choices available for further developing their talents into strengths.

Evidence of Effectiveness

Evidence of the effectiveness of strengths-based approaches exists within business, positive psychology, and higher education venues. For example, Harter and Schmidt (2002) demonstrated that employees whose supervisors have provided opportunities for them to capitalize on their strengths exhibit higher levels of engagement and greater productivity than do those where favorable conditions for growth are not consistently offered. Within the field of psychology, Seligman, Steen, Park, and Peterson (2005) conducted an intervention in which people were asked to think of a new way to use their signature strengths every day for one week. Employing a randomly assigned placebo as a control, they found those in the treatment group experienced significant increases in well-being and decreased depressive symptoms 6 months after the intervention. Among first-year students in higher education, similarly controlled empirical studies demonstrated that a strengths-development approach contributes significantly to a growth mind-set and greater feelings of control over one's own academic success (Louis, 2011) as well as to greater levels of engaged learning, higher grades, and enhanced satisfaction with college (Cantwell, 2008).

In a random-assignment control-group study of advising, Schreiner (2004) compared a strengths- to a needs-based assessment approach. Students working with faculty practitioners using a strengths-based approach reported greater satisfaction with advising, greater benefit from the specific exercises used, and higher GPAs at the end of the semester and one year after the conclusion of the study than did those who received advising based on needs assessments. In addition, the strengths-based advising group experienced a freshman-to-sophomore persistence rate that was 12% higher than that of the needs assessment group, a statistically significant difference.

Challenges

As noted by Schreiner and Anderson (2005), advising directors may encounter four challenges from advisors contesting the adoption of a strengths-based approach. First, advisors may resist a change in the status quo, which is a normal response, but advisors who support either a survival-of-the-fittest or deficit-remediation paradigm may exhibit particular reticence to change. Investing training time in a discussion of these models and providing evidence of the efficacy of a strengths-development approach, directors may open the minds of advisors trained in a different perspective. In response, some advisors may suggest that a strengths-based approach is too time consuming to be practicable. By emphasizing that all effective advising takes time and that the strengths-based approach replaces existing strategies with more effective ones, directors may alleviate concerns.

Second, some advisors lack confidence or expertise with the new instruments or strategies. Administrators can address their uncertainty by a) assuring advisors that they need not be experts on the instruments but simply prepare and ask questions that will help students independently discover their strengths and b) giving advisors the opportunity to learn about their own strengths and how to utilize them to become even better advisors.

Third, practitioners may consider talent identification the end goal, rather than focus on strengths development. Research indicates that simply helping students identify personal strengths may unintentionally send the message that individual success is dependent primarily on the presence of certain personal qualities rather than on the effort required to develop and use talents appropriately (Louis, 2011). Therefore, advisors need to frame strengths as individual predispositions that can be developed as opposed to innate characteristics that students possess. By making them aware of resources and opportunities available on and off campus for strength development, advisors assist students in cultivating their strengths and applying them to the tasks they face.

Fourth, some advisors will invoke myths about a strengths-development paradigm. Under the most pervasive of misperceptions, some believe that strengths-development strategies replace all strategies designed to address weaknesses. Faculty members who strongly believe that students should focus on their deficits may be particularly inclined to view a strengths-based advising approach as insufficient to address areas where students need improvement. However, the strengths-development approach does not ignore weaknesses; rather, through strengths-based advising students address weaknesses from a position of strength.

Both strength-based advocates and those opposed can agree that weakness is defined by characteristics that interfere with the success or performance of an individual or others in the environment (Buckingham & Clifton, 2001). Administrators can point out that such weaknesses can be addressed by helping students identify and use their strengths to improve in these areas. For example, a student who needs to improve reading comprehension and who possesses empathy can identify with the characters in a story, visualizing the situation and feeling the emotions described, to better understand the author's point. By starting with the strength (in this case, empathy), the student gains motivation and confidence to address a challenge (reading). The specific strategies characteristic of a strength likely lead the student in the direction of success (Schreiner & Anderson, 2005).

Steps in Strengths-Based Advising

Five steps in strengths-based advising tend to work best in sequence. In this section, I describe the steps and the intended outcomes of each.

Step 1: Identify Students' Talents

Strengths-based advising begins with an identification of students' talents. This process of discovery builds rapport with students as advisors focus on the individual and his or her potential contributions to the learning environment. Several methods may help advisors in this process. Although the use of a specific instrument is not necessary, many advisors find the concrete information available from a strengths assessment to be helpful. The assessment results allow advisors to initiate conversation with students; they also validate and affirm students' experiences and provide both student and advisor with a common language for talking about strengths.

This step of strengths-based advising builds positive emotions in students as they learn about aspects of themselves that can equip them for success in college as well as in their lives outside of college. These positive emotions, in turn, enhance students' problem-solving skills and creative thinking (Fredrickson, 2009).

Step 2: Affirm Students' Talents and Increase Awareness of Strengths

After identifying students' talents, the advisor increases students' awareness and appreciation of those assets and helps them see how they can be further developed into strengths. Some students do not value their talents or show reluctance in acknowledging their capabilities because they consider such competencies unexceptional. Other students have been criticized for the unique aspects of their strengths: Gregarious individuals may have been labeled by teachers as troublemakers; women may have received negative feedback for being assertive or competitive; men may have been ridiculed for expressing empathy. Especially with those hesitant to embrace their talents, advisors need to help advisees see their talents as unique and affirm them as assets in building a foundation for college success. This critical affirmation process cues students to deploy their strengths as they face challenges or rebound from failures (Steele, Spencer, & Lynch, 1993).

In addition to affirming their talents, advisors can help students learn how to develop positive habits into strengths. In the first step in the formula for success, the student identifies the talents and aspects of life that energize her or him and then determines the level of effort needed to multiply aptitudes into strengths. Only when the dominant talents are refined and honed by the skills and knowledge students gain from the learning environment can strengths emerge. Recent research on brain plasticity, which describes how the human brain changes physically and chemically as a result of practice, supports the legitimacy of this description of success progression (Bransford, Brown, & Cocking, 2008). The more a skill is practiced, the faster the neural pathways connect. Areas of the brain used during such practice become larger and more fully developed. This insight into the way the brain changes as a result of effort and practice can help students see that such effort enables them to develop strengths to succeed in college; thus, their academic success is under their control.

Step 3: Envision the Future

After identifying students' talents and increasing their awareness of the ways they can be developed into strengths, advisors implement the third step of strengths-based advising by discussing with students their aspirations and how developing their talents can help them reach their goals. This step is not primarily about career planning or major selection, but about the kind of person a student wants to become. In this envisioning phase, self-efficacy and intrinsic motivation are generated by the process of articulating what Markus and Nurius (1986) call *possible selves*—those aspects of oneself that one most wants to embody in the future. Some students, particularly those from disadvantaged backgrounds, may express a highly motivating possible self in negative terms about an unwanted future; that is, they may disclose their biggest fears about a future self they want to interdict. Whether positive or negative, a concrete and vivid depiction of one's possible selves can encourage students to take specific steps in the present to create (or avoid) that future self.

This envisioning process creates an image of a bright future for students that helps them persevere during difficult times. Psychologists have demonstrated that visualizing one's best possible self leads to more positive emotions and higher levels of motivation that can motivate students to take action to reach valued goals (Cross & Markus, 1994). Pizzolato (2006) noted that utilizing the possible-selves approach may particularly benefit students historically underrepresented in higher education.

Step 4: Plan Specific Steps for Students to Reach Goals

Designing a plan for reaching the student's goals constitutes the fourth step of strengths-based advising. Helping students connect their passions and strengths to their future selves often opens their minds to possibilities for academic majors and careers they had not previously considered (Bloom et al., 2008). In this step, the advisor focuses on cocreating a specific plan that a student can implement, with both short- and long-term goals important to the student and congruent with her or his values and strengths.

This step of strengths-based advising utilizes strategies that Lopez et al. (2004) labeled *hope building*. According to statistically significant findings in research, levels of hope in college students predict their grades as well as their persistence to graduation, even after the researchers controlled for preexisting levels of ability and demographic characteristics (Snyder, Shorey, Cheavens, Pulvers, Adams, & Wiklund, 2002). Building hope involves helping students a) identify an educational goal that is meaningful and realistically attainable for them, b) develop multiple pathways for reaching the goal, and c) brainstorm ways to handle obstacles and remain motivated in the face of challenges. The strengths that students have identified throughout the advising process become pathways to their chosen future selves. By providing the essential encouragement and support that can sustain the motivation necessary for reaching their goals, advisors can help students reframe potential obstacles to success as challenges to be overcome with effort (Schreiner, Hulme, Hetzel, & Lopez, 2009).

Step 5: Apply Students' Strengths to Challenges

Teaching students to transfer strengths from one setting to another, such as from the playing field or the theater to the classroom, comprises a critical component of strengths-based advising (Schreiner & Anderson, 2005). In the final step, advisors assist students in identifying ways to apply specific talents to new situations or challenges.

By reminding students that they have successfully dealt with challenges in the past, advisors not only offer encouragement but call to mind the specific ways students achieved past successes as well as energize and motivate them to tackle the current difficulty. Rather than communicating one strategy for success, advisors reveal that the secret to success lies in capitalizing on one's strengths as the best means for addressing and overcoming challenges.

The Skills and Tools of Strengths-Based Advisors

The practice of strengths-based advising requires a set of tools, skills, and strategies that advisors can acquire through a variety of training opportunities. Strengths-based advising is primarily a philosophical approach, and although instruments may be helpful in the process, it does not require the use of specific measures. The three major tools advisors will need include a) methods for identifying and affirming students' talents, b) strategies for helping students envision and plan for their best possible future, and c) techniques to assist students in applying their talents and strengths to new situations and challenges.

Instruments and Methods for Identifying and Affirming Student Talents

Identifying students' talents is at the heart of strengths-based advising because those aptitudes form the foundation for planning and success. An instrument to identify talents can accelerate the conversation about strengths and provides advisors with hypotheses about students' talents that they can confirm in dialogue with the student. The results from such instruments can be affirming to students as external objective validation of the attributes they possess. In addition, assessing students' strengths as they enter college sends a powerful message about the priority the institution places on learning about students and the contributions they will make to the university environment. Kuh (2008) noted that this talent development philosophy grounds the advising practices in institutions where students are highly engaged.

Three instruments were designed specifically to identify talents and strengths and can be used in a higher education setting: *StrengthsFinder 2.0* (The Gallup Organization, 2007), the *Values in Action Inventory of Strengths* (Peterson & Seligman, 2004), and *Realise2* (Centre for Applied Positive Psychology, 2010). Each instrument was created based on unique perspectives and for specific purposes. For example, *Strengths-Finder 2.0* measures strengths of competence and provides students with 5 signature themes of talent that can be used to succeed. It features 34 possible signature themes identified from a Gallup study of excellence and describes "areas where the greatest potential exists for strengths building" (Hodges & Clifton, 2004, p. 256). A web site designed for college students and educators (http://www.strengthsquest.com) provides a wealth of support materials as well as access to a textbook and to the instrument for a fee.

The *Values in Action Inventory of Strengths*, in contrast, measures strengths of character, providing students with five signature character strengths valued across cultures as elements of a well-lived life. Materials on its web site (http://www.viacharacter.org) are free and geared primarily to adults but could be adapted for use with college students. *Realise2* is a newer assessment from the United Kingdom that measures strengths based on responses to questions about the tasks that a person does well and that energize him or her. The assessment is available for a fee on the web site (http://realise2.cappeu.com/4/), which outputs an in-depth profile and personal action plan guide.

Advisors may also choose to use instruments with which they are already familiar, such as the *Myers-Briggs Type Indicator* (Myers & Briggs Foundation, 2003), the *DiSC* (Inscape Publishing, 2003), or the *College Student Inventory* (Stratil, 1988). In using these types of instruments, advisors emphasize the positive aspects of the results as the assets students can leverage or develop further for success.

Advisors who cannot access a particular instrument to identify strengths can ask students questions in the advising session that will enable them to discern their talents. For example, advisors can ask students about past accomplishments and explore with them the strategies that led to their successes in these previous situations. They can ask students about their most recent educational experiences (Hovland et al., 1997) or about the characteristics that students believe best describe them. The following advising questions allow advisors to probe for strengths:

- What did you learn with the greatest ease in high school?
- What have your teachers complimented you about most often?
- What was your favorite class in high school?
- What subjects did you enjoy studying the most?
- What can you do for hours on end?
- What fascinates you?
- What are you like when you are "at your best"?
- Tell me about a good day you have had recently; what made that such a good day?

Specific exercises advisors can use to affirm students' strengths and raise their awareness of the talents they bring to the college environment are focused around targeted questions and homework tasks. Advisors can ask students the following questions:

- How have you used your talents to succeed in the past?
- In what settings or circumstances do you most often use these abilities?
- What brings out your best or helps you thrive in college?
- What strengths resonate most with you and how have you seen them in action?
- What have you sometimes been teased about or criticized for? How could this be a shadow side of a talent that helps you achieve excellence? What would it take for others to perceive it as a strength rather than as a problem?

As a task to complete outside the advising session, advisors can encourage students to confirm their strengths with the significant people in their lives, such as family and friends who know them well. Sometimes students are not accepting of their own strengths until others affirm them. Hearing stories from family members about early life experiences in which their strengths were evident conveys to students that the ingredients for success are already within them (Schreiner & Anderson, 2005).

Strategies for Envisioning and Planning

The strategies for helping students envision and plan for a possible future include exercises for imagining possible selves (Markus & Nurius, 1986) and strategies for accentuating hope (Lopez et al., 2004). Questions advisors can ask to help students envision their future include the following:

- What are you most looking forward to while in college?
- What do you see yourself doing as a result of being a college graduate that you cannot do now?
- Where do you want to be five years from now?

○ How would you describe the person you want to become? What is that
person like? What is that person able to do? What kind of relationships does
that person have? What will it take for you to grow toward becoming that
person?

Advisors also can ask students what they have always wanted to do or what
they would do "if money was not a concern and you knew you could not fail."
This approach is similar to Burg and Mayhall's (2002) "miracle question"
(p. 82) that leads students to explore possibilities they have not previously
considered.

In addition to advising questions, two exercises help students imagine their possible
selves. In the roadmap exercise, students think about their life as a journey and draw
a road to their future that contains a fork in it. The upper fork represents their "best
possible selves" if everything in life goes well and they accomplish all their goals. The
lower fork represents their "most feared selves," the result of life that does not go as
planned, revealing the most deleterious outcomes. Students describe each fork in vivid
detail and then determine the actions needed to travel the road of the "best possible
self."

In another possible selves exercise, students draw a tree with branches for each of
their possible selves. The possible selves tree is used as a metaphor to help students
examine the key roles they will assume in life, their possible selves, and the overall
condition of their tree. Then they set goals related to the actions they need to nurture
their trees and create an action plan for reaching those goals (Markus & Nurius,
1986; Oyserman, Bybee, Terry, & Hart-Johnson, 2004).

Using any of the above techniques for helping students envision and clearly conceptualize their future goals, advisors assist them in designing an action plan to reach
those goals based on successful strategies of hope building identified by Lopez et al.
(2004). Hope consists of three elements: a) a clearly articulated, specific, and realistic
goal that the student is motivated to attain; b) specific pathways or strategies for
reaching that goal; and c) the ability to initiate and sustain the motivation needed to
deploy those strategies. The action plan should focus on the goals identified in the
possible selves exercises as most valuable or salient to the student. Articulating
the goals in measureable, observable action terms will help the student determine the
realistic prospects for reaching them and knowing when they have been achieved;
breaking each goal down into manageable steps will allow for both short- and long-
term objectives to be identified. Then the advisor brainstorms with the student multiple pathways for reaching the goals, accentuating the student's strengths as specific
pathways toward goal attainment.

Additionally, the advisor asks the student to identify potential obstacles and how
to respond to them. Campus resources and sources of social support in the student's
life are also identified at this stage. Finally, the advisor helps the student identify the
best strategy to pursue each week and agrees to check in with the student in one
week to see the student's progress.

Techniques for Applying Strengths to Challenges

In the final phase of strengths-based advising, students apply their strengths to new situations, particularly to the challenges they face in college. By this point in the process, students are familiar with their strengths and have developed personally meaningful goals and are working toward achieving them. However, challenges are inevitable and obstacles to success abound. Advisors need to help students develop the key skill of transferring strengths from one context to another.

After asking about specific ways they overcame past challenges (What strengths did they use? What else helped them?), advisors brainstorm with students about ways to use one of their talents to address a current problem and thus create a specific response to the challenge while offering encouragement based on previous successes. In an international study, researchers found that high achievers invented ways of using their strengths to address challenges (Buckingham & Clifton, 2001). Thus, advisors should not skip this step with students. They need to brainstorm at least one idea to capitalize on a talent. By doing so, advisors provide students with a reminder that they have the solution within them and that they have been successful before—which can energize and motivate them to tackle the current challenge.

Training Strengths-Based Advisors

Because strengths-based advising represents a paradigm shift, particularly for many faculty members, advisor training is a necessary first step toward creating the best advising for students. Such training can be offered as a full-day workshop or in multiple smaller modules. Key ingredients in the training include a) an introduction to the strengths philosophy; b) an exercise to identify one's own strengths as an advisor and gain practice with tools or questions used to help students identify their strengths; c) the steps of strengths-based advising and the questions or exercises available to facilitate each step; and d) practicing with strengths-based advising strategies in case studies or role plays.

To introduce the strengths philosophy and provide evidence of its effectiveness, facilitators may need to spend more time training faculty members than professional advisors. Addressing faculty concerns, such as their lack of familiarity or confidence in using a particular tool to identify student talents, may also prove time consuming. Faculty advisors who are comfortable with the strengths philosophy can conduct the workshop to make it particularly effective with fellow faculty members.

Strengths-Based Advising Scenario

Students struggling academically present a common challenge to academic advisors. The following scenario demonstrates ways that advisors can utilize strengths-based advising to help students address difficult situations.

Scenario I

A first-generation college sophomore, Riley, says to an advisor, Skylar, "I'm having trouble in two of my classes. I don't understand what the professor is talking about in one of them, but it's a required course in my major. The other is only a gen ed course, but I keep getting low grades on the writing assignments. I was always good in writing in high school. If I do poorly, this will lower my GPA, and I just got off academic probation last term. I want to stay in my major, but I don't know if I can pass this one course and that would really disappoint my family. What do you suggest I do?"

○ ○ ○

The advisor, Skylar, who adopts a strengths-based approach, asks Riley to identify the areas going well in the other two classes: "What classes seem easier to you?" Strengths-based advisors do not initiate the conversation by bringing up the areas where students are struggling. Instead, they focus on positive topics to help students identify specific academic tasks in which they have achieved some success.

Riley replies, "I'm getting good grades in my public speaking and psychology classes."

Skylar asks for elaboration: "What specific academic tasks do you do well in those classes?"

"I think it's easy to participate in class discussions and group projects, and I am pretty good at giving talks. . . . I like psychology class, especially writing the reflective journal entries about class topics."

Skylar digs deeper, asking a series of questions that begin with "Which strengths are you using when participating . . ." and following with specific instances Riley has mentioned: "in class discussions?" "engaged in group projects?" "giving oral presentations?" "writing journal entries?" Finally, Skylar asks Riley to summarize: "What energizes you when you're doing these things?"

Expressing an ability to relate well with other people and persuade them to engage in an activity, Riley responds readily, "Getting up in front of people, telling stories. I understand what makes people tick . . . and I'm fascinated by why people do what they do." Riley describes the enjoyment of thinking about and analyzing everyday phenomena.

Skylar asks, "How are the difficult classes different from psychology and public speaking?" Riley explains that in the difficult classes the professors lecture and do not utilize any group projects or class participation. Based on Riley's additional comments, Skylar surmises that the projects require analytical and research-based writing rather than reflective journaling. Wanting Riley to invent ways to use personal skills in challenging situations, Skylar follows up by asking, "Which of your strengths might be useful in those classes?"

"Well, maybe I could study with other students in the class and create my own group experience."

Acknowledging this as a good start, Skylar pushes for more ideas: "What can be done to understand the professors better? Have you been in this situation before—where it was really important to understand someone but you had difficulty doing so?"

Riley laughs before explaining, "Definitely! When I took my first job and my boss was from Korea, I had trouble understanding his English at first."

"So what did you do to understand him?"

"I watched his gestures and listened to his tone of voice."

"Why not use the same technique in the classroom?" Skylar advises Riley to watch the instructor's body language to determine the important points, which are likely to be on an exam.

"What else did you do to understand your boss?"

"I learned the job by listening carefully and by asking questions of the workers who had been there awhile. It took some time to figure him out!"

"Exactly!" Skylar exclaims. "The more you listen carefully and watch body language, the easier it will be to understand your professors. Also, I suggest writing down key words to look up after class, and be sure to read the assigned text and discuss it with others before class. You'll find the same strategies that worked for you in your first job are likely to work in these classes as well."

Skylar then changes tack: "What about those papers that require analytical, research-based writing? How do you prepare your speeches, particularly the persuasive ones?"

"I spend a lot of time searching the Internet for evidence to support my arguments."

"This strategy should help you with analytical papers too. Why don't you prepare your papers as if you're making an oral presentation? Record yourself making the presentation and then transcribe it. Take the transcript to the Writing Center for help in organizing it into a research paper."

Before leaving the office, Riley agrees to organize a group of friends in the course with the unclear instructor and arrange for them to meet the day before each class to talk about their assigned reading and compare notes from previous lectures. Skylar offers to e-mail the following week to check on Riley's progress with these plans and to set up another appointment to talk about choices for a major.

Summary

A strengths-based approach to advising offers a unique lens through which to view students and the advising process. Rather than assessing only student needs or the gaps that exist between student skills and the demands of the college environment, advisors using a strengths-based approach first address student motivation. When students are aware of their strengths and learn to apply them to the challenges they face in college, they will be motivated to set goals, achieve at a higher level, make positive choices, and complete required tasks.

In many ways, emphasizing student deficits and needs puts the focus on the student who is not there. In a strengths-based approach, the advisor works with the student who is there—the one who brings talents into the room as a foundation for addressing the future. Rather than conveying to students that one pathway leads to college success, a strengths-based approach encourages them to capitalize on their unique gifts to become the best version of themselves and gain the most they can from their college experiences. In the process, not only do students achieve success, but advisors thrive as well.

References

Aspinwall, L. G., & Staudinger, U. M. (Eds.). (2003). *A psychology of human strengths: Fundamental questions and future directions for a positive psychology*. Washington, DC: American Psychological Association.

Bandura, A. (1997). *Self-efficacy: The exercise of control*. New York, NY: W. H. Freeman.

Bloom, J., Hutson, B., & He, Y. (2008). *The appreciative advising revolution*. Champaign, IL: Stipes.

Bransford, J. D., Brown, A. L., & Cocking, R. R. (2008). Mind and brain. In K. Fischer & M. H. Immordino-Yang (Eds.), *The Jossey-Bass reader on the brain and learning* (pp. 89–108). San Francisco, CA: John Wiley and Sons.

Buckingham, M. (2007). *Go put your strengths to work*. New York, NY: Free Press.

Buckingham, M., & Clifton, D. O. (2001). *Now, discover your strengths*. New York, NY: Free Press.

Burg, J. E., & Mayhall, J. L. (2002). Techniques and interventions of solution-focused advising. *NACADA Journal, 22*(2), 79–85.

Cameron, K. S., Dutton, J. E., & Quinn, R. E. (Eds.). (2003). *Positive organizational scholarship: Foundations of a new discipline*. San Francisco, CA: Berrett-Koehler.

Cantwell, L. S. (2008). Human strengths: Differences that bring us together. In S. J. Lopez (Ed.), *Positive psychology: Exploring the best in people: Discovering human strengths* (pp. 37–54). Westport, CT: Praeger.

Centre for Applied Positive Psychology. (2010). *Realise2*. Retrieved from http://www.cappeu.com/realise2.htm

Clifton, D., Anderson, E., & Schreiner, L. (2006). *StrengthsQuest: Discover and develop your strengths in academics, career, and beyond* (2nd ed.). Princeton, NJ: Gallup Press.

Clifton, D. O., & Harter, J. K. (2003). Investing in strengths. In K. S. Cameron, J. E. Dutton, & R. E. Quinn (Eds.), *Positive organizational scholarship* (pp. 111–121). San Francisco, CA: Berrett-Koehler.

Cross, S. E., & Markus, H. R. (1994). Self-schemas, possible selves, and competent performance. *Journal of Educational Psychology, 86*, 343–348.

Diener, E., & Biswas-Diener, R. (2008). *Happiness: Unlocking the mysteries of psychological wealth*. Hoboken, NJ: Wiley Blackwell.

Fredrickson, B. L. (2009). *Positivity*. New York, NY: Crown.

The Gallup Organization. (2007). *StrengthsFinder 2.0*. Retrieved from http://sf2.strengthsfinder.com

Harter, J. K., & Schmidt, F. L. (2002). *Business-unit-level relationship between employee satisfaction, employee engagement, and business outcomes: A meta-analysis* (Gallup Technical Report). Omaha, NE: The Gallup Organization.

Hodges, T. D., & Clifton, D. O. (2004). Strengths-based development in practice. In P. A. Linley & S. Joseph (Eds.), *Positive psychology in practice: From research to application* (pp. 256–268). New York, NY: John Wiley and Sons.

Hovland, M. J., Anderson, E. C., McGuire, W. G., Crockett, D., Kaufmann, J., & Woodward, D. (1997). *Academic advising for student success and retention*. Iowa City, IA: Noel/Levitz.

Inscape Publishing. (2003). *What is DiSC?* Retrieved from http://www.discprofile.com/whatisdisc.htm

Kuh, G. D. (2008). Advising for student success. In V. N. Gordon, W. R. Habley, & T. J. Grites (Eds.), *Academic advising: A comprehensive handbook* (2nd ed.) (pp. 68–84). San Francisco, CA: John Wiley and Sons.

Kuh, G. D., Kinzie, J., Schuh, J. H., & Whitt, E. J. (Eds.). (2005). *Student success in college: Creating conditions that matter*. San Francisco, CA: Jossey-Bass.

Linley, P. A., Willars, J., & Biswas-Diener, R. (2010). *The strengths book*. Coventry, UK: CAPP Press.

Lopez, S. J., Snyder, C. R., Magyar-Moe, J. L., Edwards, L. M., Pedrotti, J. T., Janowski, K., . . ., & Pressgrove, C. (2004). Strategies for accentuating hope. In P. A. Linley & S. Joseph (Eds.), *Positive psychology in practice* (pp. 388–404). Hoboken, NJ: John Wiley and Sons.

Louis, M. C. (2011). Strengths interventions in higher education: The effect of identification versus development approaches on implicit self-theory. *The Journal of Positive Psychology, 6*(3), 204–215.

Markus, H., & Nurius, P. (1986). Possible selves. *American Psychologist, 41,* 954–969.

Myers & Briggs Foundation. (2003). *MBTI basics*. Retrieved from http://www.myersbriggs.org/my-mbti-personality-type/mbti-basics/

Oyserman, D., Bybee, D., Terry, K., & Hart-Johnson, T. (2004). Possible selves as roadmaps. *Journal of Research in Personality, 38,* 130–149.

Peterson, C., & Seligman, M. (2004). *Character strengths and virtues: A handbook and classification*. New York, NY: Oxford University Press; Washington, DC: American Psychological Association.

Pizzolato, J. E. (2006). Achieving college student possible selves: Navigating the space between commitment and achievement of long-term identity goals. *Cultural Diversity and Ethnic Minority Psychology, 12*(1), 57–69.

Rath, T., & Conchie, B. (2008). *Strengths-based leadership*. New York, NY: Gallup Press.

Ryan, R. M., & Deci, E. L. (2000). Self-determination theory and the facilitation of intrinsic motivation, social development, and well-being. *American Psychologist, 55*(1), 68–78.

Saleebey, D. (1996). The strengths perspective in social work practice: Extensions and cautions. *Social Work, 41*(3), 296–305.

Saleebey, D. (2006). Introduction: Power in the people. In D. Saleebey (Ed.), *The strengths perspective in social work practice* (4th ed.) (pp. 1–24). Boston, MA: Pearson.

Schreiner, L. (2004). *Affirming students' strengths: A campus-wide approach to student success and retention* (Report to the Fund for the Improvement of Post-secondary Education P116B000306). Washington, DC: U.S. Department of Education.

Schreiner, L. (2010). The "thriving quotient": A new vision for student success. *About Campus, 15*(2), 2–10.

Schreiner, L. A., & Anderson, E. C. (2005). Strengths-based advising: A new lens for higher education. *NACADA Journal, 25*(2), 20–29.

Schreiner, L., Hulme, E., Hetzel, R., & Lopez, S. (2009). Positive psychology on campus. In S. J. Lopez & C. R. Snyder (Eds.), *Oxford handbook of positive psychology* (2nd ed.) (pp. 569–578). New York, NY: Oxford University Press.

Seligman, M .E. P., & Csikszentmihalyi, M. (2000). Positive psychology: An introduction. *American Psychologist, 55*, 51–82.

Seligman, M.E.P., Steen, T. A., Park, N., & Peterson, C. (2005). Positive psychology progress: Empirical validation of interventions. *American Psychologist, 60*(5), 410–421.

Shushok, F., & Hulme, E. (2006). What's right with you: Helping students find and use their personal strengths. *About Campus, 11*(4), 2–8.

Snyder, C. R., Rand, K. L., & Sigmon, D. R. (2002). Hope theory. In C. R. Snyder & S. J. Lopez (Eds.), *Handbook of positive psychology* (pp. 257–276). New York, NY: Oxford University Press.

Snyder, C., Shorey, H., Cheavens, J., Pulvers, K., Adams, V., & Wiklund, C. (2002). Hope and academic success in college. *Journal of Educational Psychology, 94*(4), 820–826.

Steele, C. M., Spencer, S. J., & Lynch, M. (1993). Self-image and dissonance: The role of affirmational resources. *Journal of Personality and Social Psychology, 64*(6), 885–896.

Stratil, M. (1988). *The College Student Inventory*. Retrieved from https://www.noellevitz.com/student-retention-solutions/retention-management-system-plus/college-student-inventory

Weick, A., Rapp, C., Sullivan, W. P., & Kisthardt, W. (1989). A strengths perspective for social work practice. *Social Work, 34*(4), 350–354.

8

ACADEMIC ADVISING INFORMED BY SELF-AUTHORSHIP THEORY

Janet K. Schulenberg

[Academic advisors] are positioned to facilitate a transformative experience for students—to help them make meaning around how the accordance or discordance of previous and current learning relates to their educational goals and aspirations.

—Kincanon, *Translating the Transformative*, 2009

Many theoretical lenses contribute to an academic advisor's endeavor to facilitate student learning. Self-authorship theory, a relatively new developmental perspective on human psychosocial maturation, is a particularly powerful lens for academic advising because it focuses on the way individuals understand the world and make decisions within it. In particular, it emphasizes the development of an individual's capacity to balance critical evaluations of information, personal beliefs and values, and relationships with others when setting goals and taking action. This kind of complex thinking is a distinctive learning goal of higher education (e.g., American Association of Colleges and Universities [AAC&U], 2002), and advisors have a significant role in helping students achieve it (Baxter Magolda & King, 2008; Lowenstein, 2011; National Academic Advising Association, 2006).

Although self-authorship involves multiple aspects of an individual's development, in general it is characterized by a shift from less dependence on an authority to an intrinsic understanding of self that guides decision making. Self-authored individuals can balance external influences to develop their own internally generated beliefs, goals, and plans of action.

> A self-authored student will not blindly follow parental expectations or expect advisors to tell her or him the major that will be best, nor will a self-authored student single-mindedly follow a gut feeling or passion. . . . Rather, the self-authored student will consider both external expectations and internally defined goals and values. (Pizzolato, 2006, p. 32)

Self-authorship theory is part of a family of constructive-developmental theories in cognitive psychology, which as a whole represents a major theoretical tradition within academic advising. Like other developmental theories, self-authorship lends itself quite naturally to advising applications and points toward certain strategies that can be used to encourage students to more aggressively engage the developmental process. Because advising situations naturally include discussions of how students come to know themselves and their world, personal beliefs, and relationships with others, self-authorship theory forms a particularly applicable advising strategy to help students grapple with complex situations and gain empowerment to make difficult decisions. The theory highlights the educative role of academic advising by reminding advisors that discomfort is an important part of learning.

Self-authored decision making is consistent with the learning outcomes expected of students of higher education (Baxter Magolda, 2009b; Hodge, Baxter Magolda, & Haynes, 2009). Many individuals and organizations have articulated expected outcomes of higher education, including the ability to interact with diverse others in solving complex problems and to become actively contributing citizens skilled in critical thinking (e.g., AAC&U, 2002; Council for the Advancement of Standards of Learning and Developmental Outcomes, 2009).

> In a turbulent and complex world, every college student will need to be purposeful and self-directed in multiple ways. Purpose implies clear goals, an understanding of process, and appropriate action. Further, purpose implies intention in one's actions. Becoming such an intentional learner means developing self-awareness about the reason for study, the learning process itself, and how education is used. Intentional learners are integrative thinkers who can see connections in seemingly disparate information and draw on a wide range of knowledge to make decisions. They adapt the skills learned in one situation to problems encountered in another: in a classroom, the workplace, their communities, or their personal lives. (AAC&U, 2002, chap. 3, para. 3)

The skills involved in self-authorship directly relate to those articulated in the AAC&U statement, particularly those involving self-awareness and integrative thinking. Consistent with the outcomes desired of higher education, the orientation toward self-authorship includes an individual's ability to handle complex information, interact with diverse others, and make nuanced decisions that acknowledge both intrinsic desires and external realities. "Promoting self-authorship enables learners to learn *how* to learn and think for themselves rather than *what* to learn" (Baxter Magolda, 2009b, p. 2).

The Basics of Self-authorship Theory

The concept of self-authorship was first articulated by Kegan (1994) to describe a person's capacity to balance multiple external pressures to create an internally defined identity that guides complex decision making. A self-authored individual habitually and critically evaluates his or her values, beliefs, social relationships, and externally imposed expectations to manage an internally consistent identity (Baxter Magolda, 2009a). The process of developing self-authorship is not linear, nor is it a once-and-done process. Rather, it involves shifts in perceptions and behavior patterns after much practice (Baxter Magolda, 2009a). Self-authorship requires development along three dimensions: the cognitive (coming to know information or phenomena), intrapersonal (considering one's own beliefs and values), and interpersonal (maintaining healthy relationships) (Baxter Magolda, 2009a).

Self-authored decisions are not egocentric ones. Rather, they reflect the construction of mutually beneficial, authentic relationships (e.g., ending destructive relationships or managing decisions to meet the needs of all parties involved) (Baxter Magolda, 2008; Baxter Magolda & King, 2004). Made by those with a clearly defined sense of self, these decisions are not self-serving. Self-authorship represents the development of "an internal belief system that allow[s] [the individual] to consider but not be overwhelmed by external influence, a coherent identity that yield[s] the confidence to act on wise choices, and mature relations to collaborate productively with colleagues" (Baxter Magolda, 2008, p. 269). For example, a student may still decide to study a subject that her parents expect her to pursue, but that decision reflects self-authorship when made with an awareness of external expectations and based on an internally controlled sense of self. Scholars of self-authorship often refer to this internal belief system as *listening to one's internal voice* (see, e.g., Baxter Magolda, 2009a; Pizzolato, 2004).

Baxter Magolda (1992, 2001, 2009a) conducted a longitudinal study focused on the development of self-authorship among traditional-aged college students into adulthood. She further elaborated various elements of self-authorship, including the conditions that promote it in individuals. Those not engaged in self-authored ways of knowing follow external formulas and make decisions without thinking critically about them. College students in this developmental phase tend to believe in immutable truths, employ right-wrong and good-bad dichotomies, and expect authorities to provide answers and directions. Students entering college often have not yet met the challenge of developing an internally consistent identity that allows them to develop and achieve realistic, self-driven goals. In particular, Pizzolato (2008) noted that students' initial goals are often "inherited from others, particularly parents" (p. 20). Students use gut instincts, rather than a critical evaluation of their motivations, expectations, and realities, to generate decisions. Particularly relevant to academic advising, students often choose academic and career paths for extrinsic reasons and later find the outcomes unfulfilling or dissatisfying.

While in college, students often do quite well by following external formulas, meeting instructor requirements to earn good grades, following degree requirements to make appropriate progress to graduation, choosing majors that satisfy family members' agendas. Eventually, however, individuals may encounter situations in which external formulas no longer sufficiently lead to satisfactory decisions. Baxter Magolda found that graduates in their twenties begin grappling with problems arising in work and relationships (Baxter Magolda, 2001). She referred to this experience of significant dissonance as *the crossroads* (p. 38). Individuals may be thrust into the crossroads when confronted with questions that a clear-cut right-or-wrong response cannot answer, encounter a new situation with no commensurate path to follow, or realize that following formulas leads to ungratifying destinations. The recognition of this dissonance, the hallmark of the crossroads, characterizes the beginning of self-authorship.

Students come to the crossroads when external formulas conflict with internal voices. However, students in the crossroads do not always embrace change because they may fail to recognize the dissonance of the crossroads or choose to leave it unresolved (Baxter Magolda, 2001). Individuals encounter the crossroads at different points. Some never recognize it or act on it while some encounter and respond to it fairly early. For example, those from oppressed or marginalized groups may enter the crossroads before their twenties and develop self-authored decision making sooner than their majority or commonly represented peers (Abes, Jones, & McEwan, 2007; Costello, 2010; Pizzolato, 2004; Torres & Hernandez, 2007; Torres, Reiser, LePeau, Davis, & Ruder, 2006).

This discovery supports the suggestion that self-authorship could be provoked if individuals receive appropriate challenge and support (Baxter Magolda, 2008; Pizzolato, 2006). Pizzolato (2003) identified a particular point—*the provocative moment*—when a student in the crossroads takes action. She suggested that college educators, including academic advisors, can create these conditions for students. Pizzolato (2005) described one student's provocative moment:

> After the acceptance letters from various colleges came home prior to freshman year I had to make this decision [whether to attend college], because as a member of my family you MUST work for the family, like my father and his father. I had to choose. My options were to go to school or carry out the business. . . . I thought about myself and . . . I became more confident in the fact that I am independent of my family's business and will become my own entity unassociated with the business. (p. 629)

As individuals build skills in coordinating their beliefs, identities, and social relations, they build habits that move them through other elements of self-authorship (Baxter Magolda, 2008). "Becoming the Author of One's Own Life" represents an element in which individuals actively work on developing "internal perspectives and self-definition" (Pizzolato, 2003, p. 798). As this thinking pattern becomes more habitual, individuals build *Internal Foundations* on which they consistently employ their internally defined perspectives to evaluate situations and guide action (Pizzolato, 2003, p. 798). Participants in Baxter Magolda's (2009a) longitudinal study became comfortable with this type of self-authorship in their thirties. Individuals continue to move in and out of each of these self-authorship elements over a lifetime as they encounter different challenges.

Reflective Conversations

Baxter Magolda's (2008) work stresses that "self-authorship evolves when the challenge to become self-authoring is present and is accompanied by sufficient support to help an individual make the shift to internal meaning making" (p. 271). Learning environments that promote self-authorship share particular characteristics: While offering support through collaborative relationships, they consistently challenge learners to grapple with ambiguity and to see themselves as knowledge constructors (Baxter Magolda & King, 2004). Baxter Magolda (2002) described support for self-authorship as "good company" for the developmental journey. She and other authors have noted that due to the supportive, relationship-oriented nature of their work, advisors are ideally situated both to provide good company and to provoke students to tackle questions that lack clear-cut answers (e.g., Baxter Magolda & King, 2008; Pizzolato, 2006).

Academic advisors regularly engage students in handling decisions with multiple possible outcomes, such as those associated with choice of major, challenges to past self-understandings of academic strengths, and changes in interests and goals. Because the majority of college-aged students follow external formulas, they often look to advisors, faculty members, and parents as authorities who can provide the definitive directions for success (Baxter Magolda & King, 2008). In addressing complicated areas of student inquiry, advisors can employ reflective conversation techniques that encourage students to think through complex situational issues and identify their own interpretations and solutions (Baxter Magolda & King, 2008). However, advisors need to refrain from offering solutions to problems and instead focus on helping students discover their own paths to success. For example, in a reflective conversation about choice of major, an advisor might ask, "What has surprised you about X? How has it changed the way you think about Y?" or "What is the most important thing you've learned about your academic interests so far?" Such queries help students situate themselves as knowers as they attempt to make meaning of their experience as they are living it.

The critical role of reflective conversation easily reconciles with prevailing notions of quality academic advising. However, when pressed for time, advisors find that telling, rather than asking and listening, feels like a more efficient use of appointment time. By keeping self-authorship as a theoretical focus, the advisor is attentive to the role of collaborator and reflective conversation partner, and thus encourages students to build more complex ways of knowing. Such conversations can challenge students to wrestle with the complexities in their decisions while talking through the issues without experiencing judgment. For example, Bob confesses in an advising session that his math skills are not as good as he initially thought. As someone with experience relevant to the student's challenge, Sharon collaborates with Bob to identify the differences between his collegiate and high school experiences. Perhaps Bob discovers that his expectations about the appropriate amount of study time built in secondary school no longer applies, he has not adapted to the collegiate teaching style, or he finds the subject less than intellectually compelling. Each of these attributions for Bob's difficulty warrants a different conversation and a unique student action. Academic advisors can provide a safe, nonjudgmental space for frank conversations where students identify their own interpretations.

Advisors can challenge students to recognize crossroads moments by initiating provocative conversations. Perhaps Bob does not consider his math skills a problem, but Sharon notes that his algebra midterm grade is significantly lower than his marks in other classes. Sharon might encourage Bob to talk about the classes in which he feels successful and direct him to speculate about the reasons for the good outcomes. After recognizing Bob's academic achievements, Sharon shifts the conversation to the courses in which Bob is struggling. Without such supportive provocation, Bob may never have mentioned his math performance. However, by encouraging Bob to address a disappointing grade, Sharon helped move him toward self-authored habits of reflection.

As Baxter Magolda's work suggests, and Pizzolato's research elaborates, movement out of the crossroads and toward becoming an author of one's own life requires dissonance and discomfort. Disequilibrium is a particularly critical aspect of self-authorship theory, and advisors and other higher education personnel should make students feel unsettled sometimes; they should present students with problems and dilemmas they cannot readily solve or reconcile. For example, when meeting with a student choosing a major primarily because she believes it will lead to a job acceptable to her parents, an advisor can ask for evidence-based reasons that such a major would offer a satisfying postgraduation career.

When situated with proper support from a reflective and collaborative relationship, individuals may address dissonance, an aspect that distinguishes application of self-authorship theory from other related developmental perspectives. Pushing students to feeling uncomfortable runs contrary to customer service principles set forth at some universities and the helping-oriented impulses of advisors; however, to help students see and navigate the crossroads, the advisor must nudge the student into new territory by challenging extrinsic motivations and simplistic interpretations of situations. Done with appropriate support, this challenge can lead the student to develop higher levels of self-authored abilities, consistent with the learning outcomes of higher education.

The Learning Partnerships Model

Baxter Magolda and King developed the learning partnerships model (LPM), which translates self-authorship theory into particular actions that can be used in educational settings to encourage self-authorship (Baxter Magolda, 2009b; Baxter Magolda & King, 2004). This model encourages practitioners to balance challenge with support and emphasizes the central role of the learner to exercise both freedom of choice and responsibility in action (Baxter Magolda, 2009b). The LPM is based on three basic principles: validate students as knowers, situate learning in students' experiences, and define learning as mutually constructing meaning. While all of these principles can be addressed through reflective conversation, they can also be implemented through other strategies that encourage reflection, such as minute papers or questions asked in preparation for an advising appointment (Kincanon, 2009).

Validate Students as Knowers

As a locus of learning in higher education, academic advising presents the opportunity for students to see themselves as able to construct knowledge and possess ideas inherently their own (Pizzolato, 2008). Engaging in reflective conversations, advisors can help students recognize and validate their role as knowledge constructors. Through reflective, collaborative conversations students accept multiple ways to view any situation, recognize the complexity of knowledge, and appreciate their own role in its construction (Pizzolato, 2008).

As students discuss their interpretation of experiences and construct meaning from them, advisors serve as collaborators in supporting the self-authorship process. They support students addressing challenges, providing a safe space in which to reflect and make meaning and serving as a sounding board for ideas. Before advisees reach the crossroads, advisors must build a trusting relationship to ready students to engage in a provocative moment. They can employ principles of positive psychology (such as those included in motivational interviewing, as discussed by Judy Hughey and Robert Pettay in chapter 5, and appreciative approaches to advising, highlighted by Jenny Bloom, Bryant Hutson, and Ye He in chapter 6) to help students remember ambiguous situations they successfully negotiated toward satisfying outcomes. In this reflection, students need to detail the reasons they had been successful in previous situations and devise a plan to use those behaviors to tackle current challenges (Pizzolato, 2008).

However, to implement strategies consistent with validating knowledge creators, advisors need administrative support. Of paramount importance, advisors and students need time and space to build relationships that enable significant conversations (Pizzolato, 2008). Therefore, advising loads must be balanced with advisors' other duties to accommodate appropriate appointment length and availability. To build authentic relationships, Pizzolato (2008) suggested, based on research results, that student appointments should span at least 30 minutes, and each student needs access to multiple appointments in a semester if desired.

Situate Learning in Students' Experiences

In any learning setting, students should be encouraged to use their existing knowledge and experience as a foundation for interpreting new situations. Academic advising inherently focuses on student experiences, and therefore advisors enjoy a significant opportunity for engaging in self-authorship development via LPM principles. Once empowered as knowers, students can identify the obstacles that might hinder achievement of their plan and collaborate with advisors to identify possible strategies to overcome roadblocks (Pizzolato, 2008). For example, a student struggling in a math class, like Bob did, needs to identify strategies to meet the specific difficulties related to the course or topics covered. The advisor who simply refers the student to tutoring or a study skills class does not necessarily help the student uncover the fundamental problem with math. In addition to offering appropriate referrals, the advisor who helps the student unpack the particular source of the challenge also provides the groundwork for determining solutions unique to her or his circumstance, thereby situating the solution directly in the advisee's own personal experience. In addition, as students develop the habit of critically evaluating a situation, ferreting out root causes, and identifying specific strategies to meet the challenges at hand, they develop the self-authorship skills that translate to the higher-level problem solving and critical thinking expected as outcomes of higher education.

Define Learning as Mutually Constructing Meaning

In reflective conversations, advisors contribute perspectives to help students reach nuanced interpretations of their experiences. In this role, the advisor is not an expert, but a partner who is also learning from and with the student. Advisors encourage students to seek additional knowledge from others (e.g., faculty members, peers, professionals in their target career area) and then help them think through these multiple perspectives to identify their own interpretations and plans of action. For example, when working with someone selecting a major, the advisor may help the student separate family perspectives from those of peers and develop his or her own interpretation of a good fit. With advisors as collaborators (i.e., good company on the road to self-discovery), students articulate future goals based on their own self-understanding and consider how their current actions relate to their goal attainment (Pizzolato, 2006). As students recognize and practice using their internal voices, they become increasingly trusting of themselves (Baxter Magolda, 2008).

Translating Theory to Advising Practice

Self-authorship theory can be translated into practice in many advising situations, particularly those that require students to make decisions and set goals. Baxter Magolda (2008, p. 283) encouraged educators to

○ assist students in building their internal foundations through reflective conversations;

○ help reduce the distraction of external pressures, such as peers, family, or social expectations so students can find their own voice;

○ encourage students to act on their internal voice, trust it, and align beliefs with action.

By keeping these practices in mind, advisors can help students recognize crossroads issues and may be able to pose questions that trigger provocative moments.

Examples of Self-authorship Practice

Taylor enters college as an engineer because he performed well in high school math classes and his teacher suggested that engineering may be a good major for him. Candace enters college as a pre-med major because she wants to help people. Rachael wants to make a lot of money as a dentist and plans a biology major despite disliking science and math.

All three students have made a decision without significant reflection on the academic focus they have chosen, their interests in the subjects they will be studying, or realistic notions of the career paths they imagine. All three follow external formulas: Parents, teachers, or societal stereotypes defined the terms. An academic advisor can draw on principles of self-authorship theory to challenge these students to consider and articulate the reasons for their academic focus and support them to make choices with awareness of both external and internal motivations. For example, prior to attending orientation, their advisors could ask Taylor, Candace, and Rachael to research the skills and knowledge they will learn in their targeted majors. At orientation, the advisors could initiate brief reflective conversations about the reasons the chosen study areas attracted their interest and subsequently challenge them to think about their motivations and perceived knowledge of these majors. Throughout the semester, the advisors continue to prod the students toward self-authorship. For example, Taylor's advisor could suggest an in-depth exploration of the engineering curriculum, especially regarding the ways the physics requirement will influence his learning, while Candace's advisor could challenge her to define more fully her ideas about the meaning of "helping people."

After a semester, Taylor recognizes that engineering is not a good major for him. After talking to his father, who works in finance, he asks his advisor to switch his major to business. He emphasizes that he needs to make the change immediately so that he can register for the proper classes the following semester. Self-authorship theory suggests that Taylor reached a crossroads, potentially containing a provocative moment that could propel him to greater self-awareness. His advisor could capitalize on Taylor's dissonance to prompt further research and expand the realm of possibilities before jumping to a new major. The advisor might ask questions that encourage Taylor to reflect on his motivations and past experiences: "What did you learn from your experience in engineering?" "How can you use that information to help you make your next decision?" Through reflective conversation, the advisor could help him separate the influence of adult authorities and his own motivations, and thereby help Taylor develop a more future-focused orientation (Pizzolato, 2006). Advisors can help students anticipate possible obstacles and make plans to overcome them; for example, Taylor is inclined to make decisions without reflection on his own interests.

In an alternative scenario, in which customer-service impulses overshadow the opportunity to use the crossroads moment, the advisor could simply switch Taylor's major and thus ameliorate Taylor's discomfort without requiring significant reflection from him. However, according to self-authorship theory, the advisor best helps Taylor by having him pause and reflect on his past and present decisions, evaluate them critically, and carefully plan with self-awareness the transition from one discipline to another.

Candace performs poorly in the math and science courses needed for medical school, and she begins to doubt her choice of major and career path as well as her future in college. Distraught at not being a doctor, Candace does not know how else to help people, and she places little value on a nonscience education. Helping students deal with failure is an important role for academic advisors, and Candace's advisor helps her recognize the skills, knowledge, and growth she can acquire from higher education generally and the liberal arts and professional fields specifically. Employing self-authorship theory, the advisor understands the challenge to Candace's sense of self and pays particular attention to being good company as Candace grapples with an ambiguous future. The advisor engages Candace in a series of conversations that focus on her evolving understanding of her own intellectual identity and the role higher education plays in her plans. Using appreciative and motivational techniques in the reflective conversation, the advisor specifically helps Candace identify her strengths, interests, and personal values, thereby validating her as a knower and a learner (see, for example, chapter 5 on motivational interviewing and chapter 6 on appreciative advising). The advisor could ask Candace to describe situations in which she helped people: Perhaps she is often a sounding board for friends as they talk out problems or wrote articles that highlight social problems for her high school newspaper. The advisor can help Candace recognize these as significant experiences worthy of her attention and develop a plan that would help her connect them to potential alternative majors.

Rachael is failing both chemistry and algebra, and seeks help from an advisor to change her course sections because she thinks the ways these classes are taught is causing her difficulty. Through self-authorship theory, the advisor recognizes that Rachael is seeking external answers in reaction to a challenge to her preexisting notions of her academic strengths. Rachael blames the teaching methods instead of facing the dissonance created because she is studying subjects in which she has no intrinsic interest. An academic advisor might challenge Rachael to see alternative explanations for her current struggle, including her own actions and interests as relevant factors. By asking how she is interacting with course material out of class, the advisor can help Rachael undertake a shift in learning style and emphasize the out-of-class, independent study needed for collegiate success.

While the advisor can recognize the discord between Rachael's lack of interest in math and science and her goal to become a dentist, Rachael cannot see it. Rachael identified a career goal on the basis of one criterion—financial expectations—and then used it to make an equally one-dimensional academic goal—biology. The advisor can challenge Rachael to recognize the dissonance between her goals and her interests by engaging her in goal reflection (as per Pizzolato, 2006), specifically charging her to examine multiple dimensions of the complex problem she has encountered. For example, the advisor can ask Rachael to describe her motivations for this particular course of study and examine the relationship between her responses and the curriculum she is pursuing: "Are you learning things you find rewarding and important?"

The advisor might suggest that Rachael research the prerequisite courses and GPA requirements for dental school admission so they can discuss her interests in completing those classes at the level expected. The advisor may also encourage Rachael to reflect more thoroughly on her career aspirations by shadowing a dentist and specifically inquiring about realistic expectations for life in dentistry school. The advisor might further prompt Rachael to reflect on her motivations to earn a high salary and research the related salaries of careers outside of dentistry. Through these self-authorship–inspired strategies, Rachael can develop a more nuanced understanding of her goal. If Rachel completes her assignments and feels the increased dissonance characteristic of the crossroads, she may experience a provocative moment in which she grapples with the newly acquired learning about herself and undertakes more complex decisions than she had previously considered.

In all these cases, self-authorship theory helps advisors recognize particular learning opportunities and suppress their instincts to solve problems quickly for students. It is particularly important in high-pressure settings such as those in which advisors have large case loads, at points in the semester where students make last-minute decisions, or when a student makes a decision while experiencing tense relations with parents. Academic advisors have unique and powerful opportunities to encourage self-authored habits by engaging students in a series of reflective conversations, but they must recognize the opportunity and allow students to feel discomfort. Students, of course, will ultimately choose whether to take advantage of opportunities for self-authorship development, but as educators, advisors must provide the challenge and support students need to engage increasingly complex ways of thinking.

Self-authorship Advising Scenarios

Advising Scenarios I and II illustrate ways that advisors can implement self-authorship theory in select cases. These cases represent a small set of the crossroads advisors will help students negotiate as they discover themselves along the road to adulthood.

Scenario I

A first-generation college sophomore, Riley, comes to an advisor, Skylar, and says "I'm having trouble in two of my classes. I don't understand what the professor is talking about in one of them, but it's a required course in my major. The other is only a gen ed course, but I keep getting low grades on the writing assignments. I was always good in writing in high school. If I do poorly, this will lower my GPA, and I just got off academic probation last term. I want to stay in my major, but I don't know if I can pass this one course and that would really disappoint my family. What do you suggest I do?"

∘ ∘ ∘

Self-authorship theory helps Skylar recognize that Riley is dealing with dissonance. Rather than jumping into the conversation with solutions, such as suggestions to visit office hours and tutoring centers or take advantage of course-drop policies, Skylar allows Riley to experience discomfort, consistent with practices that foster self-authorship development. Awareness of Riley's dissonance as an opportunity for growth allows Skylar to help Riley practice complex thinking and construct interpretations of the situation, apply personal beliefs and values, and reflect on relationships.

After recognizing the importance of not fixing the problem for the student, Skylar, informed by self-authorship theory, initiates a reflective conversation, asking Riley to identify the causes of present troubles, develop goals, and create action plans that help to meet those goals. First, guided by practices derived from self-authorship theory such as LPM—validating the student as a knower, situating learning in the student's experience, and defining learning as mutually constructing meaning—Skylar prompts Riley to reflect on past challenges and successes through the following questions:

○ What created the situation that got you into academic probation?

○ What changes did you make that helped you recover?

○ What major courses have you really enjoyed? What about those courses made them such good experiences for you?

Through this reflective conversation, Skylar can help Riley recognize the importance of interpreting situations and taking actions that affect outcomes.

Second, Skylar can use this multifaceted challenge as an opportunity to help Riley practice complex problem solving that directly draws on past personal experience. Initially Riley must separate the multiple aspects of the situation by focusing on one challenge at a time. The following conversation prompts may help Riley move in a new direction:

○ Let's talk about the course in your major first. Describe that course to me.

○ What should you be learning in that class and how does it relate to the rest of the major?

○ What about the class is making sense to you?

○ What do you mean by "not understanding the professor"?

Skylar may suggest that Riley list particular reasons for struggling in class and then brainstorm ways to overcome those challenges. As a collaborative partner, Skylar should offer suggestions and alternative explanations as warranted:

○ Let's see if we can figure out why this class is included in the major. . . . Let's look at the syllabus together to see what you're supposed to take away from it.

○ What did the instructor say to you when you inquired about this?

Third, after co-examining the situation with Riley, Skylar could shift focus to the next issue:

○ Let's talk about your gen ed class. What's going well for you in that class?

○ You say the writing assignments are the cause of your current challenge. What made you good at writing in the past? How is what's being asked of you now different from what was expected in high school?

Again, Skylar can use reflective conversation to help Riley identify the particular reasons for struggling and brainstorm ways to overcome the challenges.

Finally, throughout the discussions, Skylar needs to help Riley reflect on decisions, construct internally meaningful interpretations, and find empowerment to set goals and take action. As self-authorship theory suggests, many college-aged individuals give priority to external authorities. Particularly, students need to practice paying attention to their internal voices and give their own values and beliefs a prominent position in driving decision making. By providing good company, Skylar helps Riley examine motivations and separate inner and outside voices, thus increasing Riley's ability to mediate external pressures while focusing on the tasks that can be affected by action.

Scenario II

A second-year student, Ali, comes to Drew to discuss withdrawing from school: "I'm really not doing well this term. It's not the courses or the professors—I just don't feel like I fit in. A few of my friends left after last year, and I haven't really found any new ones. My new roommates are not really like me, so they kind of stick together by themselves. I'm not in any clubs or anything like that, although I do work off campus. Also, I feel my parents and I have spent lots of money, but I'm not sure it's worth spending more if I'm not that interested. Do you have any suggestions? What do you think I should do?"

○ ○ ○

Self-authorship theory helps Drew recognize that Ali is dealing with a potential crossroads moment. While grappling with identity and commitment to goals, Ali has started to experience dissonance. Drew understands the importance of giving Ali the driver's seat in negotiating the college journey.

Drew can use self-authorship principles to engage in reflective conversation that helps Ali examine expectations and motivations. Drew could ask the following questions:

○ When you were deciding what to do after high school, what made you choose college?

○ How did you come to choose this institution?

○ What would you do if you left?

Drew and Ali can collaborate to identify Ali's voice in coming to past decisions and separate internal motivation from external influences. Was Ali following formulas in choosing to attend college? What does Ali hope to gain from the collegiate experience?

By applying techniques derived from self-authorship theory, Drew can help Ali identify motivations more clearly and work to identify actions that will lead to satisfying outcomes.

Summary

Self-authored decision making is consistent with the higher-level learning outcomes expected of postsecondary education. In particular, the characteristics of self-authored decision making are the same as those that characterize intentional learning and integrative thinking (AAC&U, 2002). However, most students do not make substantial progress in self-authorship until well after graduation (Baxter Magolda, 2009b). Therefore, Baxter Magolda (2009b), alone and with King (2004), emphasized the role of college educators in promoting self-authorship development during college, and suggested that students require both challenge and support from educators:

> Promoting self-authorship during college requires finding the delicate balance between guiding learners and enabling them to be responsible. Too much guidance affirms reliance on external formulas. Yet enabling responsibility must be balanced with guidance until learners develop the internal mechanisms to act responsibly. (Baxter Magolda & King, 2004, p. xxiii)

Academic advisors, often in a strategic position to offer that challenge and support by applying principles from LPM, can help students attain greater levels of self-authorship in their college years. They encourage students to see themselves as active constructors of knowledge and push them to practice their critical-thinking skills by examining challenges in their lives. Such practice promotes habitual use of complex decision-making skills needed in an educated citizenry.

Like other psychosocial developmental theories, self-authorship theory helps advisors understand student decision-making patterns. In particular, it provides a model for illustrating ways individuals develop habits of making increasingly complex interpretations of experience and internally meaningful plans of action through balancing information, personal beliefs, and relationships with others. As important, it points to specific actions educators can take to promote student engagement in the developmental process. Particularly for academic advisors, this theory highlights the developmental necessity of discomfort and helps practitioners realize that sometimes promoting dissonance, rather than diffusing it, proves most helpful to college students. It aligns with the contemporary perspective of academic advising as an educational endeavor, but runs counter to customer service–oriented, satisfaction-based measures of advising quality. Enacting self-authorship principles in academic advising settings requires discipline from the academic advisor to suspend the impulse to quickly resolve students' situations and assuage their anxieties. It also requires administrative structures that provide the time needed to develop collaborative relationships and assessment methods based on the recognition that immediate student satisfaction is not a sufficient measure of quality advising (Nutt, 2003).

Academic advisors can offer good company to students practicing complex thinking and decision-making skills. Through reflective conversation, they support students working through challenges and encourage them to pause and engage with the provocative moments they encounter. As students and advisors relate through conversations founded on a trusting, collaborative relationship, academic advising provides a critical venue in which students can partake in the iterative, cyclical, back-and-forth process of habitual self-authorship.

References

Abes, E. S., Jones, S. R., & McEwan, M. K. (2007). Reconceptualizing the model of multiple dimensions of identity: The role of meaning-making capacity in the construction of multiple identities. *Journal of College Student Development, 48*(1), 1–22.

Association of American Colleges &Universities (AAC&U). (2002). *Greater expectations: A new vision for learning as a nation goes to college.* Retrieved from http://www.greaterexpectations.org/

Baxter Magolda, M. B. (1992). *Knowing and reasoning in college: Gender-related patterns in students' intellectual development.* San Francisco, CA: Jossey-Bass.

Baxter Magolda, M. B. (2001). *Making their own way: Narratives for transforming higher education to promote self-development.* Sterling, VA: Stylus.

Baxter Magolda, M. B. (2002). Helping students make their way to adulthood: Good company for the journey. *About Campus, 6*(6), 2–9.

Baxter Magolda, M. B. (2008). Three elements of self-authorship. *Journal of College Student Development, 49*(4), 269–284.

Baxter Magolda, M. B. (2009a). *Authoring your life: Developing an internal voice to navigate life's challenges.* Sterling, VA: Stylus.

Baxter Magolda, M. B. (2009b). Promoting self-authorship to promote liberal education. *Journal of College & Character, 10*(3), 1–6.

Baxter Magolda, M. B., & King, P. M. (2004). *Learning partnerships: Theory and models of practice to educate for self-authorship.* Sterling, VA: Stylus.

Baxter Magolda, M. B., & King, P. M. (2008). Toward reflective conversations: An advising approach that promotes self-authorship. *Peer Review, 10*(1), 8–11.

Costello, J. G. (2010). *Exploring the connection between same-sex friendships and the development of self-authorship in black undergraduate women* (Unpublished doctoral dissertation). Boston College, Boston, MA.

Council for the Advancement of Standards Learning and Developmental Outcomes. (2009). *Council for the Advancement of Standards Learning and Developmental Outcomes.* Retrieved from http://www.cas.edu/wp-content/uploads/2010/12/Learning-and-Developmental-Outcomes-2009.pdf

Hodge, D. C., Baxter Magolda, M. B., & Haynes, C. A. (2009). Engaged learning: Enabling self-authorship and effective practice. *Liberal Education, 95*(4), 16–23.

Kegan, R. (1994). *In over our heads: The mental demands of modern life.* Cambridge, MA: Harvard University Press.

Kincanon, K. (2009). *Translating the transformative: Applying transformational and self-authorship pedagogy to advising undecided/exploring students.* Retrieved from

http://www.nacada.ksu.edu/Resources/Clearinghouse/View-Articles/Transformational
-Theory-in-Academic-Advising-.aspx

Lowenstein, M. (2011, September 28). Academic advising at the University of Utopia. *The Mentor: An Academic Advising Journal.* Retrieved from http://dus.psu.edu/mentor/2011/09/university-of-utopia/

National Academic Advising Association. (2006). *NACADA concept of academic advising.* Retrieved from http://www.nacada.ksu.edu/Resources/Clearinghouse/View-Articles/Concept-of-Academic-Advising.aspx

Nutt, C. L. (2003). Creating advisor-training and development programs. In *Advisor training: Exemplary practices in the development of advisor skills* (Monograph No. 9) (pp. 9–11). Manhattan, KS: National Academic Advising Association.

Pizzolato, J. E. (2003). Developing self-authorship: Exploring the experiences of high-risk college students. *Journal of College Student Development, 44*(6), 797–812.

Pizzolato, J. E. (2004). Coping with conflict: Self-authorship, coping, and adaptation to college in first-year, high-risk students. *Journal of College Student Development, 45*(4), 425–442.

Pizzolato, J. E. (2005). Creating crossroads for self-authorship: Investigating the provocative moment. *Journal of College Student Development, 46*(6), 624–641.

Pizzolato, J. E. (2006). Complex partnerships: Self-authorship and provocative advising practices. *NACADA Journal, 26*(1), 32–45.

Pizzolato, J. E. (2008). Advisor, teacher, partner: Using the learning partnerships model to reshape academic advising. *About Campus, 13*(1), 18–25.

Torres, V., & Hernandez, E. (2007). The influence of ethnic identity on self-authorship: A longitudinal study of Latino/a college students. *Journal of College Student Development, 48*(5), 558–573.

Torres, V., Reiser, A., LePeau, L., Davis, L., & Ruder, J. (2006). A model of first-generation Latino/a college students' approach to seeking academic information. *NACADA Journal, 26*(2), 65–70.

9

PROACTIVE ADVISING

Jennifer Varney

Historical Context

Proactive (formerly known as *intrusive*) advising involves intentional institutional contact with students such that personnel and students develop a caring relationship that leads to increased academic motivation and persistence. Research literature on student retention suggests that contact with a significant person within a postsecondary institution is a crucial factor in a student's decision to remain in college (Heisserer & Parette, 2002). Oft quoted, Habley (1994) stated that academic advising is the only structured activity on the campus in which all students have the opportunity for ongoing, one-to-one interaction with a concerned representative of the institution (p. 10). In fact, advisors often find themselves best suited to make important student connections, and by showing interest in their lives and circumstances, they may encourage students to stay in school. In addition, contacting students in a preventative mode may help them anticipate challenges and learn problem-solving skills and strategies (Upcraft & Kramer, 1995).

In an all-too-familiar situation, Emily begins a college program full of excitement and nervous anticipation of the classroom experience. She wants to purchase books weeks before they are available and arrives the first day of class with several notebooks and a fistful of newly sharpened pencils. Weeks go by and all seems fine until one day she does not come to class. She attends the next day, but not the following two. Before long, Emily has stopped attending altogether. While many institutions initiated proactive programming, such as first-year seminars and early academic warning to help address the needs and issues of students, like Emily, during the most vulnerable first semester, planners must recognize that academics do not constitute the only reasons that students stop attending classes and withdraw from the institution. Could a proactive approach have been useful to Emily?

Development of the Proactive Advising Approach

Proactive advising as an advising strategy first appeared, as *intrusive advising*, in the work of Glennen (1975), who sought to blend the practices of advising and counseling into a form of student intervention that allows advisors to provide students information before they request or realize they need it. Often service based, with advisors providing needed assistance and institutional information to students, it promotes relationship building similar to that generated in counseling sessions.

In the mid-1970s, at the University of Nevada at Las Vegas, Glennen gathered a group of faculty members to work intensively with first-year and transfer students. All these faculty volunteers wanted to become involved with students in a close professional-mentoring relationship. The planners centralized academic advising and the student records departments, allowing advisors to give students detailed information on potential obstacles as they progressed along the degree completion pathway and on employment opportunities upon graduation. As untrained counselors, the faculty received guidance on education and counseling practices and techniques as well as instruction on conducting group sessions.

The University of Las Vegas advisors handled preadmission counseling, matriculation into the university, and individual scheduling for all students. They reviewed the files of students, including data on their academic and family histories and any physical or mental issues noted, and identified special concerns that could hinder the students' learning process. Advisors ensured that the course schedule reflected the students' interest, abilities, and goals. During the semester, students participated in intrusive advising sessions where advisors addressed institutional and academic policies and curricular options. Most importantly, they developed relationships with students identified as at risk for being placed on academic probation. By the end of the first year, 74% of students seen for academic deficiency had passed their classes (Glennen, 1975, p. 2). Other results included a reduction in attrition by first-year students and a marked decrease in the number of students seeking psychological counseling. The finding indicated that the faculty volunteers helped students handle problems proactively before reaching crisis levels.

Proactive Advising Defined

Proactive advising is based on three approaches taken from advising research (Earl, 1988, p. 1):

1. Academic advisors can be trained to identify students who need preenrollment assistance, such as those with poor high school grades, performance deficiencies at previous institutions, or who self-identify as feeling apprehensive about certain academic areas.
2. Students respond positively to direct contact in which potential problems are identified and resources for help are offered.
3. Students who do not initially feel they fit with the institution learn success strategies and skills to help them find their place.

Earl (1988) described the intrusive model of advising as

> a deliberate, structured student intervention at the first indication of academic difficulty in order to motivate a student to seek help. By this definition, intrusive advising utilizes the systematic skills of prescriptive advising while helping to solve

the major problem of developmental advising, which is a student's reluctance to self-refer. (p. 1)

Intrusive advising utilizes the good qualities of prescriptive advising (experience, awareness of student needs, and structured programs) and of developmental advising (relationship to a student's total needs) (p. 1).

Intrusive advising, according to Glennen (1975), implies a "disposition to thrust oneself into the affairs of others or to be unduly curious about another's concern" (p. 2). However, in an academic setting this approach suggests a type of advising in which the advisor purposefully becomes involved with the student from both academic and holistic perspectives. Because of the somewhat negative connotation associated with the word *intrusive*, the National Academic Advising Association advocates the use of the more positive term, *proactive,* when describing this theory of advising.

Advising is proactive if

> it results in an academic adjustment; that is, the adjustment involves the student's ability to self-refer and assume responsibility for academic performance, and it is not solely the result of advisor provisions of specific information about academics and performance. To a great extent, [proactive] advising is also invasive in that it is personal rather than merely professional, and it is dependent on how information is relayed rather than on the information itself. (Molina & Abelman, 2000, p. 6)

Proactive advising has also been described as having a

> more personal than professional approach. It incorporates intervention strategies that allow the advisor to become an active part of the student's life, which, in turn, helps the student to stay motivated. This personal relationship encourages students to be more responsible for their own academic performance. (Cruise, 2002, p. 1)

Necessary Conditions for Proactive Advising

For advisors to proactively interact with students, they need adequate information, good insight, sound judgment, and all of the skills adequate for a counseling relationship with students (Glennen, 1975). Because academic advisors work to develop a student relationship in which they can disseminate information, listen to problems, and give advice, their involvement with the student needs to extend past the readily observable to the root of student concerns and issues. Glennen suggested that, under the proactive advising approach, institutional personnel take the initiative in working with students and do not wait until students come forward after experiencing difficulties.

Advisors who use the proactive advising approach often require students to make frequent appointments over the course of the semester to monitor student progress, identify potential stumbling blocks, offer options, make referrals, and motivate students toward academic success (Spann, Spann, & Confer, 1995, p. 104). Because of the steady and relationship-based contact with students, advisors create opportunities to develop a close relationship and rapport with them, become familiar with their abilities and challenges, discuss their progress, and refer them to programs and services to meet their specific needs. In return, "entering students find a supportive advocate and ally with whom they feel secure in discussing academic and personal concerns" (Spann et al., p. 104). Thomas and Minton (2004) described intrusive advising as based on the philosophy that "the counselor and the student share responsibility for student academic success or failure" (p. 1).

Proactive advising involves more than just putting students in classes: Students matter, and the advisor, understanding students' well-being or lack of it, affects students' academic success (Thomas & Minton, 2004). In this model, advisors express active concern for the welfare of every student, which requires directed advisor actions to reach the student at specific points throughout his or her academic career.

Building a Literature Base for the Proactive Advising Approach

Earl (1988) observed that the proactive approach allows advisors to get to the heart of student difficulties and recommend appropriate interventions. He described the proactive model of advising as an action-oriented approach that involves and motivates a student to seek help when needed, before it is too late for the student to change course. Proactive advising approaches include a continuum of strategies that promote advisor interest in and involvement with the activities of the student, such as culminates in increased student motivation. Heisserer and Parette (2002) offered the definition of *proactive advising* as "intensive advising intervention with an at-risk student in particular is designed to (a) facilitate informed, responsible decision-making, (b) increase student motivation toward activities in his/her social/academic community, and (c) ensure the probability of the student's academic success"(p. 74).

Proactive advising involves intentional interactions with students before a negative situation cannot be ameliorated. Proactive advising does not equate to hand holding or parenting, but rather to active concern for students' academic preparation; it is a willingness to assist students in exploring services and programs to improve their skills and increase academic motivation (Upcraft & Kramer, 1995). Earl (1988) suggested that

> the difficulty with most advising-student contacts is that they take place precisely at the most frantic time for both advisors and students: the registration period. By being proactive at the beginning of a semester advisors can counsel students during a low advising work cycle rather than just at advising time. (p. 1)

Garing (1993) observed that development of proactive advising relationships requires "structured strategies of intervention by advisors at specified times throughout the students' semesters in college" (p. 97). This type of communication and the relationships it builds may prove beneficial to student retention, as the link between student and advisor is strong and supportive. Tinto (1999) asserted that academic advising creates the very core of successful institutional efforts to educate and retain students. Advisors need to do more than scheduling and registration if advisees are to gain meaning from the experience. Proactive advisors must take the time to teach students how to be advised. Their efforts may help students feel more connected to the institution as well as benefit them long after they have graduated. The proactive advisor, according to Thomas and Minton (2004), understands that "retention and success are not only impacted by academic preparedness but also by students' personal and social issues" (p. 3).

Heisserer and Parette (2002, para. 26) also suggested that proactive advising may positively "affect retention rates and increased number of credit hours completed (Bray, 1985; Brophy, 1984; Nichols, 1986); increased GPA demonstrated by students (Schultz, 1989; Spears, 1990); and use of study skills, time management strategies, and classroom attendance (Spears, 1990)." Students reap the following additional benefits from proactive advising: They "(a) are more inclined to keep up with their work if they know an academic advisor will contact them; (b) have fewer financial worries; (c) receive necessary connections to university retention services; and (d) are referred to needed support services, thus communicating that someone at the institution cares about them" (Holmes, as cited in Heisserer and Parette, 2002, para. 25).

To summarize, proactive advising is characterized by

- deliberate, structured student interventions;
- purposeful involvement with the student;
- student assumption of responsibility for academic success and performance;
- a personal relationship with the goal of the advisor becoming a part of the student's life;
- considerations that reveal personal aspects not readily observable about the student;
- efforts to reach out to the student before she or he asks for help;
- teaching the student how to be advised;
- inquiries into the causes of the student's concern.

Proactive Advising and Retention

Academic advising can directly affect the persistence of students and probability of graduating, or indirectly influence grades, intentions, or satisfaction with the student role (Allen & Smith, 2008). As an integral component of student retention efforts, quality advising should not be left to chance (Tinto, 1999). Glennen, Farren, Vowell, and Black (as cited in Glennen, Farren, & Vowell, 1996) found that a

> sound academic advising program can assist the university in improving its retention rate by involving faculty advisors, professional counselors, student affairs professionals, administrators, admissions recruiters, residence hall personnel, financial aid

workers, librarians, clerical workers, and security officers. While reduction of student attrition is not the only goal of an advising program, increased retention does result from the expanded services and teamwork in services provided to students. (p. 38)

Most students know they have an advisor but may be unaware of how and when to contact the advisor or the objectives advisor can help them accomplish. Heisserer and Parette (2002) observed that "the only variable that has a direct effect on student persistence is the quality of a relationship with significant member(s) of the college community (cf. Losser, 1985; Noel, 1976; National Academic Advising Association, 1994)" (para. 21). Because the advisor is often the person best suited to form a significant relationship with the student, ". . . intrusive advising strategies can be especially useful when advising to build student resiliency" (Miller & Murray, 2005, para 17).

Table 9.1 shows some retention-related issues (Hill, 2010) and proactive advising strategies.

Proactive Advising and At-Risk Students

"An estimated 30% of entering freshmen exhibit deficiencies in college-level reading, writing, and math" (Fieldstein & Bush as cited in Molina & Abelman, 2000, p. 5), and "evidence suggests that academic skills are declining in the overall population of students" (Jones, Slate, Blake, & Holifeld as cited in Molina & Abelman, 2000, p. 5) in secondary schools. In addition to lacking adequate academic preparation, many students matriculate as the first in their families to attend college, receive low levels of parental support, and cannot anticipate the college experience (Molina & Abelman, 2000, p. 5). In addition, "approximately 40% of all students who enroll at 4-year institutions fail to earn a degree, and nearly 57% of this group leaves before the start of the second year" (Molina & Abelman, 2000, p. 5).

The advisor must identify factors that may inhibit students' success and create an early strategic framework to mitigate them. Some educators view poor academic performance as the result of inadequate cognitive and motivational strategies that subsequently hinder successful adjustment to the challenges of college life (Kirk-Kuwaye & Nishida, 2001). These students often exhibit inadequate coping systems and lack of information on where or how to seek help with college and life problems. However, when these at-risk students connect with advisors and resources, their persistence rates improve. The high-involvement model described by Kirk-Kuwaye and Nishida (2001) to identify these students includes notification of poor academic performance as well as required meetings with academic advisors. The advisors strive to change student study behavior and patterns as well as help them achieve personal fulfillment in the institution. Despite concerns that students might resist mandatory advising to discuss grades, student feedback indicated feelings of relief that advisors called them and gave them the opportunity to discuss their academic challenges.

Table 9.1. Factors that affect retention and proactive advising strategies

Retention Factor	Proactive Advising Strategy
Students need to feel integrated into the program and school.	Find connection points with students that are not exclusively academic and connect them with support services and social organizations and opportunities.
Pedagogy and instructor training affect retention efforts.	Develop relationships with faculty members and share academic insights with their students.
Family obligations may interfere with school priorities.	Encourage students to share relevant information in a safe space, help them manage school and family obligations, and refer them to counseling services if needed.
Students need support throughout their academic careers.	Provide support from preenrollment through graduation; connect with relevant support services as appropriate.
The nature of interactions between students and the institution exerts influence on student decisions to stay.	Student interaction begins long before the first class meeting; be the link to support services and promote positive student interactions.
Students satisfied with the institutional environment are more likely to remain enrolled.	Be vigilant and responsive to students' needs; anticipate challenges through relationship-based, proactive advising.
Specific student situations and behaviors create barriers to retention.	Use student relationships to help them develop positive habits and strategies to overcome academic, social, and family challenges that may impede their academic performance.
Best practices encourage students to stay in school.	Encourage students to engage in their education and help them to find ways to be a proactive part in their own learning experience.

Note: Retention factors from Hill (2010), pp. 10–11.

Molina and Abelman (2001, p. 6) identified four factors contributing to poor academic performance. See Table 9.2.

Similarly, using a fishbone diagram from Braussard, Ritter, McManus, Collett, Love-Goodnight, and Tucker (1992), Beatty (1994, p. 70) described an approach for determining the cause of at-risk characteristics. Specifically, four areas form barriers for any student, but they exert particular impact on those academically at risk:

- student characteristics—self-esteem, motivation, energy, personal crises;

- faculty and staff—teacher disinterest, class size, lack of recognition in class;

Table 9.2. Molina and Abelman's matrix of factors affecting retention

Internal/uncontrollable factors: health problems, learning disabilities, inability to master college course work	External/stable factors: unhealthy family or social environments that prevent students from adequately performing in their courses
Internal/controllable factors: poor time management, lack of class attendance	External/unstable factors: transient in nature, like when students change classes or instructors

Source: Molina and Abelman (2001), p. 6. Used with permission of the National Academic Advising Association.

- curriculum—language problems, lack of basic skills, inability to keep up with the work or pass tests; and
- family—lack of money for college, appreciation for education, communication, and monitoring of truancy as well as need for student to be a caretaker at home.

Three phases of an effective advising intervention process as identified by Boylan (1980, pp.10–11) include

- introducing students to the rules, regulations, and services of the institution and providing a clear explanation of the academic management tasks expected of the students. Advisors can intervene through clear articulation of course load and withdrawal policies as well as registration and financial-aid filing deadlines.
- monitoring the progress of students to determine how well they use provided information. For example, are students registering for classes? Are the classes appropriate? How are the students' grades? Do any classes need to be repeated?
- acting based on the information advisors collect. For example, does the student seem to have trouble writing? Is she or he doing very well in some of the courses in the program but not others? Is the major the correct fit for the student? How can the student find needed support and services for the areas identified by the advisor?

At-risk students, in particular, may benefit greatly from the proactive approach as they may not know the ways to deal with unexpected situations. Vander Schee (2007) described an insight-oriented form of proactive advising. He suggested that advisors discover the nonacademic factors preventing students from reaching their full academic potential, including their financial situation, family interactions and dynamics, and social situations, and then encourage students to develop an internal locus of control that will help them discover the relationship between their own actions and academic success. For example, a destructive relationship with a family member or friend may take up an extraordinary amount of a student's time and emotional energy, which could distract from academic pursuits. Understanding the issues, students gain insight into reasons they are not performing to their full academic potential and how they can adjust their thoughts and actions to maximize their performance (Vander Schee, 2007).

An important way to monitor student progress, according to Winston, Ender, and Miller (1982), involves the use of contracts, which offer an effective method for monitoring student progress. Negotiated between students and advisors, contracts specify activities (participating in tutoring, attending a learning skill workshop, etc.), a time frame for completing the assignment, and the level of success expected. Such contracts "provide a structure often needed by underprepared first-year students to motivate them to take responsibility for improving their academic performance" (Winston et al., 1982, p. 108).

Proactive Advising Strategies

To become more proactive, advisors can engage a number of strategies. For example, they should develop a solid and comprehensive understanding of the institutions and the resources available to students as well as know those staffing these services. Although advertised in many places on campus and on the school's web site, relevant resources often elude students trying to navigate the wealth of information available and find the specific services that will prove most beneficial at the appropriate time. Because students can easily become overwhelmed by the amount of available guidance and referral information on campus, advisors need to help them identify and connect quickly to the most appropriate resources. According to Miller and Murray (2005, para. 17), preadmissions assessment tools (e.g., ACCUPLACER, COMPASS, etc.) determine student skills and abilities that proactive advisors can incorporate into effective advising sessions, and the following student programs, resources, and groups offer appropriate assistance for students with specific needs: TRIO/SSS, Gear Up, writing and math centers, learning and study skills classes, college survival courses, orientation, career development centers.

The following strategies for proactive advisors, also from Miller and Murray (2005), offer guidance for practitioners:

- employ open-ended questioning techniques e.g., "What subjects did you enjoy studying in the past?" with follow-up questions such as "What methods did you find successful in studying this subject?"
- identify student strengths as well as skill deficits;
- be direct, emphatic, and prescriptive when designing a plan to overcome skills deficits (Ender & Wilkie, 2000);

- recommend courses appropriate to students' current skill levels mixed with course options in areas of previous success;

- match student learning style with the teaching style used in the course; use caution in recommending on-line classes or satellite classes;

- help students determine the time of day that will best optimize learning e.g., determine if the student is a "morning person";

- help students set short and long-term goals and develop action plans to achieve their goals (Ender & Wilkie, 2000) . . . ;

- explain the importance of meeting deadlines and regular class attendance . . . (para. 17).

In another proactive strategy, advisors remain available for students whenever or wherever reasonably possible. They could make use of phone, e-mail, and in-person appointments, as well as Skype, Facebook, Twitter, or any other virtual gathering place for students. Distance learners might also appreciate virtual advising sessions via webinar-style platforms. Advisors could hold "tea with the advisor" or other similar online information sessions in which students have opportunities to connect both with the advisor and with each other.

Proactive institutions also should monitor student progress (e.g., employ an early alert system) with the goal of ensuring that students are making satisfactory progress by quickly identifying those struggling. With institutional support, including academic advisors who reach out to them, students gain needed assistance before academic problems become too overwhelming to handle effectively. By sending messages of support and congratulations to those making adequate or exceptional progress, advisors encourage students to continue putting forth effort and making good decisions. Finally, advisors should not be afraid to contact students before they contact the advisor: College students get sidetracked with many distractions; advisors need to compete with diversions!

The manner in which the information is relayed significantly affects the academic performance and persistence rates of at-risk students. Proactive interventions, including the following strategies, outperform those that are impersonal, prescriptive, and nonnegotiable:

- insistence on personal contact,

- generation of student responsibility for problem solving and decision making, and

- assistance in identifying resolvable causes of poor academic performance.

Research by Abelman and Molina (2002) shows that at-risk students who participated in the most proactive interventions experienced higher cumulative GPA and retention rates than those who received less proactive interventions. Their study suggests that any amount of proactive contact with at-risk students is better than none.

Proactive Advising Starts with Inquiry

Garing (1993) suggested that during the inquiry phase of enrollment advisors initiate relationships via student interviews, answer in-depth questions regarding curricula and other program nuances, and develop student admission materials. When information about advising is included in matriculation material, potential students receive encouragement to cultivate relationships with their advisors. The sooner students understand the help they can expect from their advisors, the more effective the advising relationship created. Although building advising relationships generates challenges for advisors with high case loads, they can successfully connect with advisees via customized individual departments and through targeted student-outreach efforts. Forming relationships early is vital to both advising parties, but especially for students who may have overstated their academic abilities and understated their areas of challenge.

Advisors often play a critical role in new-student course registrations. They may provide in-depth information on educational program planning and scheduling, outlining the expectations for the student–advisor relationship, ensuring students register for appropriate courses based on preadmissions assessments, and double-checking that students know where and when the advisor will be available. For institutions in which advisors specialize in certain programs, teaming up admissions representatives and faculty members provides support such as preferred course sequencing, compatible course pairings, and class suggestions for students of various backgrounds.

Critical Outreach Points for Proactive Advising

Effective communication stands as the cornerstone of any advising practice. Academic advisors help students identify short- and long-term goals and make suggestions and recommendations around both sets of objectives while closely monitoring student progress and any concerns that students express over time.

Garing (1993, pp. 101–103) noted four critical times for advisors to connect with students:

1. During the first 3 weeks in an academic program, students make academic and personal adjustments, identify areas in which they may need support, and gain comfort in asking for help. They also may exhibit a better understanding of the expectations of their courses and areas of possible challenge. Even if they present without immediate needs, proactive intervention may help students lay plans for handling possible difficulties. Advisors may choose to conduct this intervention in groups, individual sessions, or through written notes, e-mails, or any other form of student-preferred means of communication.

2. At the next critical time for outreach, the middle of the first term, students typically have received grades and feedback in their classes and can assess their current progress as well as predict how the semester might end. By this time,

the students likely have developed areas of comfort with some subject matter and types of assignments, which may help them complete the current term and register for future courses.

3. Preregistration follows as the third critical time for student intervention as students face important decisions and benefit from advisor guidance. Advisees also may need assistance in analyzing if the selected major constitutes an appropriate fit or if other majors or potential careers should be explored. Undecided students likely need help choosing possible career pathways and appropriate courses.

4. Between semesters is the fourth critical time because underprepared or at-risk students may have a higher tendency of dropping out of college, making advisor contact especially important between terms. Poor grades, family responsibilities, financial obligations, and lack of contact with the university might lead to feelings of isolation and losing sight of college plans. Contact with an advisor could keep the relationship strong while the student is off campus. This type of proactive contact is particularly important for students completing their programs from a distance, as they may never come to a physical campus yet need to feel connected with someone at the institution.

Once advisors gain familiarity with the student's strengths and areas of challenge, they can refer her or him to appropriate campus resources. Tutoring programs, math and writing centers, and study skill services provide excellent resources for students with academic preparation issues. The career center also serves as an additional resource for students unsure of their major and potential career fit. Time management workshops and stress management seminars can prove helpful for those challenged with setting and keeping goals (Spann et al., 1995).

Advisors must consider student learning style when making recommendations if they are to assure that resources and services best meet student needs. In an ideal decision-making situation, the student considers the teaching styles of professors before course enrollment or advisors direct students to services where they can learn ways to adapt their learning styles to match those of the instructor. When well-constructed, academic course syllabi help students choose classes that fit with their learning styles because they shed light on the ways instructors structure and teach the course as well as articulate the nature of the learning outcomes expected. For example, a lecture course with essay question–based exams would not compatibly fit with a student with a preferred visual-learning style and who experiences difficulty writing on an abstract level (Spann et al., p. 106).

Creating a Proactive Communication Schedule

A way to schedule and keep track of the critical outreach points in students' educational–life cycle is through the use of a communications calendar and strategy.

Figure 9.1. Communications calendar

OCTOBER						
Sunday	Monday	Tuesday	Wednesday	Thursday	Friday	Saturday
					Send reminder of office closure Monday	1
2	3	4 Registration opens: send message via e-mail or text	5	6	7	8
9	10 Call students on academic warning to check in	11	12	13 Send special requirements lists	14	15

Figure 9.1 shows a communications calendar, and the following example shows the steps needed to create a communications strategy:

1. Design the overall strategy
    a. What are the goals?
        i. Example: Conduct one significant student-outreach activity each week
            1. Webinars, Skype sessions, phone calls
            2. Group advising sessions
    b. How often will students receive proactive communication?
        i. Weekly?
        ii. Monthly?
    c. Which students?
        i. Divide students by major, class (first year, second year, transfer, etc.), at risk, major changers
        ii. Create messaging geared to specific cohorts
    d. Message topics?
        i. Important dates (registration, petition to graduate)
        ii. New classes
        iii. Networking opportunities, lectures, programs
2. Integrate a special communications plan for new or entering students
    a. Include preterm welcome messaging
    b. Send support materials, webinar recordings

c. Include a series of communications that keep students informed and engaged before they begin their first classes

d. Include messaging on change management, finding balance with school and work, and similar nonacademic support

3. Incorporate the strategy in a comprehensive communications calendar

Proactive Advising Scenarios

Scenario I

A first-generation college sophomore, Riley, comes to an advisor, Skylar, and says, "I'm having trouble in two of my classes. I don't understand what the professor is talking about in one of them, but it's a required course in my major. The other is only a gen ed course, but I keep getting low grades on the writing assignments. I was always good in writing in high school. If I do poorly, this will lower my GPA, and I just got off academic probation last term. I want to stay in my major, but I don't know if I can pass this one course and that would really disappoint my family. What do you suggest I do?"

o o o

A proactive advisor, Skylar will help Riley navigate through the difficult classes by helping to determine the exact nature of the problem. Starting with questions about the class, professor, and feedback given on assignments, Skylar guides Riley in discerning if the low grades are a result of poor writing skills, as Riley suggests, or a misunderstanding of the assignment and material.

With the root of the problem identified, the proactive advisor makes appropriate referrals. In this case, Skylar directs Riley to the Tutoring Center and Academic Support Services and suggests that they work on articulating the problem clearly so that Riley can ask for the most appropriate assistance. The proactive advisor makes calls to colleagues in resource offices introducing the student and giving some background information (with student consent). In this case, Skylar also thinks that Riley would benefit from connecting with peer mentors or similarly experienced students in Riley's major who can share experiences, struggles, and successful strategies for overcoming problems specific to the academics of the program.

Finally, the proactive advisor schedules communications with the student at regular intervals. Skylar needs to be as specific and detailed as possible (noting days, time, and contact methods), as well as outline expectations of information that Riley will need to bring to advising meetings. By helping Riley understand the root cause of the situation and learn strategies to move beyond the temporary obstacle, Skylar provides strategies that Riley can use when faced with the next academic challenge.

Scenario II

A second-year student, Ali, comes to Drew to discuss withdrawing from school: "I'm really not doing well this term. It's not the courses or the professors—I just don't feel like I fit in. A few of my friends left after last year, and I haven't really found any new ones. My new roommates are not really like me, so they kind of stick together by themselves. I'm not in any clubs or anything like that, although I do work off campus. Also, I feel my parents and I have spent lots of money, but I'm not sure it's worth spending more if I'm not that interested. Do you have any suggestions? What do you think I should do?"

o o o

As with Scenario I, the proactive advisor in Scenario II begins by helping the student get to the root cause of concern. Drew senses that Ali feels disconnected from the university, but Ali must determine if this is the sole reason for feeling that leaving may be a good idea. Taking a proactive stance, Drew considers Ali's history:

- What have previous advising sessions been like? What concerns did Ali discuss in the past? Did Ali show any behaviors that caused concern? What referrals had Drew made?

- What about Ali's interactions with faculty members: How is Ali performing in class? Does the record indicate unexplained or drastic change in Ali's grades? Have either faculty or staff members noted any concerns? Has the resident assistant or others made comments about Ali?

- How is Ali handling the workplace? Is a work situation creating stress or a change of perspective about school? Does Ali indicate any dissatisfaction about school discussed by others in the workplace?

Drew looks for any information that could point to the reasons that Ali is unhappy as well as suggest connection points within the school. Because the advising notes show little information about Ali's work situation, Drew decides to ask about it: "Do other students work there?" When Ali replies that most of them are either not enrolled or ready to graduate, Drew suggests that by volunteering on campus, possibly at freshman orientation, Ali can identify with others in a similar college lifestyle. "What do your roommates like to do?" Drew continues, "Can you suggest participating in an activity that you all might enjoy?" After they discuss ways to get Ali connected, Drew suggests that Ali stick with school through the semester while looking at building relationships and getting involved from a different perspective. Finally, Drew and Ali set a schedule of times to check on the intentional connections Ali is making.

Summary

When communicating effectively with students, advisors learn advisees' strengths and areas of potential weakness and show genuine interest in them and their concerns. The proactive advisor builds mutually satisfying relationships with students that enable students to grow and develop academic independence and success. High advisor involvement effectively provides assistance to students experiencing academic difficulty and especially for those having trouble asking for help. Proactive advising interventions involve enhanced personal contact and

○ generate student responsibility for problem solving and decision making,

○ assist the student in identifying resolvable causes of poor academic performance,

○ offer negotiated agreements or contracts for future actions, and

○ outperform interventions that are impersonal, prescriptive, and nonnegotiable (Molina & Abelman, 2000, p. 13).

The proactive advisor concentrates on "developing the interpersonal skills of effective listening, questioning, and referral [that] is vital for advisors in order for one-to-one academic advising to be successful" (Nutt, 2000, p. 223) as well as use of appropriate self-disclosure regarding personal experiences as a way to build and inspire trust with the student. Research suggests that the single most important factor in advising students is helping them to feel that the institution cares about them (Heisserer & Parette, 2002). This trust and care will provide the foundation for a long and effective positive and proactive advising relationship. See Table 9.3 for a summary of the key points and strategies of proactive advising.

Table 9.3. Summary of proactive advising: Critical aspects, reasons, and tactics

Critical Point	Reason	Tactic
Start early.	Start students on a strong path.	Begin in preadmissions, start of term.
Develop relationships with students; think in terms of a counseling relationship.	Academics are not the only reason that students are unsuccessful in school.	Reach out, contact, and connect.
Use the relationship to help students get past obstacles and setbacks.	Students need a caring connection at the school, someone to help them identify challenges and advocate for themselves.	Get to know students. Help them see aspects of themselves that they may not currently appreciate. Capitalize on student strengths.
Be the student connection to the institution.	Students need a strong point of connection, someone who cares.	Be that person.

References

Abelman, R., & Molina, A. (2002). Style and substance reconsidered: Intrusive intervention and at-risk students with learning disabilities. *NACADA Journal*, 22(2), 66–79.

Allen, J. M., & Smith, C. L. (2008). Importance of responsibility for and satisfaction with academic advising: A faculty perspective. *Journal of College Student Development*, 40(5), 397–410.

Beatty, J. D. (1994). Advising special groups within the undecided student population. In V. N. Gordon (Ed.), *Issues for advising the undecided college student* (pp. 67–83). Columbia: University of South Carolina, Division of Continuing Education, National Resource Center for the Freshman Year Experience.

Boylan, H. R. (1980). Academic intervention in developmental advising. *Journal of Remedial and Developmental Education*, 3(3), 10–11.

Cruise, C. A. (2002, October 28). Advising students on academic probation. *The Mentor: An Academic Advising Journal*. Retrieved from http://dus.psu.edu/mentor/old/articles/021028cc.htm

Earl, W. R. (1988). Intrusive advising of freshmen in academic difficulty. *NACADA Journal*, 8(2), 27–33.

Garing, M. T. (1993). Intrusive academic advising. Academic advising: Organizing and delivering services for student success. *New Directions for Community College*, 82, 97–104. doi: 10.1002/cc.36819938211

Glennen, R. E. (1975). Intrusive college counseling. *College Student Journal*, 9(1), 2–4.

Glennen, R. E., Farren, P. J., & Vowell, F. N. (1996). How advising and retention of students improves fiscal stability. *NACADA Journal*, 16(1), 38–46.

Habley, W. (1994). Key concepts in academic advising. In *Summer institute on academic advising session guide*. Manhattan, KS: National Academic Advising Association.

Heisserer, D. L., & Parette, P. (2002). Advising at-risk students in college and university settings. *College Student Journal*, 36(1), 69–84. Retrieved from http://www.freepatentsonline.com/article/College-Student-Journal/85007770.html

Hill, C. (2010). Eight suggestions to help you get your retention act together now. In *Strategies for increasing online student retention and satisfaction* (Faculty Focus Special Report). Retrieved from http://www.hawcc.hawaii.edu/distancelearning/StrategiesForIncreasingOnlineStudentRetention&Satisfaction.pdf

Kirk-Kuwaye, M., & Nishida, D. (2001). Effect of low and high advisor involvement on the academic performances of probation students. *NACADA Journal*, 21(1&2), 40–45.

Miller, M. A., & Murray, C. (2005). *Advising academically underprepared students*. Retrieved from http://www.nacada.ksu.edu/Resources/Clearinghouse/View-Articles/Academically-underprepared-students.aspx

Molina, A., & Abelman, R. (2000). Style over substance in interventions for at-risk students: The impact of intrusiveness. *NACADA Journal*, 20(2), 5–15.

Nutt, C. L. (2000). One-to-one advising. In V. N. Gordon & W. H. Habley (Eds.), *Academic advising. A comprehensive handbook* (1st ed.) (pp. 220–237). San Francisco, CA: Jossey-Bass.

Spann, N. G., Spann, M. G., Jr., & Confer, L. S. (1995). Advising underprepared first-year students. In M. L. Upcraft & G. L. Kramer (Eds.), *First-year academic advising: Patterns in the present, pathways to the future.* Columbia, SC: National Resource Center for the Freshman Year Experience and Students in Transition and the National Academic Advising Association.

Thomas, C., & Minton, J. (2004). *Intrusive advisement: A model for success at John A. Logan College.* Retrieved from http://occrl.illinois.edu/articles/intrusive-advisement-a-model-for-success-at-john-a-logan-college/

Tinto, V. (1999). Taking retention seriously: Rethinking the first year of college. *NACADA Journal, 19*(2), 5–9.

Upcraft, M. L., & Kramer, G. (1995). Intrusive advising as discussed in the first year academic advising: Patterns in the present, pathways to the future. *Academic Advising and Barton College,* 1–2.

Vander Schee, B. (2007). Adding insight to intrusive advising and its effectiveness with students on probation. *NACADA Journal, 27*(2), 50–59.

Winston, R. B., Jr., Ender, S. C., & Miller, T. K. (Eds.). (1982). Academic advising as student development. *New Directions for Student Services, 17,* fmi-fmi, 1–108. http://onlinelibrary.wiley.com/doi/10.1002/ss.v1982:17/issuetoc

VOICES FROM THE FIELD

INCREASING FIRST-YEAR STUDENT ENGAGEMENT THROUGH MID-YEAR SELF-REFLECTIONS

Reprinted from *Academic Advising Today*

Holly E. Martin

For many students, their first year of college is a time of significant transition and the beginning of self-direction. They devote their first semester to handling the transition and needed academic and personal adjustments. After the experience of their initial term, first-year students are generally more willing to actively engage in their education and receive advice that may help them reflect on their academic interests, growth, study strategies, and progress toward their developing goals.

In one method for assisting students in self-reflection and significant conversation, advisors ask students to complete a short online questionnaire before their first advising session of the second semester. Results from the survey help the student and advisor not only assess student progress toward goals, but revise and brainstorm strategies tailored to reaching those objectives.

By filling out the questionnaire before an advising session, the advisor and advisee can review it together with the student's responses already before them so they can discuss the answers and raise important questions rather than undertake an initial question-answer session. Student responses, however lengthy or brief, often provide evidence of a student's early academic growth and successes that illuminate the student's developmental stage, study skills abilities, changes of interest, and referral needs. Presubmission of the questionnaire allows advisors and students to concentrate on those responses most pertinent to students at that point in their academic careers.

Advisors within the First Year of Studies at the University of Notre Dame use the online *Self-reflection Questionnaire* to help expand second-semester advising discussions into areas that promote academic engagement. The questionnaire consists of short, plainly worded questions that mirror First Year of Studies learning objectives. Prior to the student's return to campus for the second semester, the completed responses can be electronically returned to advisors. In its first year, over 75% of first-year students voluntarily completed the First Year of Studies questionnaire.

In the questionnaire, first-year students are asked the following:

1. In what ways have you grown intellectually over the last four months?
   This question helps students take note of their growing skills and interests. In advising sessions students and advisors identify and celebrate intellectual growth and build on it.

2. What are your academic strengths?
   As students think about their interests and strengths, advisors find answers to this question helpful in discussing possible majors and programs. While concentrating on the positive, advisors can offer specific suggestions for improvement.

3. Which classes have you found most interesting and why?
   Advisors need to know the reasons that students find some courses more engrossing than others. These insights into students' learning habits provide insight into their developing interests.

4. Which classes have been most challenging, and how did you handle those challenges?
   Through responses to this question, advisors explore how students rise to academic difficulties. They also offer additional opportunities to celebrate past achievements and brainstorm student-specific suggestions for further study-skills development.

5. Are you comfortable sharing your thoughts and ideas with peers in class?
   Advisors assist less secure students in understanding that they will become more comfortable sharing their ideas in class as they become more confident in their knowledge of the subject area. Tips concerning preparations for joining discussions constitute a natural part of the conversation.

6. Have you taken advantage of opportunities to learn outside of the classroom? Please give examples.
   Students generally interpret this question to mean the use of professors' office hours, review sessions, or tutoring centers. While advisors should encourage such positive behaviors, they should also point out that attending campus art events, joining volunteer and club activities, and participating in other forms of on-campus opportunities are at the heart of learning outside of the classroom. At this point in an advising session, the advisor should know the student well enough to suggest specific events or activities that might interest him or her.

7. Is there a topic on which you might like to do research? How did you become interested in it?
   Except in the physical and social sciences, through which students may participate in ongoing research projects, few first-year students are ready to identify research topics. Therefore, this question challenges students to think about areas they might find most interesting as they move forward in their

education. In other words, it encourages them to think of their education as more than fulfilling externally prescribed requirements.

8. Are you becoming the person you want to be?
   This question prods students to think about their education in the context of the whole person, but it also provides students the opportunity to indicate pressing personal difficulties that may be affecting their academic work.

9. What would you like to learn in the remainder of your first year?
   In response to this question, students consider specific academic goals for the upcoming semester. Advisors and students work on personalized goals and strategies based on the information gleaned from their conversation.

The mid-year *Self-assessment Questionnaire* helps students build upon an analysis of their own experiences. Many students have never been asked to think about these kinds of questions before; they have focused on grades and requirements, not on the bigger, long-term impacts of their decisions. These questions challenge them to focus on their own learning to date, including their likes and dislikes, strengths, goals, and strategies that have been effective for reaching those goals. The answers provide a place for advisors to start productive conversations.

In addition to the students' high school records and tests, first-semester grades, and impressions gathered from earlier conversations, the brief mid-year self-reflection exercise helps guide advising discussions. Answers to questions provide insight into students' development levels so advisors can work with them more effectively. More specifically, pre-advising session questionnaires assist advisors in identifying students who feel academic or personal anxiety, show advanced academic interests, and exhibit academic strategies that are (or are not) serving their needs. While this tool focuses conversations on student appraisals of their own academic lives, their self-reflections can also help advisors note emerging trends among all of their first-year students.

Mid-year self-reflections can help students become more directly engaged in their own education. When kept with students' records or portfolios, they offer a clear view as students look back on their first-year goals, strategies, and experiences.

This article was reprinted with permission from *Academic Advising Today* (2011, Dec.), *34*(4). NACADA.

10

ADVISING AS COACHING

Jeffrey McClellan

As evidenced by their wide use within educational institutions and corporations across the United States and their growing use internationally, academic advising and leadership–personal life coaching have emerged as two practical and popular methods for promoting learning and growth. Their practicality and popularity are largely due to the simplicity with which practitioners operationalize them and the outcomes they achieve. Both methodologies share a common history and sensible structure that make them valuable in helping relationships.

In recent years, the coaching revolution has begun to intersect with academic advising. An interest group dedicated to academic coaching and advising as coaching has gained popularity within the National Academic Advising Association. The emergence of this interest group corresponded with an increased recognition that the practices of effective professional coaching clearly parallel those of academic advising. The philosophical, historical, and practical similarities between the two practices create the basis of the relationship between coaching and advising. Both fields largely evolved in the past century out of the need to provide practical guidance to their clientele. Both possess a broad theoretical base drawn largely from the social sciences. Therefore, I offer an exploration of the practical significance and utility of coaching approaches in academic advising and strategies for implementing them to strengthen advisor–student relationships, promote student learning outcomes, and facilitate the advising process.

Coaching and Advising: History and Similarities

Though rooted in historical apprenticeship and mentoring practices dating back centuries, coaching as a profession likely emerged as an outgrowth of the use of professional developmental counselors hired to assist executives in the workplace and life coaches in adult education programs as well as leadership development programs (Judge & Cowell, 1997; Kampa-Kokesch & Anderson, 2001; Skiffington & Zeus, 2002; Smith, 2008). Unfortunately, the exact history of executive or leadership coaching as a professional practice is difficult to trace and appears to have arisen, in its current form, within the past 20 to 30 years (Kampa-Kokesch & Anderson, 2001).

The theoretical roots of coaching, however, include an eclectic combination of psychology, management, education, and athletic training research and practices.

Notwithstanding the tremendous popularity and growth of executive coaching as a practice, the term remains somewhat ill defined (Joo, 2005; Kampa-Kokesch & Anderson, 2001). The literature suggests that *leadership coaching* represents a one-on-one counseling or consultative practice designed to facilitate the learning and development processes of leaders and followers in the workplace through the use of either internal or external, professional or peer coaches. The use of focused inquiry designed to facilitate decision making and action planning and to promote accountability typically lead to the learning and development outcomes of coaching (Bono, Purvanova, Towler, & Peterson, 2009; Boss, 2000; Ducharme, 2004; Frisch, 2005; Goleman, Boyatzis, & McKee, 2002; Hall, Otazo, & Hollenbeck, 1999; Joo, 2005; Kampa-Kokesch & Anderson, 2001; Mobley, 1999; Orth, Wilkinson, & Benfari, 1987; Skiffington & Zeus, 2002; Stern, 2004; Wasylyshyn, 2003).

Because coaching is a one-on-one development process, the end goal often involves the alteration of behavior to improve performance in a professional setting (Bono et al., 2009). This outcomes-oriented focus has resulted in a diverse array of philosophical and practical approaches to the practice of coaching (Bono et al., 2009; Cocivera & Cronshaw, 2004; DeLuca, 2008; Ducharme, 2004; Feldman & Lankau, 2005; Kilburg, 2004; Orem, Binkert, & Clancy, 2007; Passmore, 2007; Peltier, 2001; Peterson, 2007), just as the practice-based orientation of advising has led to similarly diverse approaches. This variety also inspires many coaches to become highly eclectic in the methods they use to support their clients.

In spite of the many theoretical frameworks, personal philosophies, tools, and approaches used by different coaches, practitioners engage in the coaching process in relatively similar ways. Typically, the process begins with some form of relationship building and initial needs assessment followed by more formal assessment and feedback. After discussing feedback with the client, both participants engage in goal-oriented planning to address concerns or build strengths. Implementation, or active learning, and follow-up round out the process (DeLuca, 2008; Freas, 2000; Goldsmith, 2000; Grayson & Larson, 2000; Kampa-Kokesch & Anderson, 2001; Thach & Heinselman, 2000).

In their review of the coaching literature, Kampa-Kokesch and Anderson (2001) discussed seven empirical studies, a number of which focused on measuring and identifying the outcomes of executive coaching. They found coaching benefited the organization and the client by contributing to increased skills, learning, productivity, sustained behavior change, awareness, and performance improvement. Additional literature reviews and research articles have revealed similar conclusions (Boss, 2000; Feldman & Lankau, 2005; Joo, 2005; McGovern et al., 2001; Olivero, Bane, & Kopelman, 1997; Orenstein, 2006; Schlosser, Steinbrenner, Kumata, & Hunt, 2006; Schnell, 2005; Stoberr, 2005; Waldman, 2003; Wales, 2002).

Although a process-based technique that represents a natural extension of the developmental advising model, coaching practices can be applied successfully to any philosophical approach to academic advising. In fact, those who adopt an advising-as-teaching approach can easily use coaching because advising and coaching share extremely similar theoretical, procedural, and technical aspects. Both are grounded in an eclectic blend of theoretical concepts drawn from the social sciences. Both are intensely practice oriented. Both focus on promoting the growth, learning, and development of their clients largely through one-on-one inquiry-based processes grounded in facilitated decision making and accountability. Finally, both embody three practice-oriented levels of advising as coaching: developmental programming, individual advising, and decision making.

The Three Levels of Advising as Coaching

A careful review of the process-oriented literature of both coaching and advising reveals that the fields share very similar processes that intersect at three levels. Each of these levels, characterized by distinct structures and goals, relates to different areas of advising programs.

Level 1: The Developmental Program

Level 1, as illustrated in Figure 10.1, shows the ongoing relationship of the advisors and students over time as students progress through their degrees to the completion of their long-term educational goals. Depending on the philosophical approach of advisors (developmental, teaching, career, etc.), a student's personal, career, and ongoing learning goals may also guide the procedural work at this level.

Clearly, in the first stage of the Level 1 process the participants initiate contact. The advisor and student must come together as a result of some effort on the part of one or the other. The nature of the first conversation, whether student initiated out of need or the result of some proactive advising effort, may impact the characteristics of relationship building.

Relationship building should, of course, be an ongoing element at all stages of the advising process. However, those first few moments of the initial encounter prove particularly important, and the advisor should make a significant effort to make a good impression, build trust, and break down barriers (Bloom, Hutson, & He, 2008; Gladwell, 2005; Lyons, 2000). Ongoing relationship building is central to the effectiveness of all coaching interventions and will likely continue over multiple sessions.

The third stage in this program-level process, assessment, requires an advisor to strive for understanding of the student, specifically the abilities and resources they possess or lack in relation to the pursuit of educational and life goals. Advisors may employ quantitative means, such as a self-report survey, or qualitative inquiry methods, such as a structured interview. Regardless of the approach taken, the advisor's goal remains to acquire a greater understanding of the student, such as

Figure 10.1. The program-level advising-as-coaching process

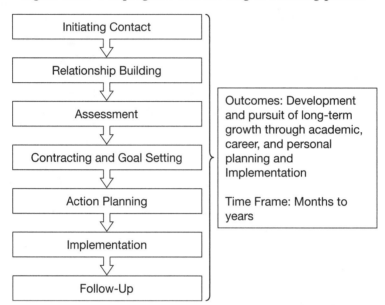

personality, learning style, study habits, self-efficacy, interests, and the like, to better nurture the relationship over time. This stage could require multiple meetings.

Once the advisor and the student understand the resources, abilities, and interests of the advisee, they engage in contracting and goal setting. At this stage, the parties frame the advising relationship within boundaries that reinforce the roles and responsibilities of each. Advising syllabi are particularly valuable at this stage. The participants also focus on specific goals and thereby generate a clear direction on how to proceed. At this point, student goals could be more or less abstract because the advisor–advisee team repeats the process at each meeting in efforts to clarify and achieve the student's goals.

In the next stage, action planning, the advisor and student begin developing career and education plans. They then work on implementation such that the student pursues personal goals in accordance with these plans. With the final goal of further clarifying and achieving the student's goals and revising his or her plans as necessary, the advisor then follows up with the student to evaluate progress and revisit the plans. Advisors may need to conduct assessment on these program-level processes over multiple individual sessions, stages of development, and implementation steps.

Advisors wishing to employ coaching at the program level should focus on the advising program structure. For example, in the initiating-contact stage, leaders might consider whether to set up a proactive or responsive approach to contacting students. Table 10.1 shows the coaching decisions identified with each advising stage outlined in Figure 10.1.

Table 10.1. Application of advising as coaching at the program level

Stage	Questions About Coaching Approach
Initiating contact	Will advisors be proactive in contacting students? When will the initial contact take place?
	Who will make this contact? Advisors or administrative staff?
Relationship building	What standards or guidelines affect relationship building between students and advisors?
	How much initial contact time should be dedicated to relationship building?
	What information, if any, will be collected from the student? How will this information be used to build the advisor–advisee relationship?
Assessment	What methods will be used to gather information about students?
	What specific instruments, assessments, or surveys will be used (*Myers-Briggs Type Inventory* [2003], *Strong Interest Inventory* [Gallup, 2007], etc.)?
	When and how will this information be collected and discussed with the student?
Contracting and goal setting	Will contracting be formal or informal?
	What information should be included in an advisor-student contract or syllabus?
	Are goals standardized via program outlines or developed uniquely between advisor and student?
	What standardized or individual goals or outcomes, if any, should be articulated?
Action planning	What available process or tools can facilitate action planning?
Implementation	What tools and resources can students access to implement their plans?
Follow-up	How frequently will advisors follow up with students to monitor progress and revise plans as necessary?
	Will follow-up visits be initiated by advisors, students, or both?

Level 2: The Individual Session

The second level represents the process through which advisor–student interaction unfolds in an individual advising session. At this level of coaching, the immediate needs of a student come into focus as they relate to the pursuit of long-term goals. Thus this process should further the program-level coaching process. Consequently, an advisor can direct the individual session entirely toward moving the student forward in relation to one or more of the stages of the program-level process. See Figure 10.2.

Figure 10.2. The individual session advising-as-coaching process

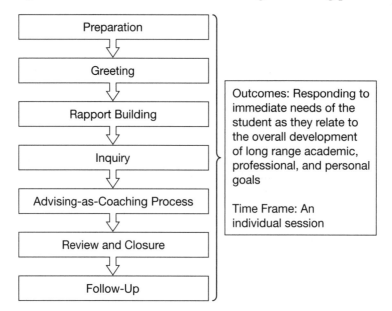

This advising session process begins with careful preparation. An advisor should adequately get ready by reviewing previous session notes and gathering materials based on any pre-session conversation with the student. While this stage does not frequently appear in the advising-process literature, it nevertheless serves as a significant step in integrating this session-level process within the program-level process (Nutt, 2000), and so the advisor should not lose sight of the big picture while preparing for an individual session. The advisor should greet the student and initiate rapport or relationship building, which is continued throughout the session. The advisor then makes inquiries to ascertain and clarify the student's needs. The session reaches the advising-as-coaching stage, which involves the provision of guidance through the facilitation of student decision making. Then the advisor follows up prior to the next session in which the process begins again.

Throughout these steps the advisor carefully situates immediate assistance in the context of the student's long-term goals. Current challenges, insights, and experiences must inform, and alter as necessary, the goals and academic plans of the student. In addition, the student's goals, plans, and past experiences should guide decision making about actions for addressing immediate needs. Thus, just as immediate challenges may alter the coach's and client's focus for a time, each advising session should ultimately move the advisee in the direction of long-term objectives.

As they consider ways to implement coaching at the individual level, advisors may wish to address specific questions that relate to each stage of the process. See Table 10.2.

Table 10.2. Application of advising as coaching at the individual session level

Stage	Questions About Coaching Approach
Preparation	How much preparation time should be dedicated to each visit? What information should be reviewed?
Greeting	What kind of greeting is culturally appropriate? Does the way in which advisors greet students demonstrate interest in them and their concerns?
Rapport building	What approaches are appropriate for advisors to use in building rapport with students?
Inquiry	What training do advisors need to demonstrate active listening and effective questioning? What steps may insure that advisors dedicate sufficient time in understanding student needs and concerns before they begin to engage in the advising-as-coaching process?
Advising-as-coaching process	When should advising as coaching be used in place of a more prescriptive advising approach? Do advisors understand and know how to use the advising-as-coaching process?
Review and closure	What standards should be communicated to students at the conclusion of a session?
Follow-up	What policies and procedures should guide and support advisors in keeping commitments made within individual sessions?

Level 3: The Decision Facilitation Process

The third level represents the short-term decision-making process and action planning of the individual advising-as-coaching process. At this level of engagement advisors can draw most on coaching practices. Indeed many of the other approaches to advising discussed within the other chapters of this book and the advising literature in general are based on coaching practices at this level, including developmental advising (Creamer & Creamer, 1994; Crookston, 1972/1994/2009; Gordon, 1995), advising as teaching (Lowenstein, 1999, 2005), career advising (Gordon, 2006), appreciative advising (Bloom et al., 2008; Bloom & Martin, 2002), solution-focused counseling and advising (Mayhall & Berg, 2003), strengths-based advising (Schreiner & Anderson, 2005), and self-authorship advising (Baxter Magolda & King, 2008; Pizzolato, 2006).

With a focus primarily on facilitating decision making and promoting accountability, advisors build on the inquiry undertaken at the previous two levels, deepening it to identify and understand the student's dreams, goals, or problems. After clarifying these aspects of the student's life, the advisor as coach encourages the student to articulate attempts already made to address challenges or achieve the dream as well as the impact of any actions taken to date.

Based on an understanding of the dream or problem and an awareness of past attempts at enacting achievements or solutions, the advisor as coach brainstorms with the student to identify possible subsequent approaches. The goal is to develop as many alternatives as possible. However, an analysis of alternatives at this point should be avoided, as assessment of ideas tends to diminish the creative thinking essential at this stage (Bradford, 1976; Schein, 1998; Yukl, 1998).

Once the advisor and advisee list possible alternatives, the advisor as coach asks the student to select options most likely to achieve the desired dream or resolve the problem. The pair then establishes specific goals and develops an action plan for achieving these goals. Then the advisor encourages the student to seek support from others, as appropriate, to implement the plan. Finally, the student implements the plan and the advisor follows up to monitor progress and insure accountability. The implementation and follow-up processes are critical elements at the decision-making level. See Figure 10.3.

Like other advising strategies, the advising-as-coaching model includes activities, particularly in the implementation and follow-up stages, that span the boundaries of a typical single-session advising situation. Nonetheless, these important elements of the decision-making process merit inclusion at this level. Furthermore, at this point,

Figure 10.3. The decision-facilitation advising-as-coaching process

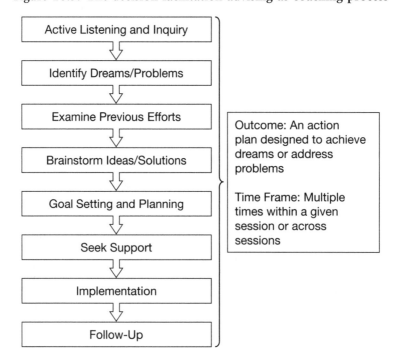

Active Listening and Inquiry

Identify Dreams/Problems

Examine Previous Efforts

Brainstorm Ideas/Solutions

Goal Setting and Planning

Seek Support

Implementation

Follow-Up

Outcome: An action plan designed to achieve dreams or address problems

Time Frame: Multiple times within a given session or across sessions the advisor as coach and the advisee integrate work at various levels. The result is a seamless, iterative series of stages in which the concepts of coaching are integrated with those of academic advising.

This level of advising is intensely practical; the advisor focuses on facilitating the decision-making process of the advisee as opposed to prescriptive advising. As a result, coaches use an inquiry-based approach to helping students. Table 10.3 provides a list of sample questions that correspond to each of the stages of Level 3.

Table 10.3. Advising-as-coaching questions used with active listening

Purpose	Questions
Identify dreams/ specific problems	What is the history of the problem? What caused it? Why does it concern you? What is the worst aspect of the problem? When do you feel the weight of the problem most significantly? What is the worst-case scenario possible as a result of the problem? What would it be like if the problem were gone? How would things be different? What do you envision as the best possible outcome in relation to this problem?
Examine previous efforts	What have you done so far to address this problem (or achieve this dream)? Are problem areas currently improving or getting worse? Why?
Brainstorm ideas/ solutions	What knowledge and skill do you need to better understand or resolve the problem? What have you thought about doing to fix the problem? What have others suggested? What have you done in the past to overcome similar problems? What would you tell someone in a similar situation? Thinking about your dream, what would make it come to life? What habits would you need to develop to accomplish your dream? May I offer some suggestions?
Goal setting and planning	Which of the options that we have discussed appear to be most viable or effective? What more would you need to do to turn these ideas into a plan? What are the action steps you need to take? When will you take them? Is your plan sufficient to achieve your goal?

(Continued)

Table 10.3. (Continued)

Purpose	Questions
Seek support	What kind of support will you need?
	Who could you recruit to help with the plan?
	How will you recruit them?
	What do you envision them doing to help?
	How will you reward them for helping you?
Implementation	When will you initiate your plan?
	When do you expect to have [a specific step in the plan] completed?
	May I contact you to check on your progress on [date]?
Follow-up	How is the situation different from when we started discussing this plan?
	What accomplishments are you most proud of so far?
	What do you want to see or do more extensively to accomplish your dream?
	What success have you had so far?
	How close are you to accomplishing your goal?
	What do you need to do next?

Obviously, the inquiry-based approach of advising as coaching promotes student responsibility and ownership of any plans and their outcomes. This emphasis, along with the accountability inherent in the process, makes this approach ideal for working with students experiencing academic difficulty. A number of the programs currently based on advising as coaching specifically address at-risk or struggling students. Nonetheless, it is an equally viable approach in any advising setting where students need to engage in decision making and action planning. To further demonstrate how advising as coaching is carried out within various contexts, the following example provides insights regarding the application of advising as coaching.

Advising-as-Coaching Scenario

Scenario II

A second-year student, Ali, comes to Drew to discuss withdrawing from school: "I'm really not doing well this term. It's not the courses or the professors—I just don't feel like I fit in. A few of my friends left after last year, and I haven't really found any new ones. My new roommates are not really like me, so they kind of stick together by themselves. I'm not in any clubs or anything like that, although I do work off campus. Also, I feel my parents and I have spent lots of money, but I'm not sure it's worth spending more if I'm not that interested. Do you have any suggestions? What do you think I should do?"

Returning from lunch, Drew, an academic advisor in the College of Liberal Arts, noted the upcoming appointment with Ali, who had e-mailed Drew a few days prior to request an appointment. Drew knew from the tone of the e-mail that Ali was struggling.	
Drew pulled up the database of student notes and reviewed the history: Ali had transitioned successfully to college the first year, had earned a 3.5 GPA in freshman courses, and seemed to have adjusted well. Planning to major in psychology, Ali appeared to be enjoying the college experience. Drew reviewed the assessments Ali had taken as a freshman, specifically the *StrengthsQuest* (The Gallup Organization, 2007) and *Myers-Briggs Type Indicator* (Myers & Briggs Foundation, 2003) results. Ali exhibited an ISFJ profile with strengths in the areas of communication, connectedness, responsibility, discipline, and empathy. Ali articulated the following goals in the first few advising sessions of the previous year: obtain a 3.0 GPA, make friends who are fun and supportive of personal and academic goals, develop a career plan, and get involved in community service. Together Ali and Drew had developed plans to achieve these goals. At the end of the year, Ali had implemented the action plans and had established friendships, earned the target GPA, and made progress on completing the psychology degree, even focusing on pursuing a master's degree in school counseling. Though not entirely sure, Drew speculates that Ali is struggling with the goals from last year.	Level 2: Preparation stage Level 1: Assessment and inquiry Level 1: Goal setting Level 1: Action planning Level 1: Implementation and follow-up
Drew was completing a review of the notes when the receptionist announced that Ali had arrived. With excitement and energy, Drew enthusiastically headed for the lobby and greeted Ali with a smile, showing a positive attitude and creating a welcoming atmosphere in both the lobby and the office. As they sat down, Drew congratulated Ali: "It is great to see you again. I must admit, I am very proud of your success last semester. You did very well in school, made some great progress on your career plan, and established some solid friendships. I hope your summer went well!"	Level 2: Initial greeting Level 2: Rapport building
After confirming that summer had been wonderful, Ali spoke energetically about the highlights. Drew moved the conversation forward by asking, "How are things since you've returned to school?" Ali's enthusiasm waned while explaining that the classes were okay, but the social scene and living situation were not ideal.	Level 2: Rapport building Level 2: Inquiry

Recognizing Ali's level of distress, Drew demonstrated empathy, restating the main points before asking for more of the details. "Is there anything exciting to you so far this semester?" Ali indicated that some of the classes were interesting, especially developmental psychology, but also reemphasized a feeling of not fitting in. "Ali, I know how important it is to you to have good friends and I know how hard you worked over the past year to establish some strong friendships. I also have to say you are exceptionally talented at setting goals and achieving them. Do you really want to drop out of school right now?" Ali indicated that "I'm just having a hard time now" and thought staying was the correct decision.	Level 3: Active listening and inquiry Level 3: Identify problems Level 3: Active listening and inquiry
Drew asked, "Can you describe for me what your ideal college experience would be like?" and took notes, with permission, of Ali's response. Drew reviewed Ali's description aloud, highlighting achievements made and some unrealized goals. Drew sensed Ali's relief in recognizing that much of the year is, in fact, going well. Drew suggested they focus on addressing the issue of friends: "What have you tried, so far, to develop friendships this semester?" Ali had hoped to make friends with new roommates, but that objective had not materialized. When prompted for other ideas, Ali mentioned some clubs of interest, which Drew wrote down before asking, "Has anyone else offered any other suggestions about this situation?" After noting Ali's answer, Drew asked, "Would you be willing to consider some of my ideas?" Ali agreed, and Drew shared some suggestions both verbally and on the list of options to try.	Level 3: Identify dreams Level 3: Active listening and inquiry Level 3: Examine previous efforts Level 3: Brainstorm ideas and solutions
Based on the list they had compiled, Drew prompted, "What do you think is a realistic goal in relation to the social challenges you're facing?" Ali felt as if making three good friends by the end of the semester was doable. "Which idea will best help you make three friends?" Ali identified a club associated with students who were interested in school counseling, some volunteer activities in the community, and said, "There are a few students in a couple of my classes that might come to a study group if I asked them." Together Drew and Ali crafted a plan outlining these options and a specific time frame for accomplishing the goals. Drew encouraged Ali to seek support from other friends, especially those made last year who had moved away, and family.	Level 3: Goal setting and planning Level 3: Seek support

With a solid plan in hand, Ali seemed more enthusiastic. "Ali, you were very successful last year in meeting your goals," Drew began a discussion of the strengths Ali had used to meet planned objectives. "I have every confidence that you can do this and support these new goals," Drew said, before offering contact information for the club advisor and the office on campus that coordinated service opportunities. They then scheduled a phone appointment for two weeks to touch base on Ali's progress.	Level 2: Rapport building Level 2: Review and closure Level 3: Follow-up
After their appointment, Drew documented the plan and noted their next appointment on the calendar. Drew also sent an e-mail to both the club advisor and the community service program coordinator to let them know that Ali would be contacting them.	Level 2: Follow-up

Summary

Scenario II demonstrates the conceptual and practical similarities between advising and coaching. Indeed, because the two are so closely related both procedurally and philosophically, advising as coaching may not seem like a unique form of advising. Nonetheless, the practical utility of coaching processes within academic advising is based on a) a framework for understanding and managing the advising process; b) a practical guide for facilitating student decision making, planning, and problem solving; and c) a means of promoting student growth and development through a self-authored approach. In the fictional case, Drew's workplace used the framework of advising as coaching to structure an advising program and provided each advisor with important information about student strengths and weakness as a way of better assisting them. Drew and other advisors also received training on each level of the model and the behaviors and practices that contribute to effectiveness at each step. They also received regular feedback from supervisors and peers, and used the model as a guide for improving their advising practice.

In addition to the professional growth Drew experiences as an advisor, advisees receive better assistance for their own personal and cognitive development. Drew's focus on facilitating and guiding the student's decision-making and planning processes allows them to develop their abilities and confidence in decision making. Follow-up sessions contribute to their growing sense of responsibility.

Furthermore, Drew's intentional focus on assisting Ali in formulating personal decisions promotes the development of autonomous decision making and self-authorship. This approach proves particularly successful if the advisor assists the student to think, as part of the brainstorming, goal-setting, and planning stages, about the people who exert influence over her or his final decision making.

The union of advising and coaching practices provides a tremendously useful framework for promoting effective advising practices. Their historical, theoretical, and practical similarities make them compatible partners, while the simplicity of their practical approaches make them easy to learn and apply. Thus, practitioners can readily implement advising as coaching to strengthen advisor-student relationships, promote student learning outcomes, and facilitate the advising process to achieve desired outcomes through a three-stage model of advising as coaching.

References

Baxter Magolda, M., & King, P. M. (2008, Winter). Toward reflective conversations: An advising approach that promotes self-authorship. *Peer Review*, 8–11.

Bloom, J. L., Hutson, B. L., & He, Y. (2008). *The appreciative advising revolution.* Champaign, IL: Stipes.

Bloom, J. L., & Martin, N. A. (2002, August 29). Incorporating appreciative inquiry into academic advising. *The Mentor: An Academic Advising Journal.* Retrieved from http://dus.psu.edu/mentor/old/articles/020829jb.htm

Bono, J. E., Purvanova, R. K., Towler, A. J., & Peterson, D. B. (2009). A survey of executive coaching practices. *Personnel Psychology, 62,* 361–404.

Boss, R. W. (2000). Preventing regression in teambuilding: A longitudinal study of the personal management interview. In R. T. Golembiewski (Ed.), *Handbook of organizational consultation* (2nd ed.) (pp. xxii, 1045). New York, NY: Marcel Dekker.

Bradford, L. P. (1976). *Making meetings work: A guide for leaders and group members.* La Jolla, CA: University Associates.

Cocivera, T., & Cronshaw, S. (2004). Action frame theory as a practical framework for executive coaching process. *Consulting Psychology Journal: Practice and Research, 56*(4), 234–245.

Creamer, D. G., & Creamer, E. G. (1994). Practicing developmental advising: Theoretical contents and functional applications. *NACADA Journal, 14*(2), 17–24.

Crookston, B. B. (2009). A developmental view of academic advising as teaching. *NACADA Journal, 29*(1), 78–82. (Reprinted from *Journal of College Student Personnel, 13,* 1972, pp. 12–17; *NACADA Journal, 14*[2], 1994, pp. 5–9)

DeLuca, L. S. (2008). An exploration of the existential orientation to coaching (Master's thesis). University of Pennsylvania, Philadelphia.

Ducharme, M. J. (2004). The cognitive-behavioral approach to executive coaching. *Consulting Psychology Journal: Practice and Research, 56*(4), 214–224.

Feldman, D. C., & Lankau, M. J. (2005). Executive coaching: A review and agenda for future research. *Journal of Management, 31*(6), 829–848.

Freas, A. (2000). Coaching executives for business results. In M. Goldsmith, L. Lyons, & A. Freas (Eds.), *Coaching for leadership: How the world's greatest coaches help leaders learn* (pp. 27–41). San Francisco, CA: Jossey-Bass/Pfeiffer.

Frisch, M. H. (2005). Extending the reach of executive coaching: The internal coach. *Human Resource Planning, 28*(1), 23.

The Gallup Organization. (2007). *StrengthsFinder 2.0.* Retrieved from http://sf2.strengthsfinder.com

Gladwell, M. (2005). *Blink: The power of thinking without thinking* (1st ed.). New York, NY: Little, Brown and Co.

Goldsmith, M. (2000). Coaching for behavior change. In M. Goldsmith, L. Lyons, & A. Freas (Eds.), *Coaching for leadership: How the world's greatest coaches help leaders learn* (pp. 21–26). San Francisco, CA: Jossey-Bass/Pfeiffer.

Goleman, D., Boyatzis, R., & McKee, A. (2002). *Primal leadership*. Boston, MA: Harvard Business School Press.

Gordon, V. N. (1995). Developmental advising. In D. S. Crockett (Ed.), *Advising skills, techniques, and resources: A compilation of materials related to the organization and delivery of advising services* (pp. 147–161). Iowa City, IA: The American College Testing Program.

Gordon, V. N. (2006). *Career advising: An academic advisor's guide* (1st ed.). San Francisco, CA: Jossey-Bass.

Grayson, D., & Larson, K. (2000). How to make the most of the coaching relationship for the person being coached. In M. Goldsmith, L. Lyons, & A. Freas (Eds.), *Coaching for leadership: How the world's greatest coaches help leaders learn* (pp. 121–130). San Francisco, CA: Jossey-Bass/Pfeiffer.

Hall, D. T., Otazo, K. L., & Hollenbeck, G. P. (1999). Behind closed doors: What really happens in executive coaching. *Organizational Dynamics*, 29(3), 39–53.

Joo, B.-K. (2005). Executive coaching: A conceptual framework from an integrative reveiw of practice and research. *Human Resource Development Review*, 4(4), 462–488.

Judge, W. Q., & Cowell, J. (1997). The brave new world of executive coaching. *Business Horizons*, 40(4), 71–77.

Kampa-Kokesch, S., & Anderson, M. Z. (2001). Executive coaching: A comprehensive review of the literature. *Consulting Psychology Journal: Practice and Research*, 53(4), 205–228.

Kilburg, R. R. (2004). When shadows fall: Using psychodynamic approaches in executive coaching. *Consulting Psychology Journal: Practice and Research*, 56(4), 246–268.

Lowenstein, M. (1999, November 22). An alternative to the developmental theory of advising. *The Mentor: An Academic Advising Journal*. Retrieved from http://dus.psu.edu/mentor/old/articles/991122ml.htm

Lowenstein, M. (2005). If advising is teaching, what do advisors teach? *NACADA Journal*, 25(2), 65–73.

Lyons, L. (2000). Coaching at the heart of strategy. In M. Goldsmith, L. Lyons, & A. Freas (Eds.), *Coaching for leadership: How the world greatest coaches help leaders learn* (pp. 3–20). San Francisco, CA: Jossey-Bass/Pfeiffer.

Mayhall, J., & Berg, J. (2003). Solution-focused advising with the undecided student. *NACADA Journal*, 22(1), 76–77.

McGovern, J., Lindemann, M., Vergara, M., Murphy, S., Barker, L., & Warrenfeltz, R. (2001). Maximizing the impact of executive coaching. *The Manchester Review*, 6(1), 1–9.

Mobley, S. A. (1999). Judge not: How coaches create healthy organizations. *The Journal for Quality and Participation*, 22(4), 57–60.

Myers & Briggs Foundation. (2003). *MBTI basics*. Retrieved from http://www.myersbriggs.org/my-mbti-personality-type/mbti-basics/

Nutt, C. L. (2000). One-to-one advising. In V. N. Gordon & W. R. Habley (Eds.), *Academic advising: A comprehensive handbook* (pp. 220–226). San Francisco, CA: Jossey-Bass.

Olivero, G., Bane, K. D., & Kopelman, R. E. (1997). Executive coaching as a transfer of training tool: Effects on productivity in a public agency. *Public Personnel Management*, 26(4), 461–469.

Orem, S., Binkert, J., & Clancy, A. L. (2007). *Appreciative coaching: A positive process for change* (1st ed.). San Francisco, CA: Jossey-Bass/Wiley.

Orenstein, R. L. (2006). Measuring executive coaching efficacy? The answer was right here all the time. *Consulting Psychology Journal: Practice and Research*, 58(2), 106–116.

Orth, C. D., Wilkinson, H. E., & Benfari, R. C. (1987). The manager's role as coach and mentor. *Organizational Dynamics*, 15(4), 66–74.

Passmore, J. (2007). An integrative model for executive coaching. *Consulting Psychology Journal: Practice and Research*, 59(1), 68–78.

Peltier, B. (2001). *The psychology of executive coaching: Theory and application*. New York, NY: Brunner-Routledge.

Peterson, D. B. (2007). Executive coaching in a cross-cultural context. *Consulting Psychology Journal: Practice and Research*, 59(4), 261–271.

Pizzolato, J. E. (2006). Complex partnerships: Self-authorship and provocative academic advising practices. *NACADA Journal*, 26(1), 32–45.

Schein, E. H. (1998). *Process consultation*. Boston, MA: Pearson Custom.

Schlosser, B., Steinbrenner, D., Kumata, E., & Hunt, J. (2006). The coaching impact study: Measuring the value of executive coaching. *The International Journal of Coaching in Organizations*, 4(3), 8–26.

Schnell, E. R. (2005). A case study of executive coaching as a support mechanism during organizational growth and evolution. *Consulting Psychology Journal: Practice and Research*, 57(1), 41–56.

Schreiner, L. A., & Anderson, E. (2005). Strengths-based advising: A new lens for higher education. *NACADA Journal*, 25(2), 20–27.

Skiffington, S. M., & Zeus, P. (2002). *The complete guide to coaching at work*. Roseville, Australia: McGraw-Hill.

Smith, E. R. (2008). A brief history of coaching. Retrieved from http://www.scribd.com/doc/7398635/A-Brief-History-of-Executive-Coaching

Stern, L. R. (2004). Executive coaching: A working definition. *Consulting Psychology Journal: Practice and Research*, 56(3), 154–162.

Stoberr, D. (2005). Approaches to research on executive coaching and organizational coaching outcomes. *International Journal of Coaching in Organizations*, 3(1), 6–13.

Thach, L., & Heinselman, T. (2000). Continuous improvement in place of training. In M. Goldsmith, L. Lyons, & A. Freas (Eds.), *Coaching for leadership: How the world greatest coaches help leaders learn* (pp. 219–230). San Francisco, CA: Jossey-Bass/Pfeiffer.

Waldman, D. A. (2003). Research briefs: Does working with an executive coach enhance the value of multisource performance feedback. *Academy of Management Executive, 17*(3), 146–148.

Wales, S. (2002). Why coaching. *Journal of Change Management, 3*(3), 275–282.

Wasylyshyn, K. M. (2003). Executive coaching: An outcome study. *Consulting Psychology Journal: Practice and Research, 55*(2), 94–106.

Yukl, G. A. (1998). *Leadership in organizations* (4th ed.). Upper Saddle River, NJ: Prentice Hall.

PART THREE

A NEW LENS: APPLYING THEORIES FROM OTHER DISCIPLINES TO THE PRACTICE OF ACADEMIC ADVISING

In fall 2005, the *NACADA Journal* was devoted entirely to theories that help advisors build their practice and explain their work. In this special issue, *Journal* authors challenged readers to look at academic advising practice through a new lens and to expand their understanding of multiple theories, both inside and outside the social sciences, that can inform practice.

Authors included in part three offer readers illustrations of advising approaches built upon practice based on theories from the humanities and social science concepts not traditionally employed in advising.

THE APPLICATION OF CONSTRUCTIVISM AND SYSTEMS THEORY TO ACADEMIC ADVISING

Terry Musser and Frank Yoder

As part of the process of professionalizing academic advising, scholars and practitioners no longer feel the need to justify the reasons a discussion of theories and philosophies applied to advising is important and necessary. However, not all advisors are familiar with the history of the field or the ways theories underpinning various other disciplines effectively apply to advising. As advising evolves as a profession, practitioners face increasingly complex situations. Once a process of selecting the correct classes, advising now involves a multilayered series of interactions that reflect a range of developmental, academic, social, personal, and institutional issues.

As providers of information, advisors inform students about the best course choices much as they did in the past, but this effort does not constitute the extent of their current responsibilities. Advisors also help teach students to negotiate the increasingly murky terrain of majors and career choices as well as a maze of institutional rules. At an interpersonal level, advisors work with students from a wide range of backgrounds with equally disparate levels of preparedness. Students arrive at college already feeling stressed, and they encounter a new culture often more open and less structured than experienced to date.

The realities of instant communication add another layer of complexity to students' adjustment to college as they often maintain close ties to their homes and communities. For example, bonds between parents and students, now often maintained daily through modern means of communication, often affect the advising relationship. When parents access student records and information, advisors may find themselves dealing with multiple opinions and divergent goals.

Bombarded with information, students often feel as if the world is spinning too fast. Advisors often speak about the growing complexity issues that arise during advising sessions—such as those involving financial challenges, personal relationships, learning to become independent adults—in addition to the more routine curricular decisions about courses, majors, and academic progress.

Theory is, therefore, becoming ever more essential to practitioners because it provides a framework of ideas to help them make sense of the shifting situations they encounter. Theory explains variations in student behavior and suggests approaches that advisors can use to guide students in positive and helpful ways. Knowing the reasons behind student reactions can free advisors to address situations proactively.

While acknowledging that theory undergirds good advising, practitioners may not immediately see ways to connect it to their daily interactions with students. Often opaque with formidable jargon, theory often seems disconnected from the realities advisors face. Consideration of theory may appear more suited to a graduate seminar in which people enjoy the time to think about and discuss such matters.

While theory that exists in a vacuum offers no value—it is most useful when applied—advisors do not arrive in their offices asking themselves, "Which theories will I apply to advising students today?" Rather, those seeking to understand its applicability ask, "How can theory make me a better advisor and improve my advising skills and knowledge?" Theory informs advising by building the foundations that support creative development of new techniques and philosophies related to academic advising. It describes approaches that have inspired new ways of thinking about the practice of advising.

Thinking Theoretically and Philosophically

Advisors may be tempted to think of themselves only as practitioners or doers and not as philosophical thinkers. While seeking out facts to inform daily work is important, the interpretation of relevant theories allows advisors to understand professional practice. While clear, black-and-white facts may fail to guide advisors, the more shadowy grays of theory and philosophy always invite examination and possible deployment.

Kieran Egan (1997) provided a comprehensive discussion of theory and philosophical thinking in *The Educated Mind* by distilling the definition of theory and philosophy and how it affects practice: "[Theories] are not facts, nor are they generalizations from facts; they are guesses, suggestions, or assertions about the nature of things, about some whole or essence, that are *based on* facts and generalizations" (p. 133). Egan believes that thinking philosophically about anything helps reduce all of the complicated thinking and influences to essential and important information that increases one's knowledge of the world. Furthermore, the skill to think philosophically helps an individual get to the heart of any matter as well as clearly identify the issue and develop viable solutions or take appropriate action (Egan, 1997, p. 134). Without a philosophical underpinning for academic advising, practitioners lack an understanding of the essential components of the complex issues at hand and risk perpetuating ineffective and inefficient advising.

Studying theory initiates good discussions and advising practices. Kendra Cherry (2011), a practitioner in the field of psychology, offers several important purposes for learning theory, saying that it

○ gives all professionals in a field a common language to share and discuss ideas, facilitating communication and understanding for meaningful discourse;

○ provides a framework for understanding human behavior, thought, and development. By having a broad base of understanding about the ways of and reasons for human behavior, people better understand themselves and others;

○ creates a basis for future research. Scholars use theories to form hypotheses that can then be tested.

The ability to think philosophically frees individuals from the constraints of past ideas, beliefs, or practices—the way others have thought about a topic—and helps them imagine a new reality for understanding and approaching a phenomenon.

As evidenced in advising publications and discussions, theories are dynamic. Advisor-scholars modify and adapt them to acknowledge new information. Hagen and Jordan (2008) described a historical journey of theoretical discovery related to the field in "Theoretical Foundations of Academic Advising," a chapter in *Academic Advising: A Comprehensive Handbook*. As recently as 2005, the *NACADA Journal*, in a groundbreaking move, devoted an entire issue to the discussion of theory and philosophy related to academic advising. When advisors share a basic understanding of underlying theories, they can more easily collaborate on developing strategies, techniques, and resources that benefit the profession.

Making the Case for Constructivism

Because a unified theory, which may be neither possible nor desirable, does not apply to the field, we propose that constructivism serves as an appropriate archetype that influences all practice and theory related to academic advising. We argue that constructivism provides a philosophy necessary to develop exemplary advising strategies and techniques that work for student populations as well as a framework upon which to build the advising approaches represented in this book.

Constructivism is a way of thinking about knowing, a foundation for building models of teaching, learning, and creating curricula (Tobin & Tippins, 1993). Although much of the literature on constructivism relates to learning theories, constructivist tenets are also associated with many fields. Duffy and Cunningham (1996) provided succinct statements about two qualities that characterize all views of constructivism: Learning is an active process of constructing rather than acquiring knowledge, and instruction is a process of supporting construction of knowledge rather than communicating information.

Educational philosopher Jean Piaget is credited as the original constructivist (Warrick, n.d.). He believed that learners create knowledge for themselves by taking a new concept or idea and linking it to constructs they already know, understand, or believe. Perhaps von Glasersfeld (1990) offered the simplest definition of constructivism, referring to as *trivial* or *personal* constructivism, when he wrote, "Knowledge is actively constructed by the learner, not passively received from the environment." In other words, no matter the information given to them, learners must construct their own meaning for it or the material will not be understood, learned, or retained. In his chapter that concludes this book and offers thoughtful speculation about the future of academic advising, Marc Lowenstein states, "While students must take responsibility for finding connections, advisors are accountable for facilitating student understanding of them." In this passage, Lowenstein supports the notion that the work of academic advisors is grounded in constructivist philosophy.

Constructivism assumes a slightly different meaning or context depending on the theorist who proposed a particular type of it. A brief description of several of these types of constructivism shows the potential applications to advising:

- *Social constructivism* was pioneered by Lev Vygotsky, who proposed that humans learn from each other, so learning should be promoted in collaboration with others (e.g., with teachers, administrators, all learners, everyone). The individual learner constructs his or her own version of the truth, but the knowledge constructed has been mediated by the collective. From the social constructivist viewpoint, the background and culture of the learner influences the entire learning process, shaping the knowledge and truth the learner creates, discovers, and retains in the learning process. (Wertsch as cited by Dougiamas, para. 34–38)

- *Cultural constructivism* suggests that knowledge and reality cannot be separated from their cultural contexts, meaning that two unique cultures will likely form different observational methodologies. "For instance, Western cultures generally rely on *objects* for scientific descriptions; by contrast, Native American culture relies on *events* for descriptions. These are two distinct ways of constructing reality based on external artifacts." (Dougiamas, 1998, para. 42–44)

- *Constructivist epistemology,* first proposed by Jean Piaget (Dougiamas, 1998, para. 24), relates to a conceptual perspective about the nature of scientific knowledge, which Piaget maintained is constructed by scholars and not discovered in the world. In other words, the concepts of science are mental constructs proposed by researchers to explain sensory experiences. Therefore, an observation explained scientifically really reflects the explanation of the scientists who studied it extensively and who have interpreted or constructed the meaning of it. Learners, in turn, must also make their own meaning of the phenomenon. (Dougiamas, 1998, para. 24–25)

- *Constructionism,* similar to constructivism, maintains that the learner creates meaning by generating, or is actively engaged in the process of generating, a product for others to see. Writing a reflection, designing a web site, or drawing a visual representation assists with the construction of knowledge. Dialogue with others also engages the learner and aids with knowledge construction. (Dougiamas, 1998, para. 45–49)

Constructivism serves as the foundation for nearly all advising approaches. Crookston (1972/1994/2009) and Perry (1970) both drew on constructivism, and their theories played important roles, directly and indirectly, in the conceptualization of advising. Crookston, for example, proposed that the advisor and student develop a relationship together by incorporating interpretation, problem solving, decision making, and evaluation skills. At the time, reflecting a new definition of advising, Crookston focused on students rather than advisors and put students in charge of determining their learning. According to Crookston, students must construct their own journey, with advisor assistance, through the academic labyrinth. Perry's theory of intellectual development influenced early thinking about developmental advising, specifically by pointing out that a person's viewpoint is shaped by her or his past relevant experiences. Perry described the intellectual positions, along a continuum, through which humans create and process meaning. That is, the theory is based on a constructivist philosophy whereby intellectual development is influenced by the individual's meaning-making process over time.

As these two brief examples from the influential founders of modern advising show, constructivist philosophy offers a common framework from which to hang the practical approaches to advising and therefore the creation of new strategies and techniques for the advising practice. We challenge the advising community to consider any and all practices related to advising in search of constructivism.

Systems Theory

Similar to constructivism, systemic thinking is a philosophical lens through which one can understand a phenomenon by looking at patterns. It provides a conceptual, visual way of considering academic advising. By thinking about the responsibilities undertaken on a daily basis as broadly and comprehensively as possible, advisors can visualize all of the elements that influence practice and come to a common understanding of the concept of advising. Thinking systemically helps scholar-advisors examine and understand the advising experience holistically. This approach also allows for the incorporation of a myriad of theories and philosophies from many fields and professions into advising practice.

Tukey (1996) argued that a systems approach to advising provides the rationale for "holding . . . broad, fundamental discussions; for coordinating unit activities; for improving staff functions; and for integrating advising into the central mission and goals of the institution" (p. 12). He further recommended the following strategies for understanding and improving academic advising:

- broadening the view beyond advising and keeping institutional ecology in mind;
- collaborating with faculty members and staff throughout the institution by crossing unit boundaries and exerting diverse influences;
- understanding the entire context of academic experiences and decisions;
- learning more about different parts of the system to work better within it (p. 12).

The four essential elements of any advising interaction—the student, advisor, institution, and external influences—provide the foundation for a systemic view of advising. Each component reveals potential issues that often influence advisor–advisee communications. Each element, with its associated topics and concepts, also opens opportunities for study and growth for the advisor. Mind maps of each element helps one to visualize academic advising.

The Advisor

Advisors bring unique values, beliefs, knowledge, and past advising experiences to the advising relationship. Reflection of their own skills and attributes informs and improves the advising relationship. See Figure 11.1.

The Student

Students, like their advisors, carry with them values and belief systems, cultural backgrounds, educational goals, and past educational experiences that influence the direction of the advising relationship. In cultivating an awareness and sensitivity to these matters, advisors are better positioned to confidently coach and guide students. See Figure 11.2.

The Institution

Figure 11.3 shows a strong network of faculty members and staff who provide educational and personal resources for students as internal components of the institution. Advisors must be familiar with the institution's vision and mission as well as the educational opportunities provided to students. The historical context of the advising system influences advising delivery and should also be understood by the advisor as it likely affects the model used by the institution.

External Influences

Finances, family dynamics, the economic outlook and career trends, and those critical aspects of life that extend beyond the immediate student–advisor relationship, and largely beyond the influence of the institution, exert a powerful effect on students' academic performance and progress toward the degree. See Figure 11.4.

The heart of any effective advising relationship involves the union of the four elements illustrated in Figure 11.5, which shows a comprehensive, visual representation of the mind map of academic advising. As illustrated in Figure 11.6, the four elements of impact on advising are deeply interwoven. Advising theories and advisors' techniques, for example, are derived from the institution's mission and values as well as from its curriculum and culture. The student's academic record, family situation, and financial aid status as well as cultural beliefs, strengths, interests, and goals influence the nature and direction of advising interactions.

Figure 11.1. The advisor mind map

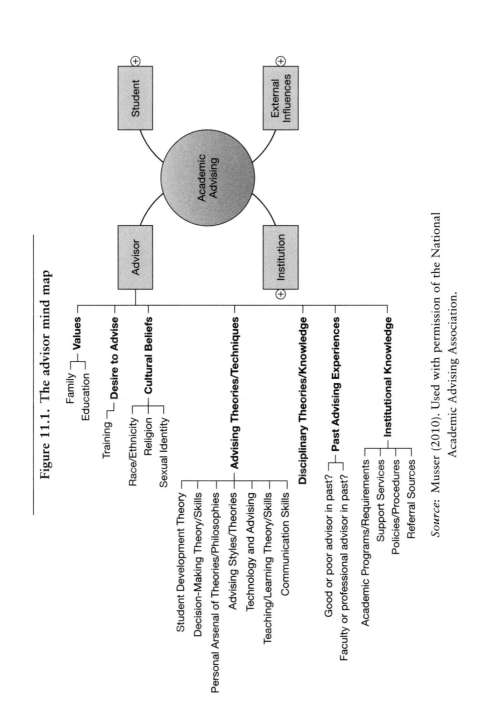

Source: Musser (2010). Used with permission of the National Academic Advising Association.

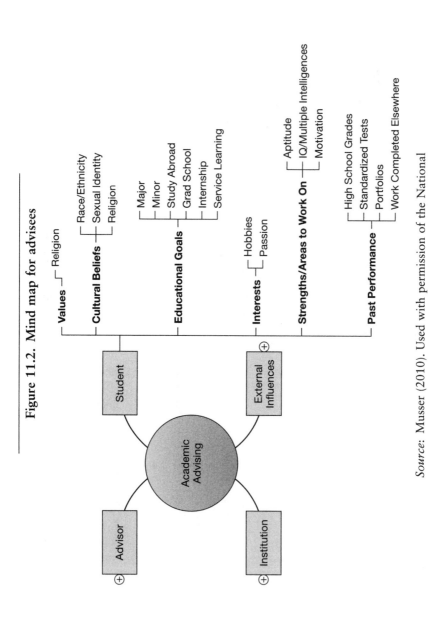

Figure 11.2. Mind map for advisees

Source: Musser (2010). Used with permission of the National Academic Advising Association.

Figure 11.3. Mind map for the institution

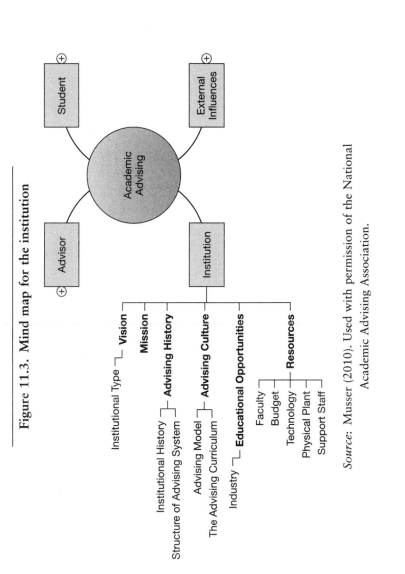

Source: Musser (2010). Used with permission of the National Academic Advising Association.

Figure 11.4. Mind map for external influences on advising

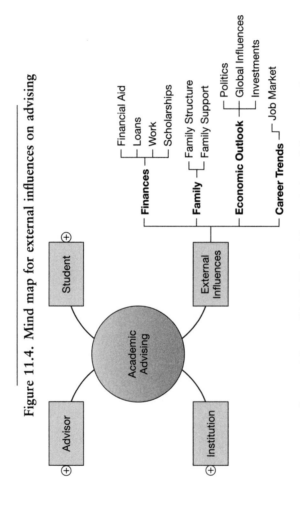

Source: Musser (2010). Used with permission of the National Academic Advising Association.

Figure 11.5. The complete academic-advising mind map

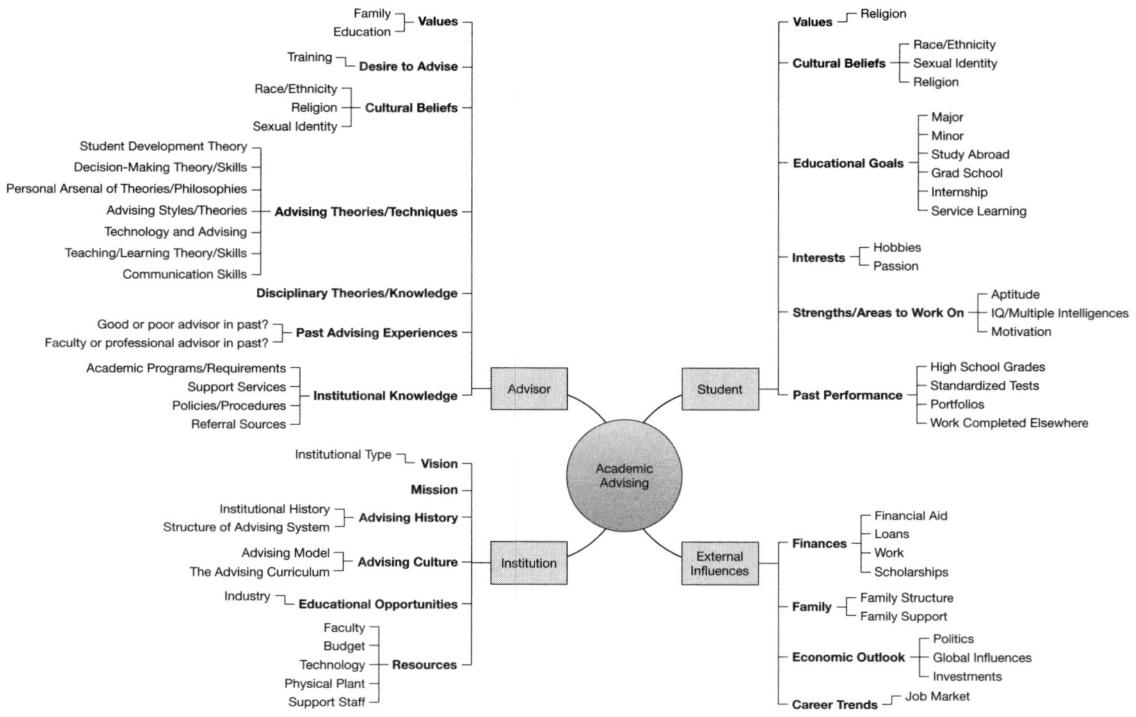

Source: Musser (2010). Used with permission of the National Academic Advising Association.

Figure 11.6. Intricate complexities of the four influences on advising per mind map

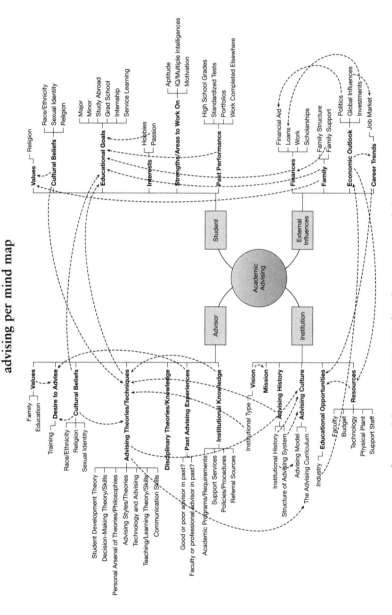

Source: Musser (2010). Used with permission of the National Academic Advising Association.

A Brief Overview of Student Development and Cognitive Learning Theories

Student development and cognitive learning theories, both with strong constructivist undercurrents, apply to students progressing through and building upon their college experiences. They put forth the important view that college experience offers a unique and profound period of change.

The study of the traditional-aged college students, largely undertaken in the mid-20th century, culminated in student development theories that describe a developmental-stage process through which students typically progress during college. Researchers have grouped the theories into three main types: psychosocial-identity formation processes, cognitive-developmental structures, and personal preference or types (Hagen & Jordan, 2008; King, 2000; Strange, 2004). Well documented in initial advising studies, in more recent years, developmental theories have also been featured in college student literature (Creamer, 2000; Hagen & Jordan, 2008; Higbee, 2005).

Perry (1970), whose research influenced early work on developmental advising, described the intellectual development of college-aged students. Stating that humans think about past experiences and that these considerations create individual meaning for various aspects of life and education, Perry proposed nine positions along a continuum, through which one progresses while learning and growing, in three main categories: dualism, multiplicity, and relativism.

People with a dualistic view of the world see in a dichotomous way, as good or bad, or black or white. They believe that knowledge is learned and understood quantitatively and based on facts, often from experts or those in authoritative roles, but they are not generally actively engaged in their own learning. Traditional-aged college students typically arrive at the academy with a dualistic view of learning. When they discover that this perspective does not necessarily hold true or they are challenged to become actively engaged with their own learning, students typically progress to the next phase of intellectual development: multiplicity.

Perry suggested that cognitive dissonance generates the impetus for students' progression to each subsequent phase. Proponents of developmental advising suggest that this dissonance can be created with sustained questioning and probing. Multiplicity, according to Perry's theory, allows students to express more than one point of view. Students in this stage accept other opinions and ideas as equally valid and they think at much deeper, more analytical levels than when in the dualistic stage.

When students realize they must become more engaged in learning and discussion about various opinions and ideas, they move into the relativism stage, where they think even more deeply to form and support unique thoughts and ideas. Students in the relativism phase of intellectual development recognize that knowledge is not only qualitative, but also contextual, because it grows from experience and circumstance.

Learning Theories

NACADA's Concept of Advising (National Academic Advising Association, 2006) describes a metaphor for advising as teaching. This document aligns academic advising with the teaching-learning component of higher education, a suggestion originally proposed by Crookston (1972/1994/2009). If teaching is accepted as a metaphor for advising, then learning theories that offer perspectives on teaching and learning have implications for advising. Although many learning theories appear in the literature, we have chosen to focus on four theorists who support our claim that advising is essentially a constructivist and teaching activity: Piaget, Vygotsky, Dewey, and Bruner.

Jean Piaget

Jean Piaget began his professional career as a child psychologist whose research concluded that children's responses to standard questions become increasingly mediated by their interactions with other children. Later Piaget developed his theory of intellectual development in which he claimed that children make sense of their environment either through assimilation or accommodation. Based on studying his own three children and others, Piaget believed that young people either make the purpose and meaning of phenomena in their environment conform to their beliefs (assimilation) or they change their mental structure of phenomena that do not initially fit with their previous knowledge and understanding (accommodation). The constant need to balance these two divergent ways of understanding their environment triggers intellectual growth in children. Piaget further developed his theory by claiming that as children age they constantly alternate between assimilation and accommodation. When learning a new concept, children grow intellectually as they reconstruct the previously known into a new understanding or meaning. Piaget proposed four stages, from birth through about 16 years of age, through which children develop intellectually:

- sensorimotor stage (birth–2 years)—babies and toddlers experience phenomena through their senses.
- preoperational stage (2–7 years)—magical thinking predominates and motor skills develop in children.
- concrete operational stage (7–11 years)—youth begin thinking logically but mostly concretely.
- formal operational stage (11–16 years)—young people develop abstract reasoning. (Boeree, 2006, para. 13–19)

According to Piaget, "The child is someone who constructs his own moral world view, who forms ideas about right and wrong, and fair and unfair, that are not the direct product of adult teaching and that are often maintained in the face of adult wishes to the contrary" (Gallagher, 1978, p. 26, as cited in Wikipedia, 2013). Piaget's three tenets—that children learn by interacting with others, must construct their own meaning for everything, and learn best when actively engaged in their education—have particular relevance for advising college-aged students and adults. According to Piaget's theory, lifelong learners continue to create meanings for new concepts and ideas through constant assimilation and accommodation as mediated by interactions with others. Based on Piaget's construct, academic advisors must find ways to help students engage in their learning, seek others with whom to interact and learn, and constantly reflect on their experiences to aid in the construction of knowledge and meaning.

Lev Vygotsky

Lev Vygotsky (1978), a Soviet psychologist at the turn of the 20th century, studied child development and the interactions with parents and others that affect it. He studied children at play and the way they internalize concepts and meanings based on their imaginative exploration. Because of his belief in the influence of culture and society on human development, the field he founded became known as *cultural-historical psychology*. He was an early constructivist as he believed that children create their own meaning based on their interactions with others within their culture.

Vygotsky was developing his psychological theories at the same time as Piaget, and although unaware of each other's work, their theories reveal very similar ideas. Vygotsky believed that the power and influence of the social interactions of children profoundly influence learning while Piaget was criticized for his lack of vision in this area. Vygotsky also believed that learning and social interaction occur simultaneously while Piaget believed learning took place after interaction.

Although many aspects of Vygotsky's (1978) theory relate to education, his ideas about learning apply most relevantly to academic advising. Vygotsky proposed that young people perform tasks within their *zone of proximal development*, meaning they function based upon familiar, understood concepts and information, and the teacher supports and pushes students to move to consider increasingly more complex ideas and information and thus supplies the *scaffolding* or support for students as they learn. When students feel comfortable with a new concept or information, the teacher pulls away the support, allowing students to work on their own. The process then repeats itself as students move through progressively more difficult subject matter.

This particular area of Vygotsky's theory, scaffolding student learning through progressively more complex stages, has implications for proactive (formerly known as intrusive) advising. Particularly for first-year, at-risk, or multicultural students, advisors must scaffold learning and adjustment, knowing when to remove support or push students to a higher level of academic complexity. Prescriptive and proactive advising techniques require the advisor to support students purposefully and force-fully as they progress into and through the university. Consistent with Vygotsky's theory, the central tools for academic advising—dialogue and interaction with knowl-edgeable adults—are important instruments for the scaffolding process.

John Dewey

John Dewey's educational philosophy directly relates to academic advising. He asserted that education should not revolve around the acquisition of a predetermined set of skills, but rather the realization of one's full potential and the ability to use acquired skills for the greater good. In *The Child and the Curriculum* (1902, p. 10), Dewey argued that effective education presents content such that students relate information to prior experiences. He was one of the earliest proponents of hands-on or experiential learning. He also suggested that the teachers become members of the community that help students seek out and understand relevant influences on their learning. As a partner in the learning process, the teacher guides students to create meaning from their learning.

Based on Dewey's writings, Russell (1999) offered specific observations for teaching applicable to academic advising. Substitute the word *advisor* for *teacher* and the word *advisee* for *learner* in the following description, and a formula for sound advising practices emerges:

> Dewey believed that learning and inquiry can't be scheduled—ample and unstructured time is needed for learners to follow their own questions and investigations. Learners are challenged through questions, discussions, suggestions, and encouragement from parents, teachers, and peers.

Jerome Bruner

Jerome Bruner (1961, 1990) developed the theory of cognitive learning, which he often referred to as *discovery learning*. He suggested that the process of learning is exemplified when the student seeks to understand an issue or concept. He emphasized that the instructor must ask relevant and personal questions that challenge the learner to seek information and think critically about the answers, and he concluded that learning ultimately accrues not from content or curriculum but from the learner's activities to discover answers.

In more recent years (1996), Bruner has written about the effect of culture and the importance of narrative to the student's educational process. For academic advisors, whose responsibility involves teaching advisees, Bruner validates the common practice of asking the right questions, not supplying the solutions, to inspire students to seek answers for themselves.

Summary

The philosophies and theories undergirding advising approaches stem from many professions and fields of study, and understanding the range of methods opens the gateway to good advising. They offer different ways of seeing, understanding, and appreciating the elements that make up the total advising endeavor.

We argue that advisors should examine their arsenals of theories and philosophies related to advising to construct individual yet socially mediated meaning and to develop new tools and strategies to improve teaching, learning, and assessment. As a result of these efforts, advisors grow adept at helping students reflect and self-assess to create unique definitions of their own academic and personal educations. Academic advisors are uniquely positioned in the academy as key guides to students in their quest to develop meaning and purpose for their educations.

References

Boeree, G. (2006). *Personality theories: Jean Piaget 1896–1980*. Retrieved from http://webspace.ship.edu/cgboer/piaget.html

Bruner, J. (1961). *The act of discovery. Harvard Educational Review*, *31*, 21–32.

Bruner, J. (1990). *Acts of meaning*. Cambridge, MA: Harvard University Press.

Bruner, J. (1996). *The culture of education*. Cambridge, MA: Harvard University Press.

Cherry, K. (2011). *The purpose of psychology theories*. Retrieved from http://psychology.about.com/od/developmentecourse/a/dev_purpose.htm

Creamer, D. G. (2000). Use of theory in academic advising. In V. N. Gordon & W. R. Habley (Eds.), *Academic advising: A comprehensive handbook* (pp. 18–24). San Francisco, CA: Jossey-Bass.

Crookston, B. B. (2009). A developmental view of academic advising as teaching. *NACADA Journal*, *29*(1), 78–82. (Reprinted from *Journal of College Student Personnel*, *13*, 1972, pp. 12–17; *NACADA Journal*, *14*[2], 1994, pp. 5–9)

Dewey, J. (1902). *The child and the curriculum*. Chicago, IL: The University of Chicago Press.

Dougiamas, M. (1998). *A journey into constructivism*. Retrieved from http://dougiamas.com/writing/constructivism.html

Duffy, T. M., & Cunningham, D. J. (1996). Constructivism: Implications for the design and delivery of instruction. In D. H. Jonassen (Ed.), *Handbook of research for educational communications and technology* (pp. 170–198). New York, NY: Simon & Schuster Macmillan.

Egan, K. (1997). *The educated mind*. Chicago, IL: The University of Chicago Press.

Hagen, P. L., & Jordan, P. (2008). Theoretical foundations of academic advising. In V. N. Gordon, W. R. Habley, & T. J. Grites (Eds.), *Academic advising: A comprehensive handbook* (2nd ed.) (pp. 17–35). San Francisco, CA: Jossey-Bass.

Higbee, J. L. (2005). Developmental education. In M. L. Upcraft, J. N. Gardner, & B. O. Barefoot (Eds.), *Challenging and supporting the first-year student* (pp. 294–297). San Francisco, CA: Jossey-Bass.

King, P. (2000). Using student development theory to inform institutional research. *New Directions for Institutional Research 2000* (108), 19–36.

Musser, T. (2010, November 30). Mind maps. Presented in T. Musser & F. Yoder, *The conceptual component of advising: Developing the purpose, values, and frameworks for why we do what we do* [Webinar]. Available at http://www.nacada.ksu.edu/ Resources/Product-Details/ID/REC002CD.aspx

Musser, T., & Yoder, F. (2010, November 30). *The conceptual component of advising: Developing the purpose, values, and frameworks for why we do what we do* [Webinar]. Available at http://www.nacada.ksu.edu/Resources/Product-Details/ID/ REC002CD.aspx

National Academic Advising Association. (2006). *NACADA concept of academic advising.* Retrieved from http://www.nacada.ksu.edu/Resources/Clearinghouse/View-Articles/ Concept-of-Academic-Advising.aspx

Perry, W. (1970). *Forms of intellectual and ethical development in the college years.* New York, NY: Holt, Rinehart & Winston.

Russell, B. (1999). Experience-based learning theories. *The Informal Learning Review, 38.* Retrieved from http://www.informallearning.com/archive/1999–0304-a.htm

Strange, C. (2004). Constructions of student development across the generations. *New Directions for Student Services, 106,* 47–57.

Tobin, K., & Tippins, D. (1993). Constructivism as a referent for teaching and learning. In K. Tobin (Ed.), *The practice of constructivism in science education* (pp. 3–21). Hillsdale, NJ: Lawrence-Erlbaum.

Tukey, D. D. (1996). Academic advising as a multisystem, collaborative enterprise. *NACADA Journal, 16*(1), 6–13.

Von Glasersfeld, E. (1990). An exposition of constructivism: Why some like it radical. In R. B. Davis, C. A. Maher, & N. Noddings (Eds.), *Constructivist views on the teaching and learning of mathematics* (pp. 19–29). Reston, VA: National Council of Teachers of Mathematics.

Vygotsky, L. S. (1978). *Mind in society: The development of higher psychological processes.* Cambridge, MA: MIT Press.

Warrick, W. R. (n.d.). *Constructivism: Pre-historical to post-modern.* Retrieved from http:// mason.gmu.edu/~wwarrick/Portfolio/Products/constructivism.html

Wikipedia. (2013). *Jean Piaget.* Retrieved from http://en.wikipedia.org/wiki/Jean_Piaget

SOCRATIC ADVISING

Janet M. Spence and Nora A. Scobie

Academic advisors often hear statements such as the following:

- ○ "I want to be a nurse because I like helping people. I have dreamed of this since I was a child, but I really hate the anatomy classes. What can I do?"

- ○ "I picked up an extra shift at work; I really need the money. As long as I keep up with the reading and take the tests, it should be okay to miss a few weeks of class, right?"

- ○ "My professor hates me! He gave me an F on a paper even though I turned it in on time. It isn't my fault that he didn't like what I wrote. It isn't fair!"

After facing these types of narratives from students, academic advisors may wonder, "What were they thinking?" Their question is at the heart of Socratic advising.

Human beings are diverse, and personal experiences make individuals unique. They live in a world of infinite possibilities, and seemingly insignificant choices can lead to many paths and determine any number of consequences and outcomes. The ability to make rational decisions, weigh options, and consider the impact on the decision maker and others is central to the realization of life goals. However, to achieve goals, persons must first undertake the difficult task of self-examination:

> The challenge to examine one's life is a difficult one. It requires a balance between solitary thought and intentional dialog with others. Socratic advising involves a series of questions asked not only to discover individual answers, but also to encourage insight into who we are, what motivates us, what is the basis for our decisions. (McIntyre, 2011, p. 1)

Academic advisors strive to help students grow, develop, and learn so that they can navigate the institution effectively, complete academic goals successfully, and reach their potential fully. The different approaches in this book help advisors meet this responsibility. Using the Socratic method, advisors teach students to use their critical-thinking skills to engage in self-reflection, make informed decisions, and resolve unexpected challenges. When students learn to use their critical-thinking skills to explore the facets of specific challenges, they can transfer and adapt those skills to address future challenges.

Although advisors want to help students grow, learn, and make informed decisions, time pressures sometimes force them to simply diagnose the problem, prescribe answers the students are expected to accept, and offer suggestions for consideration. Advisors may be able to see more students using a prescriptive approach, and students may leave the meeting satisfied with the service they received but perhaps not with the learning they deserve. Will a student who experiences only prescriptive advising know how to handle an academic challenge?

A Socratic advising approach teaches students to become self-aware thinkers who can analyze their own thought processes, beliefs, and behaviors. When students recognize inconsistent or faulty thinking, challenge long-held belief systems, and fully explore desired outcomes they become engaged learners who take responsibility for their own success. The Socratic process helps students become more autonomous, independent, and resilient.

Overview of Socratic Advising

The Socratic advising approach relies heavily upon the work of Paul and Elder (2009, www.criticalthinking.org), which helped standardize the language, terminology, and process of teaching critical thinking. Their contribution provides a concrete way for advisors to put into context the idea of advising as teaching.

In their discussion on the hermeneutic approach (chapter 13), Sarah Champlin-Scharff and Peter Hagen advocate the use of the humanities to guide understanding, inquiry, and meaning making in the advising setting. Socratic advising is similar to the hermeneutic approach in that it offers a way to view oneself, others, and the world. Socratic strategies enhance advising through the use of traditional narratives found in the humanities, but Socratic advising is more: It involves practitioners drawing multidisciplinarily from the humanities, social and behavioral sciences, and disciplines in which advisors have studied and those in which they now work.

Socratic advisors give students the tools to become self-aware thinkers and decision makers. Jayne Drake, in chapter 2 on advising as teaching, states that "the teacher's and the advisor's central responsibility is to facilitate learning." To be effective, teachers and advisors must possess knowledge of the subject, use well-planned instructional methods, and demonstrate strong pedagogical skills.

In 2010, a cohort of academic advisors at the University of Louisville collaborated with the staff of the University's Delphi Center for Teaching and Learning to develop a Socratic advising approach to help students on academic warning return to good academic standing (Academic Improvement Model Advisor Cohort I, 2010). Although created specifically to assist students in academic distress, the Socratic approach the Cohort devised can be used in almost any advising situation. Components of the Socratic advising approach articulated by the Academic Improvement Model Advisor Cohort I (2010) include

- a critical thinking framework,
- an assessment of student thinking,
- Socratic questioning,

- a proactive advising style,
- helping techniques, and
- a teaching and learning approach.

Advisors must integrate all six components to use the Socratic advising approach effectively.

History and Tradition of the Socratic Method

How did a man who never wrote anything and claimed not to have known anything of value become one of the most influential figures in history? The mystery and uncertainty that shrouds Socrates adds to his allure. Most knowledge of him is viewed through the lens of other writers, particularly his students (Taylor, 1998).

Described as a teacher, mentor, advisor, and martyr, Socrates lived and died by the belief that truth and virtue matter more than popular opinion. He challenged traditional thought and contended that the majority is not always right (Wilson, 2007). Such thinking did not always endear him to his contemporaries, but the legend that he died for his beliefs increases his appeal.

The image of Socrates as the "gadfly" of Athens is reflected in Plato's *Apology* (23a–c) in which Socrates speaks about the paradox of his wisdom. He contended that cognizance of one's own ignorance leads to wisdom and that those who believe themselves wise truly are not (Brickhouse & Smith, 2002). His ability to embrace intellectual humility made the man brilliant and secured his influence over Western philosophical thought. Advisors, too, must explore their own beliefs and acknowledge biases to ensure fair-mindedness in their work with students. Acceptance of humility over that of authority opens dialogue, thus allowing students to take an active, equal role in an interactive relationship.

As evidenced by his death, Socrates's use of the dialectic method of inquiry or *elenchus* did not make everyone comfortable. Socratic dialogue involves the examination of differing viewpoints through a series of questions and answers that spur thought and uncover ideas. Commonly used in the courtroom, this form of Socratic inquiry creates oppositional debate that pits differing perspectives against one another; one opponent may lead the other in presenting a series of contradictions that supports one particular point of view. However, not every encounter requires antagonistic interaction. The Socratic approach involves a method of negative hypotheses elimination. The examination of dissonance leads to greater understanding of one's assumptions. Through the process of uncovering faulty thinking, the best possible solution emerges.

Through the Socratic approach, advisors evaluate a student's rationale in solving problems and making decisions and then guide the advisee, through self-reflection and questioning, to improve his or her critical-thinking skills. This process results in informed decisions and well thought-out plans for addressing challenges. However, the Socratic approach in an advising setting does not yield perfect results all the time.

As Hagen (1994) stated, "The process is not all sweetness and light. Although Socrates may have always acted for the best, when he knew what was best, the same cannot always be said of our students" (p. 87). Even though advisors may uncover illogical reasons for decision making, students may still take a path, often the one of least resistance, wrought with difficulties, emotion, denial, and pride that can influence belief and action despite awareness of truth and logic. By continually and consistently challenging students to examine thought processes and belief systems, advisors provide the catalyst for gradual change. Patience and perseverance aid the advisor in fostering student learning and development.

The Anatomy of Socratic Advising

Critical-Thinking Framework

Unique to the Socratic advising approach as outlined in Paul and Elder's (2008, www.criticalthinking.org) critical-thinking framework, *intellectual standards*—clarity, accuracy, precision, relevance, depth, breadth, logic, significance, and fairness—provide a means to examine the foundations of the *elements of thought*—purpose, question at issue, information, interpretation and inference, concepts, assumptions, implications and consequences, and point of view. The elements of thought form the building blocks to all thinking processes, and the intellectual standards create the blueprints for constructing sound, coherent judgments. The Academic Improvement Model Advisor Cohort I (2010) incorporated the Paul and Elder (2008, www.criticalthinking.org) critical-thinking framework in the Socratic advising approach; however, other types of critical-thinking approaches also apply. The Paul-Elder framework features a formal structure and a discipline-neutral schema; it is used to develop certain *essential intellectual traits* in the thinker. See Figure 12.1.

The eight elements of thought, the fundamental structures of thought, characterize essential dimensions of reasoning. Used together in intimate, overlapping, and non-linear interrelationship, they shape reasoning and provide a general logic to the use of thought. Fundamental to critical thinking, the ability to assess the quality of reasoning and the universal intellectual standards, as presented in Figure 12.1, provide the criteria with which to examine thought processes and accept or reject the conclusions. The intellectual traits listed serve as outcomes or goals for cognitive development. The intellectual traits, standards, and elements, as shown in Figure 12.1, interconnect to promote improvement in understanding the mind and its function (Paul & Elder, 2008, www.criticalthinking.org). While the framework allows for the analysis and evaluation of thought, it more importantly provides a common vocabulary for those discussing, evaluating, or teaching critical thinking.

By helping students dissect their thought processes and analyze courses of action using a critical-thinking framework, advisors teach students ways to address future academic problems and to achieve desired outcomes. The ultimate goal of critical thinking is to avoid egocentrism and maximize rational thought that fosters cognitive

Figure 12.1. Paul and Elder's critical-thinking framework based on the Socratic approach to inquiry

Critical thinkers routinely apply intellectual standards to the elements of reasoning in order to develop intellectual traits.

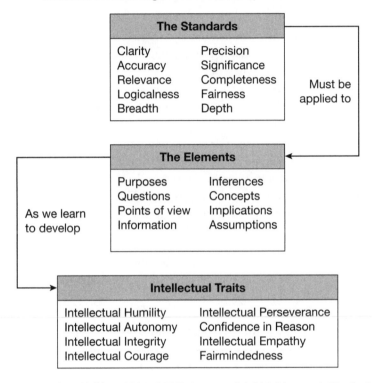

Source: Paul and Elder (2001, 2008) (www.crticialthinking.org). Used with permission.

growth. See the case study dialogue at the end of this chapter for an example of how to utilize the framework.

Assessment of Student Thinking

For advisors to help students improve their critical-thinking skills, they need to conduct an assessment of the students' levels of reasoning. Students should undertake this assessment before, during, and after the Socratic advising intervention. The Academic Improvement Model Advisor Cohort I (2010) studied the three types of thinkers described by Paul and Elder (2009, www.criticalthinking.org)—*naïve, externally focused,* and *self-aware* (p. 3)—and created the following descriptions of student thinkers, including dialogue that may characterize their thoughts, in higher education:

1. *Naïve student thinkers* are unaware. They go through their academic experience without understanding the ways institutional policies and resources affect them; in fact, they may not care about these matters. Naïve student thinkers do not analyze institutional information and often make assumptions without checking the facts. For example, naïve students may believe they are performing well academically if they have not failed a course.

2. *Externally focused student thinkers* express egotistical thought processes and adhere to an external focus. They use language indicating a belief that poor outcomes happen *to* them. They may not take responsibility for their situations and tend to blame someone for negative consequences. Externally focused student thinkers may say, "My biology professor gave me an 'F' and that put me on academic warning."

3. *Self-aware student thinkers* are fair-minded and actively seek to improve their ability to solve problems and make good decisions. They may say, "I believe I didn't make good grades this semester because I procrastinated when it came time to prepare for exams and writing papers." They have given thought to the reasons for their poor academic performance and take responsibility for the outcomes.

Of course, students can simultaneously demonstrate several characteristics described and many reflect a combination that depends upon the circumstances, the problem to be solved, or the decision to be made.

Whereas some advisors might use a strengths-based approach (see chapter 7 by Laurie Schreiner) to assess a student's talents and work to develop those skills, those using Socratic advising assess the student's level of rational thought. The Socratic advisor conducts the assessment by asking students to complete a self-reflection or by interviewing them in advising sessions. Online self-reflections sometimes prove helpful when time for advising appointments is limited, but students sometimes fail to complete the assigned self-reflection, making it difficult to complete an accurate assessment of the student's thinking until direct communication is possible. The Academic Improvement Model Advisor Cohort I (2010) created a self-reflection exercise for students on academic warning that help advisors get a feel for the students' thinking characteristics. (See Figure 12.2.)

Throughout their interactions, advisors continually gauge students' development through a rubric that tracks student cognitive growth, acceptance of responsibility, engagement in academic life, and needed improvements. The Academic Improvement Model Advisor Cohort I (2010) created a specific rubric to help measure student thinking about academic warning. See Figure 12.3.

Socratic Questioning

The art of sound Socratic questioning is fundamental to the successful application of the theory. Academic advisors should learn how to use questions to analyze student

**Figure 12.2. Student self-reflection, academic improvement model,
University of Louisville**

Academic Improvement Model

Student Self Reflection

This information is necessary for your academic advisor to help you develop a plan to return to good academic standing. Please print neatly and be thoughtful in your answers. If you need more space you may write on the back or attach another sheet of paper.

1. Full name and student ID number:

2. What is your current major? (If undecided, are there any majors you would like to learn more about?):

3. As a student on academic warning, explain what you know about the academic warning status?

4. What factors do you think led to your being on academic warning?

5. What are the strategies you intend to undertake to improve your grade point average so that you can return to good academic standing?

6. What are your expectations about your participating in the AIM program?

Note: The white space has been truncated to accommodate publication space; students could use as much space as necessary to respond.
Source: Academic Improvement Model Cohort I (2010). Used with permission.

thinking as well as help advisees gain insight into their own beliefs and explore alternative actions. With such querying, advisors move students from expressing vague concepts that lack concrete definition to articulating greater specificity and understanding.

By asking questions, advisors help students break down issues to a core with component parts, assess and clarify interests, identify educational and career goals, and discern lifestyle preferences. They help students set a coherent direction in life.

Advisors also use Socratic questioning to teach students to analyze, deconstruct, and reconstruct their thought processes, and students who engage in the process build

**Figure 12.3. Rubric for assessing student level of thinking,
University of Louisville**

Student _____   Advisor _____

Meeting (circle) 1   2   3   Date _____

1. Assessment (*Place checkmark next to appropriate description; in cases where a student may be between levels, check the midpoint box*)

a. Review the plan from the previous meeting and indicate the actions that were completed (on second page).

b. Elements and Standards of the Student's Thinking—In which category of "thinker" do most of the student's comments fall?

	Self-aware Thinker The person who is not only good at thinking, but also fair to others		External Focused Thinker The person who is good at thinking, but unfair to others		Naïve Thinker The person who doesn't care about, or isn't aware of his or her thinking
1. Information	☐ S1 Gathers complete (Depth and Breadth) information to make decisions about their academic status.	☐	☐ E1 Provides information about the behaviors of others but not their own behaviors.	☐	☐ N1 Accepts the information presented without seeking additional explanation or elaboration.
2. Questions	☐ S2 Asks significant, relevant questions related to their academic status.	☐	☐ E2 Asks superficial and/ or irrelevant questions about their academic status.	☐	☐ N2 Doesn't ask questions about their academic status. Waits to be instructed by the advisor.

3. Assumptions	☐ S3 Clearly, accurately and precisely identifies things taken for granted or assumed.	☐ E3 States assumptions about the behavior of others to a greater extent than behaviors of self.	☐ N3 Unable to identify anything taken for granted or assumed about their academic status.
4. Implications	☐ S4 Formulates clear, logical implications for their behaviors.	☐ E4 Identifies the behaviors of others as the primary reason they are on warning.	☐ N4 Does not connect behavioral choices with consequences.
5. Point of View	☐ S5 Fairly considers multiple perspectives related to their academic status.	☐ E5 Focuses primarily on the role of others that impacted their academic status.	☐ N5 Is not aware of any perspectives related to their academic warning status.

c. Intellectual Traits of the Student

	4-Exemplary	3-Developing	2-Beginning	1-Unaware
A. Intellectual Courage—Face and fairly address ideas, beliefs, viewpoints	☐ 4A Clearly, accurately, and completely identifies relevant and significant reasons s/he is on academic warning.	☐ 3A Identifies a combination of reasons based on the behaviors of self and others for why s/he is on academic warning.	☐ 2A Primarily identifies reasons based on the behavior of others for why s/he is on academic warning.	☐ 1A Does not identify reasons for being on academic warning; e.g., States I don't know how or why I am on academic warning.

Figure 12.3. (Continued)

	4	3	2	1
B. Intellectual Perseverance—Firm adherence to rational principles in spite of difficulties	☐ **4B** Consistently works their way through the complexities of being on academic warning.	☐ **3B** Expresses frustration but attempts to work their way through the complexities of being on academic warning.	☐ **2B** Quickly gives up when they encounter a difficulty as they work their way through being on academic warning.	☐ **1B** Simple, superficial thinking that does not require struggling, effort, or work to consider issues related to being on academic warning.
C. Intellectual Autonomy—Gain command over one's thoughts	☐ **4C** Consistently identifies relevant, logical plans independent of the advisor.	☐ **3C** Identifies plans to move from academic warning in collaboration with the advisor.	☐ **2C** Suggests minimal plans in addition to those from the advisor.	☐ **1C/1D** Does not have a plan to remove their academic warning status.
D. Confidence in Reason—Learn to think coherently and logically for themselves	☐ **4D** Forms realistic plans to remove their academic warning status.	☐ **3D** Develops a combination of realistic and unrealistic plans to remove their academic warning status.	☐ **2D** Develops unrealistic plans to remove their academic warning status.	

Comments:
Initial Plan:
1. Date____

	Completed?

Plan:
2. Date____

	Completed?

Plan:
3. Date____

	Completed?

Source: Academic Improvement Model Cohort I (2010). Used with permission.

a strong foundation on which to create desired goals. They also help students recognize faulty reasoning and improve their critical-thinking skills so that they make informed decisions. The case study dialogue at the end of the chapter offers specific examples of ways to use the elements of thought, intellectual standards, and intellectual traits.

Academic advisors need to be strategic in the questions they ask students. A Socratic advising toolbox of questions is helpful as advisors learn the Socratic advising approach. The questions can be organized in different ways. For example, advisors might construct a specific list of questions for each of the elements of thought and intellectual standards (Table 12.1).

Table 12.1. Socratic questioning toolbox for advisors

Elements of Thought	Topic: Academic Probation
Purpose	What is your purpose in meeting with me today? What are you trying to achieve?
Question	What are your main questions about being placed on academic probation?
Information	What information do you need to answer questions about how academic probation will affect you? How can you find the information? What information did you use to answer your questions about academic probation?
Inferences/ Conclusions	What did you learn or find out about being placed on academic probation?
Concepts	Why do you think the university places students on academic probation? What is the main idea about a student being placed on academic probation?
Assumptions	What assumptions led to your conclusions about being placed on academic probation?
Implications/ Consequences	What are the consequences of being placed on academic warning? What do these outcomes imply about achieving your goals?
Point of view	From your point of view, why do you think you were placed on academic probation? Are there other points of view that you should consider?

Table 12.1. (Continued)

Intellectual Standards	
Clarity	Could you explain a bit more about where you received your information about academic probation?
Accuracy	What are the consequences of being placed on academic probation? How can we find out?
Precision	Could you give me more details about your assumptions about academic probation?
Relevance	What issues are impacting your academic standing?
Depth	How does your plan to return to good academic standing address the complex situations that led to your poor grades?
Breadth	Do we need to consider other points of view; that is, is there another way to look at the reasons you are on academic probation?
Logic	Let's look at the logic behind the reasons you are on academic probation. At first you said you need to manage your time better so that you have more time to study, and just now you said that you are on probation because your professor would not allow you to make up an exam.
Fairness	Could you be distorting some of the information to justify your point of view?

Note. Adapted from Paul and Elder (2008) (www.criticalthinking.org), by Academic Improvement Model Cohort I (2010). Used with permission.

In Socratic questioning, advisors can use three kinds of questions to analyze student thinking (Paul & Elder, 2007, p. 14, www.criticalthinking.org). One-system questions require correct answers, whereas no-system questions call for a subjective preference or opinion. Conflicting systems questions require students to weigh multiple answers and come up with the most appropriate answer. We provide examples to give advisors insight into students' thought processes or decision-making skills.

One-System Question. "What is the minimum grade-point average required for your major?" Only one answer to this question is correct. If the student gives an incorrect answer, the advisor refers the student to research the correct answer.

No-System Question. "Why did you decide to major in nursing?" The answer, grounded in preference and opinion, cannot be assessed for correctness. If the student answers, "There are many nurses in my family and I want to keep the family tradition" or "I like to work in hospitals," then the advisor will need to ask more questions to encourage the student to further break down his or her reasoning. This exercise encourages naïve student thinkers to move toward becoming self-aware student thinkers.

Conflicting Systems Question. "What are the main factors that led to your academic warning?" The student will need to use reasoned judgment to answer the question, to weigh facts, and look at the question from multiple points of view. If the student answers, "My instructor would not let me make up an exam," then the advisor must recognize the behavior is consistent with externally focused thinking and the lack of reasoned judgment. The advisor will need to help the student correct faulty thinking. However, if the student provides a well-considered answer such as, "Many things contributed to my being placed on academic warning, such as working too many hours and not managing my time well," then the advisor can create a strategy for helping a self-aware thinker, including assistance with developing a plan to return the student to good academic standing.

Proactive Advising

When using the Socratic advising approach, academic advisors should use a proactive follow-up to gauge students' progress on completing assignments. Jennifer Varney's chapter on proactive advising (chapter 9) provides examples of this approach in working with students. According to Varney, the intrusive or proactive approach increases student motivation and persistence through intentional contacts designed to create caring, beneficial relationships between students and advisors. When using the Socratic advising approach, advisors may give students assignments (e.g., research information, identify their assumptions, or examine different frames of reference). Advisors should ask students to share their progress on assignment completion at intervals with them. When they do not hear back from students in a timely manner, advisors must proactively follow up with them. Of course, advisors can leave phone messages and send e-mails, but in many instances, these types of communications are ineffective. Sometimes advisors must place a hold on students' records so that they cannot register for courses until they have met with their advisors. This strong action becomes necessary with unresponsive students.

Helping Techniques

Just as in any successful advising approach, the Socratic method is successful only when academic advisors communicate effectively and build trusting relationships with their advisees. Helping techniques, such as those found in counseling models, assist advisors in reaching students by promoting active and reflective listening, para-phrasing, clarifying, summarizing, and information sharing employed to build trust, frame probing questions, and facilitate active discourse. Another helpful technique is silence. Giving students time to think about the question and their response can elicit the types of deep thinking and clear communication needed to implement good decision making. We recommend the following resources for advisors to review or refresh their communication skills: Corey and Corey (2007), *Becoming a Helper* (5th ed.); Evans, Hearn, Uhlemann, and Ivey (2011), *Essential Interviewing* (8th ed.); Okun and Kantrowitz (2008), *Effective Helping* (7th ed.).

Teaching and Learning Approach

A Socratic advising approach should be grounded with a teaching and learning paradigm. The Academic Improvement Model Advisor Cohort I (2010) used the NACADA Concept of Academic Advising, which includes guidance on curriculum, pedagogy, and student learning outcomes (National Academic Advising Association, 2006). See Figure 12.4. The Socratic advising curriculum is made up of student success strategies, student development theories, institutional policies and procedures, degree program requirements, and Paul and Elder's (2008, www.criticalthinking.org) elements of thought. The pedagogy involves Socratic questioning, proactive advising, helping techniques, and as shown in Figure 12.1, Paul and Elder's intellectual standards. The learning outcomes include growth among intellectual traits, the ability to engage in contemplative self-reflection, and competency in making informed decisions.

Figure 12.4. Concept of academic advising

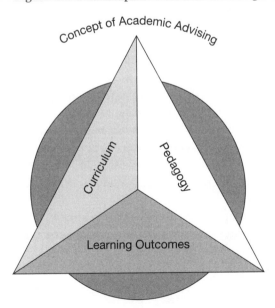

Source: National Academic Advising Association (2006). Used
with permission.

A Socratic advising approach offers an excellent tool for institutions to support a teaching and learning model of advising and an effective mechanism to define the skills advisors teach (e.g., critical thinking), ways to deliver the curriculum (through Socratic dialogue), and possible learning outcomes (e.g., greater resilience and persistence gained from improvements in intellectual habits). The Socratic advising approach requires students to research information, honestly and realistically analyze their own thinking, and develop their own solutions rather than passively receive answers to their questions. In using this paradigm, advisors challenge students to defend their position on an issue by rebutting the arguments against it. Students are forced to examine their own assumptions and uncover inconsistencies in their own logic. Rather than focusing solely on aptitudes or interests, the advisor teaches the student to analyze the reasons for her or his beliefs or behaviors and determine whether or not the reasoning behind the rationale is sound. The Socratic approach may cause advisees some initial discomfort because they may need to admit to flaws in their thinking, but dissonance can often be a catalyst for change. Therefore, advisors must enter into this exchange gradually and allow time for students to reflect.

Application of the Socratic Advising Approach

The effective use of a Socratic advising approach requires the utilization of the tools described in the section entitled *The Anatomy of Socratic Advising*, the student self-assessment rubric (Figure 12.3), the toolbox of questions (Table 12.1), and suggested assignments. Advisors may need to participate in multiple meetings with students and follow up with them as determined by the students' development in thought processes. Figure 12.5 provides a time line of a typical application of the Socratic advising approach with students who are naïve or externally focused thinkers. The three meetings outlined in Figure 12.5 take place in one semester because students experiencing academic difficulty must develop a plan to return to good academic standing as quickly as possible. Meeting with a student at three different times during the semester may challenge advisors with large advising loads, and students may find scheduling three appointments in one semester a bit burdensome. Therefore, though not ideal, an advisor might take advantage of convenient electronic communications with the student. Of course, to address long-term issues without pressing time constraints (e.g., major exploration), advisors can spread out these meetings over more than one semester.

The Socratic advising approach is applicable to almost any type of advising situation of students, including those fraught with challenges. It can be useful with the various types of advising situations.

Exploratory Students

Students exploring majors or careers may benefit from the Socratic advising approach as they examine their own assumptions about the implications for choosing

Figure 12.5. Socratic advising process

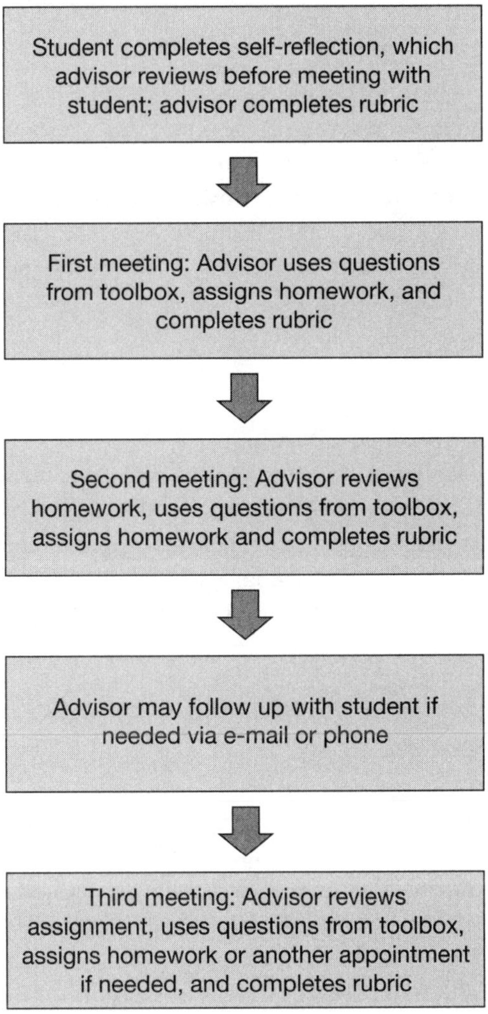

Student completes self-reflection, which advisor reviews before meeting with student; advisor completes rubric

First meeting: Advisor uses questions from toolbox, assigns homework, and completes rubric

Second meeting: Advisor reviews homework, uses questions from toolbox, assigns homework and completes rubric

Advisor may follow up with student if needed via e-mail or phone

Third meeting: Advisor reviews assignment, uses questions from toolbox, assigns homework or another appointment if needed, and completes rubric

Source: Academic Improvement Model Cohort I (2010). Used with permission.

a particular major. Through discourse and use of the critical-thinking terminology, students can articulate the depth of their knowledge about a particular field of study. They can incorporate that knowledge into self-reflection to determine if they are considering choices with realistic outcomes.

First-Year Students

First-year students face many challenges in acclimating to the institution. Through guided reflection characteristic of the Socratic approach, advisors help students examine their initial experiences at the institution and resolve inconsistencies between expectations and the realities of college life.

Transfer Students

Transfer students often face some of the same challenges as first-year students in acculturating to the institution and familiarizing themselves with institutional resources. They also need to understand how course work at their previous institution fits into the degree program they have decided to pursue. Using Socratic questioning, the advisor can probe the information the student knows and assess the relevance of past experiences to current situations.

At-Risk Students

Students at risk for academic difficulties may benefit the most from the Socratic advising approach. Struggling students often express incorrect, preconceived ideas about their lack of success and the actions needed to improve their situation. The Socratic advising approach empowers students to approach problem solving in a way that fits the challenges of postsecondary education. The case study provides an example of ways to engage a student in a Socratic dialogue.

Desired Outcomes of Socratic Advising

Advisors

Hagen (1994) asked, "Can we not expect, along with Crookston, that a successful academic advising interaction will result in varying degrees of learning by both parties?" (p. 87). Self-reflection and growth as a person and a professional are very potent outcomes of the Socratic advising method. Much like their students, advisors should consider and advance their own thinking. The Academic Improvement Model Advisor Cohort I (2010) chose the intellectual traits of humility, empathy, fair-mindedness, and integrity as foci to improve their own professional development (Paul & Elder, 2008, www.criticalthinking.org).

Repeatedly questioning value sets, beliefs, and perceptions strengthens advisors in such core competencies as self-knowledge and decision-making strategies (Folsom, 2007). Intensive training in communication and helping skills, use of assessment tools, and Socratic methodology are essential to the successful application of this approach. Additionally, advisors must be willing to examine their own beliefs, recognize shortcomings, and consider alternate points of view.

Students

Students often feel like passive observers in their own academic endeavors. Advisors can facilitate student learning, reflection, and thus empowerment through the Socratic advising approach. Socrates encountered many people who allowed their choices and beliefs to be dictated by the conventional majority; these people never questioned their ways of thinking and therefore lived passive lives (Nussbaum, 1997). If students can learn to examine the reasons for long-held beliefs and thought processes, then they can recover not only responsibility for learning but also the power to control their own futures. This process is neither failsafe nor immediate. It requires time, patience, and discipline by both advisors and advisees. If either decides to reject the ongoing dialogue, then the process stalls, at best, and fails, at worst. Therefore, advisors must understand the level of thinking students use when they initiate their relationship; if advisors push too hard, too fast, or become frustrated with the students' rate of progress, then failure is almost guaranteed.

Students engaged in the educational process and actively reflect upon their decision-making processes have the opportunity for cognitive growth and sharpened intellectual skills. "An education is truly fitted for freedom only if it is such to *produce* free citizens, citizens who are not free because of wealth or birth, but because they can call their minds their own" (Nussbaum, 1997, p. 29).

Assessment

According to Folsom, Scobie, and Shultz (2010), assessment answers the basic but essential question of whether or not the desired outcomes are met. Assessing cognitive growth and student success is complicated by the number of extraneous variables that affect both processes. Therefore, use of multiple methods most likely leads to accurate assessment of student and advisor learning.

Advisor learning can be measured by administering pre- and post-tests to assess knowledge, beliefs, and attitudes toward proactive advising, critical thinking, advisor responsibilities, and student characteristics. Assessment also provides insight into the advisors' perceived level of their own intellectual competence before and after engaging in the Socratic advising approach (The Academic Improvement Model, Advisor Cohort I, 2010). Additionally, advisors should take advantage of opportunities to meet in small groups to discuss their experiences and share effective techniques. The use of multiple indicators such as student self-reflections and advisor-administered rubrics comprise the best means of assessing student learning and cognitive growth.

Socratic Advising Scenario

Scenario I

A first-generation college sophomore, Riley, comes to an advisor, Skylar, and says, "I'm having trouble in two of my classes. I don't understand what the professor is talking about in one of them, but it's a required course in my major. The other is only a gen ed course, but I keep getting low grades on the writing assignments. I was always good in writing in high school. If I do poorly, this will lower my GPA, and I just got off academic probation last term. I want to stay in my major, but I don't know if I can pass this one course and that would really disappoint my family. What do you suggest I do?"

○ ○ ○

First, Skylar sets an open, friendly tone, and then paraphrases Riley's concerns: "I am really glad you came in to talk to me about your situation. That is a mature way to handle the challenges you are facing. Let's see if I understand you correctly: The purpose of your visit with me today is to receive advice about what you should do to address the challenges you are having in two of your classes. Is that correct?"

Riley responds, "Yes, that is correct, but I also don't know if I should change my major. If I am already having difficulty in one of my major courses I may need to change directions. I really don't want to [change] because that would be a big disappointment to my family."

Skylar recognizes the stress of Riley's dilemma: "I understand and I'm sure that disappointing your family is weighing heavily on your mind."

Offering confidence in the ability of a positive outcome, Skylar guides the conversion: "So, let's see if we can think through a couple of things. Before we start to address the challenges you are having in your two courses, a good place to start may be to take a closer look at the major you selected and the reasons you selected it. Is that okay?"

After getting Riley's agreement, Skylar says, "Okay, so tell me: What is your major and why did you select it?"

Riley explains, "My major is chemical engineering, and I picked it for a couple of reasons. I always liked my science courses in high school and got very good grades in them. My grandmother and uncle said that I would make a good engineer because my science courses always came easy to me. Besides, engineers make a very good salary and I could get a high-paying job and help my mother buy a house. Currently, she is living in an apartment. It is a very nice apartment, but she always wanted to have a big garden in her yard."

Skylar identifies Riley as a naïve thinker because the response to the main question is based on preferences, not facts or information that best supports the answer to the question. Paraphrasing to ensure accurate understanding and demonstrate engagement with Riley, Skylar summarizes, "So, you selected chemical engineering as a major because you liked your science classes in high school, they were easy for you, your family members thought engineering would be a good fit for you, and you think you could get a high-paying job so that you could help your mother financially?"

"Yes, that's basically it."

"Okay, before we move forward, let's take a few minutes to examine your thinking about your major selection. Will that be okay?"

After Riley consents, Skylar says, "Selecting your major is one of the most important decisions you will make as a college student. I am going to discuss the reasons you selected your major so we can be sure you used a logical process to select chemical engineering."

"Okay, that sounds good."

"Let's say that the question at hand is, 'Is chemical engineering the right major for me?' and I will help you use a solid, logical approach to answer that question. What assumptions are you making about chemical engineering as a major?"

"Let's see. I guess I assume because it deals with science I will make good grades in the classes."

"Can you elaborate on your thinking about that statement?"

"Yes, I loved my science classes in high school and I always made good grades. Because I made good grades in my high school science classes, I think I can do well in my engineering classes."

"Okay. Did anything else affect your decision?"

"Yes, engineers make a lot of money, and I really need the money to help my family. I guess that's about it."

To ensure that Riley has fully expressed all relevant perspectives about making money, Skylar encourages deeper reflection about the need for a good salary by asking "What else can you tell me about your desire to make good money?" However, Riley does not offer additional information outside of the previously stated family circumstances. So Skylar moves forward in a new direction: "You said that your family members think you'd make a good engineer? Did that affect your decision?"

"Oh yes, that too."

"How are your family members' opinions relevant to your decision to select chemical engineering as a major?"

"I am the first person to go to college in my family, so I am really representing our family. What they think about my college major is important to me. I don't want to let them down."

To eliminate any defensiveness Riley may be experiencing, Skylar provides reassurance: "I see. Thank you for being so candid."

"Okay, let's take a look at your assumptions and determine how they are shaping your point of view." [Riley nods in the affirmative.] "You said one of your assumptions is that chemical engineering deals with science so you will make good grades in the classes. What evidence or information do you have to support that assumption?"

"Well, I always made good grades in my science classes in high school."

"What science classes did you take in high school?"

"Science, biology, and earth science."

"Are any of those courses required in your chemical engineering major?"

When Riley says, "Well, I don't think so," Skylar asks how they can determine the answer, and Riley suggests that they turn to the online course catalog.

As they look on Skylar's computer, Riley makes the observation, "It says here that I need courses in chemistry, physics, calculus, and engineering. It looks like many of the science courses require calculus first. In high school I had up to Algebra II, but I did not take pre-calculus or calculus. I struggled with Algebra II, so I am really worried about passing calculus."

"So, by researching the specific courses required in your major and comparing them to the types of science courses you had in high school, do you still think your assumption about the easiness of courses is accurate?"

"No, I don't think so."

"Okay, let's look at your next assumption. You stated that engineers make a lot of money. What evidence do you have to support that assumption?"

"Well, I have always heard that about engineers. I don't know any engineers personally, but I've heard people say that engineers make a lot of money."

"Okay, it seems that you are making an assumption based on what you have heard. Is that correct?"

After Riley confirms this statement, Skylar asks, "Well, how can we find out an engineer's salary?"

"There must be some kind of data out there on the web. I can do a web search."

"Here," Skylar points back to the computer screen, "go ahead and use my computer. You may want to start with the U.S. Department of Education's web page."

Upon finding some useful information, Riley points out, "It says that the median entry salary for chemical engineers is $65,000. That is a lot of money to start out in a job."

"So would you say your assumption that engineers get paid well is accurate?"

Riley affirms this statement, so Skylar moves to the next point for exploration: "What about your family telling you that you would make a good engineer? Do you think their assumption is correct?"

"Well, based on how well I did in science in high school I would say 'yes,' but they do not know what science courses I will need to take as an engineer and that math is a big part of the curriculum. So, no, I suppose their assumption may not be correct."

Skylar changes direction: "I see. Well, let's focus on the implications and consequences of your selecting chemical engineering as a major. What do you think will happen if you continue to keep chemical engineering as a major?"

"Well, based on the fact that I am struggling in my first engineering course and that I am not a strong student in mathematics, it may not go well. I guess I could go back on probation and perhaps be suspended if I don't make good grades in my major courses. I just don't think I have strong enough math skills. Maybe I can't make it in engineering.

By paraphrasing, Skylar may help the student hear the consequence in another person's words and thus understand it as a real possibility: "So, you think your mathematics skills may cause you difficulties and the consequence may be an unsuccessful attempt at engineering?"

After Riley nods and quietly assents to this statement, Skylar suggests, "What if we were to look at other majors in science that do not require as much mathematics as a degree in engineering?"

Riley perks up a bit: "That would be fantastic, but what kinds of science degrees would not require as much math?"

"Well, let's research and investigate. Where do you think you could find the information?"

Again, per Riley's suggestion, they turn to the online catalog. Riley says, "Well, here are some science degrees: astronomy, biology, chemistry, geosciences, marine biology, and meteorology. I wonder what math courses are required for geosciences? I always loved my general science and earth science classes in high school." [Pause.] "It looks like it doesn't require any mathematics courses outside of the gen ed math requirement. Super!"

"Did you check to see if any of the geosciences courses have any mathematics courses as prerequisites?"

"Oh yeah, I guess I should check those. No, it looks like just geosciences courses are the only prerequisites."

"Good. What other information do you think you should review or research before you make a decision about geosciences as your major?"

"I guess I need to know more about the content of the major courses."

"That may be a good place to start. Looking at the course descriptions in your major may help you decide if these classes match your skills and will be ones that you will enjoy. Where do you think you can find that information?" "It should be on the same web page where I was just looking for the prerequisites." [Riley keeps reading.] "Here it is. Well, it says here there are 36 hours of gen ed courses, and I know I have about half of them completed. There are 42 hours in the major and the remaining are supporting courses. I'm reading the course descriptions now." [Pause.] "I think I would really like these classes and the prerequisites seem to be just fine."

"What other information do you think you should research before you make the decision to change your major to geosciences?"

"Hmm . . . Well, I think I would really like the subject matter and I believe I have the skills to do well in the courses. I'm not sure what else I need to research."

"What job qualifications and earning potential might you have after earning a degree in geosciences?"

"Oh, that's right. I guess that's pretty important too. I wonder if the Career Development Center can help me research this information."

"That sounds like a perfect place to start your research. It's getting close for our time to end this afternoon. I am going to assign you some homework. Write out a list of questions to discuss with your career coach about careers in geosciences. Make an appointment to meet with a career coach in the Career Development Center this week and then meet with me next week to tell me what you learned. If changing your major to geosciences seems like the right decision for you, I will be happy to talk with you about some strategies you can use to discuss your change of major with your family."

Riley says, "That sounds like a great plan" and thanks Skylar for the helpful suggestions. After setting up plans for the follow-up appointment, they part with Riley feeling much better about the future and Skylar expressing appreciation for Riley's hard work and honesty.

In the scenario, Skylar assessed Riley's thinking, asking questions that helped Riley covertly deconstruct and then reconstruct relevant thought patterns. Even while employing language commensurate with the critical-thinking framework (*assumptions, information, research*, etc.) of Paul and Elder (2008, www.criticalthinking.org), Skylar did not explain to Riley the strategy to engage critical-thinking skills in resolving the dilemma.

Summary

Teaching critical-thinking, decision-making, problem-solving, and coping skills defines and elevates the curriculum of academic advising. Engaging the Socratic advising approach establishes the link that Hagen (1994) advocates: "It helps us all think seriously about our field and to look for parallels that will better establish our field in our own minds as well as in the minds of other serious thinkers in the Academy" (p. 88). Combining the teaching-learning paradigm with Socratic questioning and the critical-thinking framework guides best practice in the field. Done well, Socratic advising blends the information shared, relationships built, and concepts taught.

Students engaged in the Socratic advising approach strengthen their ability to make rational, informed decisions; cope with unexpected challenges; and solve problems through critical thinking. By mastering their own thought processes, students gain the competencies necessary to question, reflect, and adapt to any situation, whether in academics or elsewhere. Thus, Socratic advising becomes far more than a service offered and offers a way to create self-directed adults fully engaged in their own futures.

Acknowledgments

We acknowledge the following individuals who participated in the Academic Improvement Model, Cohort I at the University of Louisville (2010) for their development of the Socratic advising approach: Kathryn Adamchik, Cathy Bays, Susan Best, Katherine Bixby, Paul E. Bobbitt, Virginia Brown, Vivian Lochner, Patty Payette, Margaret Rohmann, Lauren Rust, Linda Smith, and Veronica Wooten.

References

Academic Improvement Model Cohort I. (2010). [Unpublished in-house communication]. Louisville, KY: University of Louisville.

Brickhouse, B. C., & Smith, N. D. (2002). *The trial and execution of Socrates: Sources and controversies*. New York, NY: Oxford University Press.

Corey, M. S., & Corey, G. (2007). *Becoming a helper* (5th ed.). Belmont, CA: Brooks/Cole.

Evans, D. R., Hearn, M. T., Uhlemann, M. R., & Ivey, A. E. (2011). *Essential interviewing: A programmed approach to effective communication* (8th ed.). Belmont, CA: Brooks/Cole.

Folsom, P. (2007). Setting the stage: Growth through year one and beyond. In *The new advisor guidebook: Mastering the art of advising through the first year and beyond* (Monograph No. 16) (pp. 13–21). Manhattan, KS: National Academic Advising Association.

Folsom, P., Scobie, N. A., & Shultz, N. L. (2010). Assessment of training and development programs. In *Comprehensive advisor training and development: Practices that deliver* (Monograph No. 21) (pp. 33–48). Manhattan, KS: National Academic Advising Association.

Hagen, P. L. (1994). Academic advising as dialectic. *NACADA Journal, 14*(2), 85–88.

McIntyre, C. M. (2011). Peripatetic advising: How Socrates, advising, and running shoes influence student success. *Academic Advising Today, 34*(2). Retrieved from http://www.nacada.ksu.edu/ePub/AAT34-2.htm

National Academic Advising Association. (2006). *NACADA concept of academic advising*. Retrieved from http://www.nacada.ksu.edu/Resources/Clearinghouse/View-Articles/Concept-of-Academic-Advising.aspx

Nussbaum, M. C. (1997). *Cultivating humanity: A classical defense of reform in liberal education*. Cambridge, MA: Harvard University Press.

Okun, B. F., & Kantrowitz, R. E. (2008), *Effective helping: Interviewing and counseling techniques* (7th ed). Belmont, CA: Thomson Brooks/Cole.

Paul, R., & Elder, L. (2001). *Critical thinking: Tools for taking charge of your learning and your life*. Upper Saddle River, NJ: Prentice Hall, www.criticalthinking.org

Paul, R., & Elder, L. (2007). *The thinkers guide to the art of Socratic questioning*. Dillon Beach, CA: The Foundation for Critical Thinking. Retrieved from http://www.criticalthinking.org

Paul, R., & Elder, L. (2008). *The miniature guide to critical thinking: Concepts and tools*. Dillon Beach, CA: The Foundation for Critical Thinking. Retrieved from www.criticalthinking.org

Paul, R., & Elder, L. (2009). *The miniature guide to critical thinking: Concepts &*
    Tools. Dillon Beach, CA: The Foundation for Critical Thinking,
    www.criticalthinking.org
Taylor, C. C. W. (1998). *Past masters: Socrates*. New York, NY: Oxford University Press.
Waterfield, R. (2009). *Why Socrates died: Dispelling the myth*. New York, NY: W. W.
    Norton.
Wilson, E. (2007). *The death of Socrates*. Cambridge, MA: Harvard University Press.

UNDERSTANDING AND INTERPRETATION

A HERMENEUTIC APPROACH TO ADVISING

Sarah Champlin-Scharff and Peter L. Hagen

Successful academic advisors deliver truly meaningful advice, the kind that makes the advisee feel seen, valued, and understood. They deliver useful information, but also facilitate learning. When done well, academic advising supports the co-construction of an education, the product of the work done by both advisor and advisee. It requires that both student and advisor know how to interpret and understand each other, and as such, it means that advisors are charged with the task of deciphering language, making sense of students (and themselves), uncovering how students find significance, and what really matters to them, all in an effort to facilitate the co-construction of education.

While not every advising interaction requires a nuanced understanding, we suggest that meaningful advice requires more than just a general understanding of students. Of course, telling students to read assignments and attend lectures, seek out a mentoring relationship with a faculty member, and involve themselves with a nonacademic activity on campus constitutes good advice (Light, 2001). Yet, truly meaningful advice often includes something more, a deeper understanding, one that relies on the process of interpretation.

Identifying both how to approach the processes of interpretation and ways to achieve a meaningful understanding is, therefore, invaluable to the practice of academic advising. Scholars in the humanities—philosophy, literature, rhetoric, and history, to name a few—have, since ancient times, thought deeply about interpretation and understanding. Specifically, *hermeneutics,* the art or science of interpretation, provides a rich body of literature stretching back two millennia from which to draw concrete, hands-on, everyday advice that practitioners can use in their work with students. In this chapter, we offer hermeneutic theory as a source of inspiration and as a guide for the complicated process of making sense of advisees. Hermeneutics is fundamentally concerned with understanding; the following questions, among others, characterize the practice: How is understanding possible? How does one know when an understanding is accurate? What must one already know in order to understand?

Such questions are relevant to practicing advisors because they are in the business of understanding; that is, they help students build the stories of their educations, and this co-creation of identities must be solidly based in understanding, in sound interpretation.

As we focus on a hermeneutic approach to advising, several related ideas command attention. These key aspects involve use of language and experience:

- All advising is mediated through discourse: language. Scholars of hermeneutics know quite well, but practitioners may easily overlook, that language is, at best, only an indirect way for making meaning. Accurate interpretations depend not only on the words of the discourse, but on the situation and context as well.

- Advising uses narrative language. Through this use of language, students construct versions of their life stories to advisors, who tell stories about themselves and about other students and, as representatives of the ends to which higher education tends, also put forth the grand narrative of higher education. Most important, advisors help students build the story of their educations and of their lives.

- Human beings make sense of things from within the individual context of their own existence. The conditions of human existence, loosely translated as human experiences, are those through which meaning is created. When advisors deeply understand students' experiences, they become better advisors.

We begin this chapter by offering a summary of the history of hermeneutics and then focus on the work of two major contributors to the field: Martin Heidegger and Hans-Georg Gadamer. We conceptualize the process of interpretation, offer an outline of what ought to be considered in the search for meaning, and provide practical suggestions for the everyday work of advising. Without an accurate understanding of advisees, practitioners may deliver mediocre and even ineffective advice. By providing the foundation for the work of academic advising (rather than a definitive methodological approach), intended to be used alongside any number of the approaches described in this book, we hope to offer grounded support for the successful academic advisor.

Hermeneutics: Toward Interpretation

Rooted in the Greek words *hermêneuein* and *hermêneia,* translated as "to interpret" and "interpretation," hermeneutics was first used to approach biblical interpretation (Palmer, 1969, p. 12). Perhaps the most historically influential treatise on hermeneutics is Augustine's *On Christian Doctrine* (Ebeling, 1959, p. 249). Augustine (354–430) is concerned with the interpretation and understanding of Holy Scripture. He warns that one ought to be aware of the limitations of language, recognizing the indirect relationship between the written word and that to which it refers. As a result, Augustine suggests that understanding must include the precarious relationship between language and the inner thoughts and ideas it is charged to express.

Like Augustine, Friedrich Schleiermacher (1768–1834) notes the distinction between language and thought and emphasizes the particular role understanding plays in interpreting how each affects meaning. Schleiermacher's work, however, no longer privileges Scripture or the contents of any other particular text or discipline. Instead, he identifies hermeneutics as the "art of understanding," (1998, p. 5) shifting focus from the object being interpreted to the act of understanding itself.

Wilhelm Dilthey (1833–1911) anticipates a methodological approach to understanding. His hope was to legitimize the human sciences (those fields studying the inner workings of human life, now called the *humanities*) by providing a proper systematic approach to understanding, one that insists on the study of human life "in terms of itself," that is, a) from within the context of lived experience and b) by drawing on one's own experienced sense of this context. Moreover, Dilthey argues that meaning extracted from lived experience is ultimately historical. Memories of the past taken together with the anticipation of the future provide the horizon through which one makes sense of a given present moment (Palmer, 1969, pp. 100–101). Dilthey's work provides the foundation for Martin Heidegger's work on the fundamentally historical character of all human experience.

Martin Heidegger (1889–1976) shifts the focus of hermeneutics. He is not interested in determining the nature of or a methodology for understanding and interpretation (Heidegger, 1962). Instead, he explains that understanding and interpretation are primary to human existence; they characterize how human beings are in the world. Humans are beings for whom understanding and interpretation are fundamental. So, uncovering meaning, according to Heidegger, no longer centers on discovering the truth about things "out there" in the world, but instead focuses on realizing ourselves, as human beings, and the conditions within which we are in the world. Therefore, interpretation must involve recognition of the conditions of existence in the sociohistorical context within which we exist over time. Adding to this particular view of hermeneutics, Hans-Georg Gadamer (1900–2002) emphasized the centrality of language, arguing that language offers the opportunity for disclosure. As such, language is that which opens the door for interpretation and understanding.

What emerges from this brief history of the field of hermeneutics is the simple notion that interpretation is at the heart of all understanding and involves a process through which the unintelligible can be made lucid (Grondin, 1994, p. 18). As Nakkula and Ravitch (1998) noted, "Hermeneutics is about clarifying the meaning of messages—hidden messages, messages with multiple meanings, messages that carry essential importance for the ways we live" (p. xix). A hermeneutic understanding allows for a more accurate and nuanced approach to any academic advising interaction.

Hermeneutic Foundations for Academic Advising: Heidegger and Gadamer

The work of academic advising always involves, to some extent, figuring out or interpreting students. Hermeneutic inquiry provides a tool for deciphering the unknown or difficult to understand, and provides a foundation for the practice of academic advising. It offers a space to explore the process of interpretation, rather than a presentation of empirical data or demonstrative proof. We hope that hermeneutic theory will foster and support an active and ongoing interpretation of advisees.

In this section of the chapter, we focus on the work of Heidegger and Gadamer, two major voices in the field of hermeneutics. We use the advising scenarios to illustrate the concepts involved in Heidegger's and Gadamer's work as well as to demonstrate the application of this theory in the real world. Both of the problem-based scenarios are familiar to the practicing advisor. We consider that advising is a process that involves more than solving problems: It is an acculturation, a co-construction of the life of a mind, an education in and of itself. From a narrow view, hermeneutic theory can enhance one's understanding as it relates to problem resolution, but on a grander scale, it can help advisors focus on the dialogical nature of the advising relationship, which is comprised of interlocutors attempting to understand one another.

A discussion of Heidegger's work offers a detailed understanding of the conditions of human existence and prepares humans to consider how to live authentically in the world. While Heidegger's work prompts consideration of what ought to be included in the process of interpretation, Gadamer's work articulates recognition of the conditions of human existence, their relationship to living authentically, and the best course of action for interpretation itself.

Martin Heidegger

Martin Heidegger (1962) maintains that human existence is primarily a process of interpretation constituted by an ever-changing, unique sociohistorical context. Such thought involves at least four key concepts: interpretation, connectedness, world, and time (Nakkula & Ravitch, 1998). We applied these four concepts to advising Scenario I with the intent of underscoring the benefit of a hermeneutic approach to the field of academic advising.

Interpretation. At the center of Heidegger's work is the notion that meaning is not contained independently within the things "out there" in the world. That is, meaning is not some innate property discoverable through objective analysis of the external world. Instead, meaning is interpretation determined by the significance something has for an individual human being. Advising Scenario I clarifies the conception of interpretation and identifies how it can be useful to the work of academic advising.

Hermeneutic Advising Scenario I

A first-generation college sophomore, Riley, comes to an advisor, Skylar, and says: "I'm having trouble in two of my classes. I don't understand what the professor is talking about in one of them, but it's a required course in my major. The other is only a gen ed course, but I keep getting low grades on the writing assignments. I was always good in writing in high school. If I do poorly, this will lower my GPA, and I just got off academic probation last term. I want to stay in my major, but I don't know if I can pass this one course and that would really disappoint my family. What do you suggest I do?"

o o o

"What do you suggest I do?"

Easy answers spring to mind: "Study more!" "Go to the tutoring center." However, to dismiss Riley's concerns Skylar forgets that, as important as a practical fix, the problem may be foundationally rooted in how Riley understands the importance of the course, the major, or even being a college student. Instead of offering advice, Skylar might ask for deeper reflection:

- o Why have you chosen this major?
- o Why is being in college important to you?
- o What are your attitudes toward general education? Writing?

After noting Riley's concerns about degree program, academic probation, and family, Skylar considers the required course in Riley's major: What is its value, its meaning, its significance? At the very least, Riley's academic performance in the course will determine the feasibility of remaining within that particular major, and therefore, warrants the family's approval or disapproval. While historical records of course evaluations, the assignments outlined in the current syllabus, observations of other students taking the current course, and even an examination about the way in which the class is taught may prove helpful in determining important aspects of the course, none of these data would necessarily reveal the value, meaning, or significance of the course to Riley. From Heidegger's view, this course makes sense, not in terms of any innate properties it may possess (course evaluations, number of assignments on the syllabus, etc.), but from within the context of what is important to the student. Meaning is signified through the student's contextualized existence in the world. Therefore, the course is understood in terms of the way it affects Riley's academic performance and subsequent ability to continue studying in a particular major, and therefore, the family's level of approval or disapproval.

By recognizing the centrality of interpretation, advisors can focus on key areas of inquiry to generate a deeper and more nuanced understanding of advisees. To provide an advisee with useful information, advisors ought to uncover what is important and how things have significance for the advisee. Advisors should understand the impact that connections and disconnections with others, sociohistorical context, and change over time exert on the advisee.

Connectedness (Being-with). Heidegger explains that individuals exist in the world with others and as such are conditioned by their connections and disconnections (being-with): Who we love, hate, affiliate with, what groups we belong to or not, all affect the way that we interpret and make sense of things. For example, family pressures carry weight in Riley's consideration of major selection. The entire scenario may, in fact, center on the influence of this familial connection. Therefore, Skylar must draw out how Riley thinks and feels about the familial connection, framing the conversation to uncover the significance of it. Skylar should ask open-ended questions such as "How do you think your family would feel if you changed majors?" or "How do you feel about your parent's interest in your major choice?" Of course, the familial influence may have little to no effect. Responses to such inquiries allow both parties to identify the importance of the connection, or disconnection, how it plays a role in Riley's choices, and provides an indication of the kind of advice that might be helpful. Scenario II allows for a deeper consideration of these questions.

Hermeneutic Advising Scenario II

A second-year student, Ali, comes to Drew to discuss withdrawing from school: "I'm really not doing well this term. It's not the courses or the professors—I just don't feel like I fit in. A few of my friends left after last year, and I haven't really found any new ones. My new roommates are not really like me, so they kind of stick together by themselves. I'm not in any clubs or anything like that, although I do work off campus. Also, I feel my parents and I have spent lots of money, but I'm not sure it's worth spending more if I'm not that interested. Do you have any suggestions? What do you think I should do?"

Drew might suspect Ali is experiencing uncertainty about the value of education; therefore, Drew guides the discussion accordingly, but is cautious not to make assumptions about the underlying causes of Ali's difficulties. Advisors ought to structure the conversation in such a way that students are able to reflectively discover the effects of the connections and disconnections that influence the way they identify value. Therefore, Drew may need to do more than simply ask, "How do you feel about education?" and engage in open-ended conversation to seek the kind of detail that will reveal how Ali finds significance. Recognizing the effect of connections and disconnections and probing to better understand the ways they influence Ali's understanding, Drew is able to recognize how Ali makes sense of things.

Connectedness

How can practicing advisors recognize the importance of students' connections and disconnections? Advisors can ascertain this information by asking questions that allow students to reflect about the role that family and friends play in choices such as those affecting major, college, or courses. For example, "What does your best friend think about you being a business student?" "Why does your family think it is important for you to major in engineering?"

Ali is clearly influenced by the connections and disconnections experienced on campus. Drew might ask, "What are your parents' expectations?" "Why did your friends make the choices they did?" Perhaps such a disconnected student might appreciate an ally in the advising office where connections can be readily made!

World (Being-in-the-World). Equally influential to understanding and interpretation is the world within which each human being is situated contextually. Not to be confused with a physical location, *world* is the sociohistorical position within which interpretation takes place. It is not the physical universe, but the framework through which an individual makes sense of her or his experiences. Being-in-the-world involves race, class, gender, sexual orientation, ethnicity, and religion, but also education, age, hobbies, number of siblings, and experiences traveling, among other conditions.

How does sociohistorical context affect interpretation? In Scenario I, Riley tells Skylar about struggling in two classes, one of which is a degree requirement, that we will determine, for the purpose of this discussion, is psychology. Drawing out the effects of Riley's world proves challenging, so Skylar asks open-ended, probing questions designed to make Riley feel safe in answering honestly. For example, Skylar allows Riley to vent about frustrating experiences in the class. When Skylar presses for more specific information with a statement such as "I hear how frustrated you are, why do you think that is?" Riley states, "I just don't understand what my professor is talking about!" Skylar might ask about the topics studied and Riley, with space to reflect in a targeted way to identify context, explains that the readings in class are distressing because mental health issues generate feelings of concern: "My sister was recently diagnosed with an eating disorder." Later Riley explains, "I want to study the psychological aspects of my sister's disorder and continue a career in counseling."

With this new information, Skylar may want to discuss the ways that classroom experiences have affected Riley's feelings about a major in psychology. Perhaps Riley is not gifted enough in the social sciences to remain a psychology major, but with a clear understanding that Riley's sister's eating disorder has inspired the original decision, Skylar may want to help Riley find an alternative way to study the issue or work through the loss of majoring in psychology.

Details presented in Scenario I (first-generation college student, sister with eating disorder, on probation last semester, involved parents) do more than simply inhabit a space on a list of sociohistorical contextualizations. The list serves as the filter through which everything matters to Riley. World is the sociohistorical position within which humans experience things. It is the context through which meaning is disclosed; the effects of sociohistorical context are not predictable, yet recognizing the existence of each unique framework can help guide the work of advising.

Time. In popular culture the notion of time is signified as a series of individual present moments monitored by a clock. For Heidegger, time is part of the process of existence and that through which change takes place. Time is the connector of what has been, what is, and what will be—the framework for change and development. The past influences understanding of the present, which in turn shapes interpretation of the future.

Changes to one's life, world, and connections alter the way one understands, makes sense of things, and finds significance. After a recent conversation Skylar, from

Scenario I, discovers that Riley's sister expresses a belief that sessions with the psychologist are awkward and unhelpful. Skylar, using Heidegger's framework, wonders how this latest revelation alters the way that Riley values the practice of clinical psychology. Will Riley consider another profession or will this encourage a recommitment to becoming a good, helpful therapist? Either way, this new discovery will have some sort of influence on the way Riley makes sense of and values the practice of clinical psychology, coloring the commitment to the study of psychology and feelings about the topics studied to date, which will prejudice the way Riley thinks about future studies. Skylar's key task as the advisor involves finding a way to make connections between the elements of past, present, and future; thinking about how they all fit together; and how they have changed Riley's perceptions.

World and Time

Students find meaning as influenced by their own world (sociohistorical context) and from within the context of time (that through which change and development are experienced).

Advisors can come to know the student's world and the influence of time by asking biographical questions: "Where did you grow up?" "Why did you come to this college?" "Are you the oldest sibling in your family?" "What's the best thing that ever happened to you?"

Such a conception of time highlights the way in which change inevitably shifts interpretation and alters how things make sense. With mindfulness that these changes and shifts in interpretation are inevitably part of human existence, advisors should anticipate the need for continual reframing and approach each conversation with an openness that will allow for a more accurate understanding of what is important to each student.

Heidegger's explanation of the conditions of human existence underscores the importance of understanding how connectedness, world, and time shape the way each advisee finds significance in the world. Yet, Heidegger might suggest that advisors are equally conditioned, approaching advising from within their own contextualized existence. Therefore, while it is important for advisors to acknowledge and uncover how each advisee is conditioned, they must also understand how the conditions of their own existence shape their interpretation and understanding. In fact, Heidegger argues that an authentic existence requires a lived awareness of ourselves as a contextualized interpreter, and necessitates an openness toward a continually changing and ultimately finite existence. The process of advising, then, ought to include a contextualized understanding of the advisee from an advisor actively self-conscious about the ways in which her or his own contextualized understanding affects the work of advising.

Hans-Georg Gadamer

Heidegger's *Being and Time* was first published in German in 1927; by the time Hans-Georg Gadamer published *Truth and Method*, also in German in 1960, the former work was already ensconced as one of the major statements of 20th-century philosophy. Encapsulating and paying homage to Heidegger's achievement, Gadamer (1989) suggests that "understanding is the original characteristic of the being of human life itself" (p. 259). Four aspects of Gadamer's work are useful to the practicing advisor: prejudgment, hermeneutic circle, question, and I/thou.

Prejudgment. While advisors may wish to think that they enter into an advising interaction without preconceived notions, such is not the case. In fact, prejudgments are inescapably and unavoidably the way that interpretation and understanding can take place at all. They are the sum total of one's experiences with prior texts and conversational partners, and they contribute to making cogent judgments.

> To try to escape from one's own concepts in interpretation is not only impossible but manifestly absurd. To interpret means precisely to bring one's own preconceptions into play so that the text's meaning can really be made to speak for us. (Gadamer, 1989, p. 397)

In an article aimed at therapists, Chang (2010), drawing upon Gadamer, concisely expressed the usefulness of inevitable prejudgment: "Since it is impossible to escape from our preunderstanding, it is imperative to actively engage it, incorporate it, and utilize it as the basis for new understandings" (p. 23).

Advising cannot be conducted free from prejudgment; however, advisors ought not be blindly enslaved by their unexamined prejudgments. Gadamer (1989) warns against "the fundamental presupposition of the Enlightenment, namely that methodologically disciplined use of reason can safeguard us from all error" (p. 277). Therefore, even while yearning for a way to guarantee perfect advising, just as Descartes sought to philosophize without error by starting from the seemingly innocuous proposition that he existed, perfect practice is impossible. Therefore, it behooves advisors to acknowledge and constantly examine their prejudgments.

What can the practicing advisor do to become aware of prejudgments, not to erase them (an impossible task), but to engage them and incorporate them into discussions with students? We suggest that advisors examine their own lives, especially with regard to personal history, education, personality, attitudes, and values. Put in the form of questions to be answered, the following serve as examples:

1. *Review personal history with questions.* "What has the story of my life been? Where is it going?" The answers to these questions constitute how one's autobiography might be written. An advisor who answers with "My life has

been one long struggle with adversity and bad luck" might work differently with students than an advisor who answers with "My life has been pretty smooth sailing because I worked hard for peace and prosperity."

2. *Consider the influence of formal education* by asking, "What has the story of my education been?" The answers to this question will likely influence the ways the practicing advisor will deal with students. For example, an advisor who thrived in a small liberal arts college, loved general education courses, and excelled in writing may struggle with prejudgments when dealing with Riley, the first-generation student in Scenario I who is not enamored of general education requirements. If working at a large research university, this advisor may also need to work diligently to connect with advisees, especially those having difficulty with college-level writing.

3. *Know oneself.* Advisors can start their own self-discovery by answering the question of "What sort of personality am I?" Answers will vary with the system of inquiry chosen, but we recommend that advisors seek to ascertain their own personality traits and characteristics. In any case, the advisor should take his or her personality into account during interactions with students. A self-aware advisor will be less likely to dismiss a student's concerns as irrelevant because she or he will recognize that the advisee possesses unique personality traits unlike those of the advisor.

4. *Assess attitudes and values.* "What commands my respect? What do I deplore?" Answers to these kinds of questions draw on the whole of human experience: politics, religion, education, relationships, cultural background, and so forth. By becoming aware of such prejudgments, the practicing advisor can use them to engage with the student (though clearly not for the purpose of converting the student to the advisor's predilections).

Student Prejudgments

How can an advisor discover the prejudgments that the student brings to the advising session? Through questioning and being alert to even oblique responses in key areas.

Personal history: "What has your life been like up until now? Do you like the way it's headed?"

Education: "Is the story of your education headed for a happily-ever-after ending? Is there anything that would make your college experience more interesting?"

Personality: "If I were your best friend, what would I already know about you?" Even a humorous question might lead to serious knowledge about the student's personality: "So, what's it like being a Gemini?"

Attitudes/values: "Who are you going to vote for? Why?" "Why are you a Giants fan?"

Both Riley and Skylar, featured in Scenario I, bring prejudgments to the conversation. In this, as in any case, the advisor has three tasks with respect to prejudgments. First, the advisor must constantly examine her or his own prejudgments. Skylar, for example, may want to ask, "What are my impressions about first-generation students?" If a first-generation student once, Skylar may harbor strong feelings about being in that situation and urge Riley to tough it out because taking on the struggle worked for Skylar. Likewise, what are Skylar's prejudgments about the choice of Riley's major? Of general education?

Second, because the advisor is likely to be a more experienced interpreter than the student, he or she should seek to understand the student's preconceptions as well. In Scenario I, Skylar can pick up on obvious clues, such as when Riley refers to poor performance in "*only* a gen ed course." The importance of family to Riley is also manifest. Furthermore, Riley's presence in Skylar's office testifies to an open-mindedness to advice and some respect toward advising.

Third, the advisor, as the more experienced interpreter, should foreground the prejudgments—when circumstances warrant it—of both conversational partners so that each is aware of the other's prejudgments. In Scenario II, Drew might remind Ali that advisors want to see students succeed in school and are predisposed to encourage them to finish, and then ask, "Ali, are you getting pressure from family or friends to leave?"

Hermeneutic Circle. Central to the field of hermeneutics, *the hermeneutic circle* is often expressed as a paradox: interdependence in discourse between the whole and its parts. That is, one cannot understand the whole without understanding the parts, and yet the parts are not comprehensible without an understanding of the whole. However, Gadamer (1989) describes the hermeneutic circle as more appropriately an oscillation: "The movement of understanding is constantly from the whole to the part and back to the whole" (p. 291). From a broad view, this oscillation reflects the interplay between the present situation and all the previous texts and conversational partners. One sees the current text or conversational partner against the backdrop of her or his own accumulated experiences, traditions, and acculturations. Prejudgments provide an initial expectation of meaning between conversational partners.

The Big Picture

The traditions and purposes of higher education can be thought of as a grand narrative with interpretable meaning. How might the advisor help the student see the meaning of the educational journey? Students often lose sight. "Why do I have to take an arts course? I'll never use it." "Why does this course have a prerequisite? I'll never finish on time." Every practicing advisor faces such questions from time to time. Experienced advisors know that often the best response allows the student to supply the answer: "Do you expect to have a life devoid of art? How has your life been enriched already by art? What's on your iPod? Why?" To the student with prerequisite woes the advisor might ask, "Why do you suppose that this is a prerequisite?"

Many books have been written on the big picture of higher education, and the practicing advisor would do well to consult them. We recommend Rust (2011), "The Utility of Liberal Education: Concepts and Arguments for Use in Academic Advising," *NACADA Journal, 31*(1), 5–13.

> The circle, then, is not formal in nature. It is neither subjective nor objective, but describes understanding as the interplay of the movement of tradition and the movement of the interpreter. The anticipation of meaning that governs the understanding of a text is not an act of subjectivity, but proceeds from the commonality that binds us to the tradition. But this commonality is constantly being formed in our relation to tradition. Tradition is not simply a permanent precondition; rather, we produce it ourselves inasmuch as we understand, participate in the evolution of tradition, and hence further determine it ourselves. Thus the circle of understanding is not a "methodological" circle, but describes an element of the ontological structure of understanding. (Gadamer, 1989, p. 293)

By "ontological structure of understanding," Gadamer simply means that this oscillation is how understanding takes place. Meaning is constructed in the interplay between the prejudgments and traditions that the advisor and the advisee each bring to the situation and the discourses that they utter.

The second scenario, in which Ali seems disenchanted and disenfranchised, may reflect a student caught up in the hermeneutic circle and experiencing it as a downward spiral. If skilled in hermeneutics, Drew can discuss some of the grand meanings toward which higher learning tends. A discussion of the importance of the life of the mind, the meaning of the curriculum, and the as-yet-untapped cocurricular activities that have always been available may help Ali see past the parts to the whole of an education.

Question. Gadamer regards any text, any utterance by a conversational partner, as the answer to a question, such that if one can express that question she or he can truly understand the text or utterance to which it is an answer. The give-and-take of dialogue, the oscillations of the hermeneutic circle, offer insight. As dialecticians (see, e.g., Hagen, 1994), advisors are skilled in uncovering the presupposed questions underlying the words of their students, their conversational partners.

> A person skilled in the "art" of questioning is a person who can prevent questions from being suppressed by the dominant opinion. A person who possesses this art will himself search for everything in favor of an opinion. Dialectic consists not in trying to discover the weakness of what is said, but in bringing out its real strength. It is not the art of arguing (which can make a strong case out of a weak one) but the art of thinking (which can strengthen objections by referring to the subject matter). (Gadamer, 1989, p. 367)

Both of the sophomores in the scenarios can benefit from an advisor displaying the give-and-take of the skilled dialectician, the questioner. Where prescriptive advisors may presume to already know the student, those approaching advising from a hermeneutic perspective eschew such hubristic presumptions and instead practice "epistemic humility." That is, hermeneutic advisors do not presume to already know. Instead, they bring out the strengths of the student by asking increasingly probing questions.

How can the practicing advisor enhance dialectic skills? No single method works all the time for everyone, but advisors, in general, should always be alert for themes and hidden contradictions, just as when reading a novel or a poem. For example, Riley (Scenario I) brings at least one theme or central idea that Skylar can reveal through skilled questioning. Riley's college attendance may indicate courage and a yearning to make the world a better place for self and family. Such a story ends better than the one written from a sociological perspective in which the cards seem stacked against Riley.

Probing Questions

The quality of a student's education is at stake. Advisors need to dig deep to help the student see the rationale for the choice of a major or college. Sometimes oblique questions work best; sometimes the direct approach gets better information. No method applies, but the following open-ended questions may help extract from students a description of meaningful aspects of their lives:

○ Why are you in college at this point in your life? Are you here because you want to be or because someone else wants you to be?

○ What is it like to be you right now?

○ At your retirement dinner, what do you want people to say about you?

○ Who are you and what are you about?

The student from Scenario II suffers from hidden contradictions. Ali sees life playing out and accepts it complacently as experience, living out one's destiny, perhaps. As a skilled practicing advisor who is unafraid to ask probing questions, Drew may show Ali that destiny can be shaped through action: "What is your bliss? What moves you? What are the defining attributes of who you are as a person?" The answers may lead to a more involved, self-actuated life for Ali and a renewed sense of engagement with the college.

I/Thou. How shall advisors (the *I*) regard advisees (the *thou*)? Due to the thoroughly intersubjective nature of any conversation, how might advisors (as *thou*) wish to be regarded by their advisees (as *I*)? Gadamer offers three ways in which the "I" can be with respect to the "Thou." In the least satisfactory way, it is when the I experiences the thou, not as an autonomous and unique human being, but rather as an embodiment of human nature, that is predictable, and therefore controllable. Such an attitude, probably recognizable in some advisors, encourages a calculation of another's behavior. Advisors with this perspective may think of students as types and think "I know how to deal with that kind of advisee." Advisors with such unexamined use of prejudgments, not only practice unprofessionally, but also ineffectively with stilted outcomes because most students can see right through such a nongenuine stance.

The second I-thou interaction is perhaps less negatively perceived but nearly as unsatisfactory as the first: One claims to know the thou better than him or herself because the I believes him or herself to be free from prejudgments and bias; however, in these cases, the I viewpoint is often, in fact, driven by hidden, unexamined prejudgments. The advisor who piously claims to be unaffected by prejudgment and therefore able to encounter each student on her or his own terms embodies this ineffective practice. "A person who believes he is free of prejudices, relying on the objectivity of his procedures and denying that he is himself conditioned by historical circumstances, experiences the power of the prejudices that unconsciously dominate him" (Gadamer, 1989, p. 360).

The third and most useful conversational relationship with a student allows the advisor to "experience the Thou truly as a Thou—i.e., not to overlook his claim but to let him really say something to us" (Gadamer, 1989, p. 361). This application means that advisors must constantly examine and critique his or her own prejudgments and allow students to change advisors' perceptions. "Openness to the other, then, involves recognizing that I myself must accept some things that are against me, even though no one else forces me to do so" (Gadamer, 1989, p. 361). Despite the difficulty of practicing this type of relationship, any advisor with the advisee's interest at heart wants the student to also regard her or him as a conversation partner and wants the discourse to influence both participants. Advisors and advisees who interact in this way will allow the truth that emerges in the dialogue to claim them, to be changed by them.

Epistemic Humility

Why should advisors allow themselves to be changed by their students? The power that advisors possess is only appropriate if it is held in trust for the benefit of the student. Advisors willing to be changed can be assured that the trust is not being violated.

Should advisors necessarily be changed by each student who walks into the office? No. However, advisors must adopt an attitude of epistemic humility, to know, like Socrates, that one does not have all the answers. It is a stance of reverence toward the other whether he or she is in the office or on Facebook.

Does it mean that advisors cannot offer prescriptive advice or scold students sometimes? By no means. Advisors who affirm the stance of epistemic humility can still admonish a student's lackluster performance. However, knowing when to criticize for the student's good is not easy, but by adopting a stance of epistemic humility, advisors can ensure that they do not abuse the inherent power of their position over advisees.

Of course, Gadamer does not offer any specific insight into the dilemmas facing Ali and Riley. Rather Gadamer offers a way of being in any relationship with any thou: remaining open to the other and allowing oneself to possibly be changed in unanticipated or even undesirable ways by the interaction with the conversational partner.

Gadamer does not offer so much a method for the practicing advisor as an attitude to adopt, one that allows for give-and-take in the conversation with the student. The hermeneutic advisor holds him or herself reflectively in a free space, even if cluttered with tradition and prejudgments, and questions the student so that both parties are influenced through the interplay of ideas. Only in such a way can an advisor co-create an education.

Practical Applications

Advisors are generally comfortable drafting prescriptive instructions, pointing students in the right direction, helping them anticipate, and even delivering an occasional speech. They are sources of information, and their work often consists of answering questions about deadlines, requirements, and resources. However, just as with many of the approaches elsewhere in this book, we argue for practice that extends the basic role of advisors. By advocating for a hermeneutic approach to advising, we hope our colleagues will deliver advice that makes the advisee feel seen, valued, and understood. All appropriate advice is useful, to be sure, but good advice is based on an understanding of what is important to and what makes sense to the individuals being advised. This sort of guidance requires more than prescriptive delivery of information. Through application of hermeneutic theory, the advisor recognizes the difficulties associated with the opacity of language, which mediates the advising interaction, conveying thought and feeling indirectly. Interactions are clouded by language, and therefore, successful communication requires a certain amount of attention and care.

At first glance, hermeneutic theory appears convoluted and impossibly complicated; yet, it brings to light the primacy of interpretive activity and thus offers a tool for advisors to understand both their advisees and themselves. Interpretation is the modality through which we exist as human beings; as such, it serves advisors' interest to take hold and consciously involve themselves in the process. Advisors aspire to the co-construction of an education for advisees, one that involves a nuanced understanding and meaningful advice. To employ hermeneutic theory practically, advisors need to set up and engage in a two-sided conversation, recognize and probe for context, and actively embrace the process of self-reflection.

In support of two-sided conversations, advisors ought to ask open-ended and probing questions, along the lines of those we have suggested, and be prepared to actively listen. Mirroring what the advisee has communicated and asking for clarification and further information, the advisor should attempt to draw specific information from the student. For example, "Let me get this right, it sounds as if you are expressing frustration about your psychology course and that you are concerned you will not do well enough to qualify to become a psychology major. Can you tell me a bit more?"

Advisors can take to heart Heidegger's conception of contextualization and remember to search for information that helps them recognize what is important to advisees. While open-ended conversation should provide the temporal and intellectual space necessary for the advisee to feel comfortable revealing contextual information, the advisor needs to recognize important cues and prompt for further explanation. Most important, advisors should remember to look for context, details about connectedness or disconnectedness to others (parents, friends, work colleagues, social groups, etc.), information about sociohistorical position (ethnicity, religion, education, age, hobbies, number of siblings, and experience traveling, etc.), and changes to these contextualizations. For example, a conversation about an advisee's roommate can facilitate a discussion about the advisee's peer group, and in turn allow the advisor to gauge peer group influences. In another case, an advisor might ask about the local weather to uncover information about the advisee's hometown and to learn more about the way in which the advisee may be influenced to interact, understand, and function in local culture.

Of course, while lengthy, open-ended discussions are ideal for uncovering the sort of connection necessary to identify meanings for the individual, not all advisors possess the time or resources necessary to pursue this strategy. In fact, some advisors work with hundreds of advisees, maintain a part-time position, or have teaching and research that must take priority. However, we suggest that developing a hermeneutic approach is still possible through advisor self-reflection. In fact, self-reflection is central to an authentically hermeneutic approach. Recognizing where one exists contextually, identifying and being conscious of one's own prejudgments, is essential to the success of any hermeneutic interpretation. Advisors can do their best to foster open-ended, two-sided conversations (honoring both I and Thou), probe for clarification, make note of contextualizations; however, without self-awareness and reflection, advisors cannot own the process of interpretation.

Hermeneutic theory reminds practitioners of the opacity of language, the importance of context, and the centrality of self-conscious interpretation. As such, it informs a feasible approach in practice. Understanding involves recognition of the conditions within which people exist and make sense of their lives and world; understanding requires interpretation. We hope that advisors acknowledge the importance of two-sided conversation, recognition of context, and the necessity for active and ongoing self-reflection.

Summary

To advise with a hermeneutic approach is to enter the conversational exchange with epistemic humility, just as one would experience an unfamiliar written text, a never-before-heard song, or a painting that seems reluctant to yield its meaning. It is to take to heart the idea that identity creation and indeed the way we make sense of our being in the world is through narrative. It is to question how the other, the advisee, makes meaning out of his or her experience of the world. Lastly, it is to be mistrustful of method in any practice, but accepting of a stance, an orientation that values good interpretation of the discourses of advising.

References

Chang, J. (2010). Hermeneutic inquiry: A research approach for postmodern therapists. *Journal of Systemic Therapies*, 29(1), 19–32.

Ebeling, G. (1959). Hermeneutik. *Religion in geschichte gegenwart* (3rd ed.). Tübingen, Germany: Mohr Siebeck.

Gadamer, H.-G. (1989). *Truth and method* (2nd ed.). J. Weinsheimer & D. G. Marshall (Trans). New York, NY: Continuum. (Original work published 1960)

Grondin, J. (1994). *Introduction to philosophical hermeneutics*. J. Weinsheimer (Trans.). New Haven, CT: Yale University Press.

Hagen, P. L. (1994). Academic advising as dialectic. *NACADA Journal, 14*(2), 85–88.

Heidegger, M. (1962). *Being and time*. J. Macquarrie & E. Robinson (Trans.). Oxford, UK: Basil Blackwell. (Original work published 1927)

Light, R. J. (2001). *Making the most of college: Students speak their minds*. Cambridge, MA: Harvard University Press.

Nakkula, M., & Ravitch, S. (1998). *Matters of interpretation*. San Francisco, CA: Jossey-Bass.

Palmer, R. (1969). *Hermeneutics: Interpretation theory in Schleiermacher, Dilthey, Heidegger, and Gadamer*. Evanston, IL: Northwestern University Press.

Schleiermacher, F. (1998). *Hermeneutics and criticism and other writings*. Cambridge, UK: Cambridge University Press.

A NEW PATH: ENVISIONING THE FUTURE OF ACADEMIC ADVISING

In his 2005 *NACADA Journal* article [issue 25(2), pp. 65–73], Marc Lowenstein asked readers to consider the question "If advising is teaching, what do advisors teach?" In part four, Lowenstein again challenges readers, this time to imagine possible futures for the field of academic advising and for those who practice within the profession.

Lowenstein encourages readers to set professional goals. Additionally he delineates the undertakings that institutions, the advising community, and individual scholar-practitioners must consider, not only to help students succeed but to advance the academic advising profession.

ENVISIONING THE FUTURE

Marc Lowenstein

Throughout this book, readers have been reflecting on how each approach to advising relates to their own practice, where it may be useful, and how it might be adapted. At this point, each reader can draw on those reflections to address some more general questions: In my role as an advisor, what do I aspire to achieve? What is my view about the overall purpose of advising? What will advising look like in ten years? In what kind of advising profession would I like to participate in the future? How would I change the ways advising is done and organized?

In this chapter I suggest the direction for advising. I encourage readers to consider whether they are attracted to this vision of the future or whether they prefer a different direction for the profession.

A Fable

Tracy opened her laptop in her residence hall to register for her final semester. She had not seen her advisor because she did not have an advisor—no one at Future U did. Instead, being a conscientious student, Tracy opened the Ad-Vy-Zor software module attached to the registration site and ran her degree audit for the next-to-last time to verify the classes she needed. Identifying the courses, Tracy navigated to the registration page and had a rude awakening: One of the courses she needed in her major was not offered!

This had happened before, but not so close to graduation. Tracy knew to go back to Ad-Vy-Zor and click on the "course unavailable" area. She typed in the course ID and clicked on "recommend substitute." The system offered only one option. A veteran user of the system, she knew that a recommended substitute was not necessarily an *approved* substitute. So she navigated to still another module and clicked "request substitution" and supplied the necessary information. (Most of the fields were prefilled because the module accessed her open registration page and degree audit.)

At this point, Ad-Vy-Zor surveyed a highly confidential database of algorithms regarding circumstances under which various substitutions were acceptable. These rules resulted from a collaboration between information technology personnel who had trained on the Ad-Vy-Zor system and department faculty members and were approved by respective deans and the curriculum committee. The rules take into account a student's proximity to graduation: A substitution that would not be permitted for a junior might be allowed for a senior. In Tracy's case, the verdict was *Yes*. Offered this outcome, she happily clicked "accept" and went back to the registration screen to key in the new course. Meanwhile the degree audit module updated her record to show that this course met the intended graduation requirement and subsequently all the remaining red fields in her audit turned black. Tracy exited the system and headed off to the cafeteria for lunch. The whole process had taken 10 minutes.

This fable represents one possible future for advising, but not the only one. What, if anything, is wrong with this scenario? Tracy did not need to interact with a human being to meet her needs. Is that a problem? Ad-Vy-Zor is likely as consistent, reliable, and accurate as a human advisor. Certainly Tracy is satisfied. She would be less pleased if she had received a negative response, to which a human advisor could have offered sincere sympathy, a benefit that may not justify the expense of maintaining an advising center. What other advantages, if any, can advocates of human advisors cite?

At Future U, the case for the value added by human advisors was not made effectively. What might the future be like if that case is made, and how might the case be made?

A Vision, Not a Prediction

In the following depiction, I do not seek to predict the future of advising, but rather describe a possible future worth pursuing. The function of a prediction is to come true, and it is evaluated on that basis. The function of a vision is to motivate, to inspire. In this chapter, I present a cluster of ideas and goals for the advising community to consider. My central claim is that advising can potentially become the most important academic resource in higher education if only the advising community will embrace the ideas and goals set forth here and effectively articulate them to the wider academic world.

In this chapter, I describe an imagined future for advising in which colleges and universities, to take advantage of the benefits of advising, are organized differently from the way they now are ordered. I present the information in sections about

- advisors and students,
- advisors and institutions, and
- advisors and academia.

Through a series of propositions in each section, I describe one aspect of advisors' roles in this imagined world.

A Note on Sources

The practices described are not factual, so the chapter does not present (and therefore does not document) evidence that they are real. However, the ideas extend from other works, and readers who find these ideas attractive—or who do not—may wish to peruse some of these sources. In any case, credit is due to some colleagues who have made important contributions to broadening the discourse on advising, including several whose work is represented in this publication.

Hagen (1994), describing Plato's Socrates as an academic advisor, was one of the first to present a paradigm of advising rooted in a humanities discipline. Hemwall and Trachte (1999, 2005) argued that the core purpose of advising is to facilitate learning. They also called attention to the value of focusing students on an institution's overall educational philosophy as represented, for example, in its mission statement. In a previous publication (Lowenstein, 2000), I proposed that advisors enhance learning by helping students understand and articulate the logic of their curricula and furthermore (Lowenstein, 2005, 2011) suggested that this activity gives concrete meaning to the concept of *advising as teaching*.

Schulenberg and Lindhorst (2010) provided a superb context for thinking about the future of advising through a historical account of ideas about the role of advising in higher education (and how the reality has differed from the ideas) as well as an inspiring exhortation for advisors to take their rightful place as academic leaders and thinkers. In this chapter, I suggest one way advisors might advance and communicate their roles in the academy.

Advisors and Students

Because students are, of course, central to advising, my vision for the future begins with a description of advisors' relationships with advisees. In this scenario, future advising will realize the potential to be the single most important factor in each student's education. The discussions of advisors' future roles in their institutions and in higher education generally are the subsequent, logical extensions of their impact on students.

Each of the statements is at once a description of a possible future for advising and an element of a philosophy of advising that emerges from the account as a whole. The descriptions, although about the future, are rendered in the present tense for stylistic simplicity.

Advising Is a Locus of Learning, Not a Service

Advising is a locus of learning; it is not a service that directs students to the place where they can learn. Advisors have overcome the view that their work consists of helping students select learning experiences or even of helping them identify the goals of their learning experiences. Instead, they are teachers, and their advising interactions with students consist of teaching and learning. Advisors help students to make a coherent whole out of their entire education in a manner analogous to that in which a classroom instructor helps students make sense of the material in a single course. Students recognize and create linkages and logical relationships between and among their various courses, comparing and contrasting ways of knowing, understanding how one body of knowledge builds on another, reflecting constantly on how courses and groups of courses contribute to meeting educational goals, even as new experience may change those goals.

Advisors coach and facilitate this learning process, asking their students questions such as those described by Janet Spence and Nora Scobie in chapter 12 on Socratic advising, encouraging them to focus not only on facts and theories but also on intellectual skills and habits of mind, and always returning to an evolving set of learning goals and intentionally focusing on how experiences relate to these objectives. To undertake this process, advisors need a breadth of intellectual background and a set of pedagogical skills identical to those that the best classroom teachers possess, as delineated by Jayne Drake in chapter 2 on advising as teaching.

Advising Gives Meaning to Education

Learning in the advising setting gives coherence and meaning to students' educations. In the past, students often perceived their curricular requirements as a set of discrete entities, represented by boxes to be checked off of a curricular worksheet in whatever order might be permitted (more recently the boxes appear on a computerized degree audit). Too often advisors (and those who hired and evaluated them) perceived advisors' primary responsibility as helping to ensure that students did not miss any boxes, and regardless of the quality of their performance in this role, they reinforced their advisees' limited understanding and squandered an opportunity to add value to those students' educations.

Today, advisors appreciate that their work also includes helping students develop a much richer understanding of their curricula. Students and advisors spend their time together discussing how the students' learning experiences fit together across a semester and over time. Students understand that there is, after all, a rationale to the requirements they must meet; moreover they can expand on this rationale and take ownership of it by tying it to their own educational goals—and those goals, in turn, become more sophisticated over time as they are informed by new learning. With their advisors' help, students now see their course selections not only as steps toward completing requirements, but as opportunities to reinforce and complement what they have learned and to set the stage for further learning.

Advisors and students realize that an education is more than the sum of its parts. Each individual component not only stands on its own, but grows tentacles as subsequent experiences shed new light on it, illuminating the ways it can interconnect to other components. Not only is learning shaped by the context of the student's past, but the converse holds true as well: Prior learning takes on new meaning when subsequent ideas and information create a new context for it. While students must take responsibility for finding connections, advisors are accountable for facilitating student understanding of them.

Advising Is a Year-Round, Nonadministrative Enterprise

Course selection remains a locus of the advising relationship because the process offers teachable moments about a student's learning progress. However, students and advisors best accomplish goals at times other than the hectic registration period so that they can take a longer and broader view of the ways student classes and experiences fit together. Moreover, students' perspectives on their learning change throughout a semester, so a single visit is unlikely to prove optimally effective.

An unfortunate trend of the late 20th and early 21st centuries involved commoditization of higher education. Students shopped for colleges and universities, which often catered to these potential customers by packaging their product as an attractive purchase. Once they selected a college, students often continued to see themselves as consumers. As a consequence of this perspective, they tended to see everyone (with the *possible* exception of their course professors) at the institution as a service provider. They expected the registrar's web site, the bursar's office, and the cafeteria to provide services that they had already purchased. They also viewed the advisor's job as monitoring their efficient progress toward graduation.

The latest, enlightened view of advising has not completely changed consumerist attitudes throughout the university, but it has affected advisors' view of their roles and students' views as well. Advisors do not see themselves as processors of paperwork (even though, of course, they have record-keeping responsibilities), and they recognize that the experiences that students share with them are anything but routine. Advising involves very little busy work.

Advising Is Transformational

That one might experience positive change by interacting with an administrative office would never have occurred to a student in the past. Now, even if students are not immediately aware of it, advisors aspire to transform students' understanding of their education.

Advisors hope students will finish college with a more complex worldview and a richer sense of what knowledge is, how it fits together and how it changes, than they had when they entered higher education. Advisors see this student evolution as a principal goal of their work. They do not indoctrinate students—whose beliefs are their own—rather, in the Socratic sense, they serve as midwives to the students' delivery of ideas.

Advising Socializes Students to Take Responsibility

For quite some time, most faculty members have seen active learning as absolutely essential for students to master the material in their courses. Constructivism as a pedagogical theory holds that students must construct their knowledge of the course content for themselves; they do not receive that knowledge from others—not the instructor, the textbook, nor any other source.

More recently advisors, too, have come to understand that students must take responsibility for their own direction. This tenet of student obligation involves more than the traditional (and legalistic) proposition found in college catalogs that suggests that, while advisors offer help, students are responsible for knowing and following an institution's policies. Rather, advisors now understand that students' academic task in college involves constructing an overall, uniquely personal understanding of how the world works, the ways by which knowledge is gained and critiqued, the meaning of these understandings in terms of students' own lives, and the fit of students' values into a worldview. No one can create understanding of these aspects of learning for students. However, advisors can help students recognize the learning tasks ahead and repeatedly coach them through various stages of accepting the challenge and monitoring the many twists and turns of the students' changing ideas over time.

Advising Helps Students Create Meaning and See Patterns in Their Learning

Students need to see patterns in their learning. Although difficult for modern educators and students to believe, students did not willingly visit their advisors, and so some in the academy longed for the days when students were required to obtain an advisor's signature to register. Seemingly against their own interests, however, advisors opposed the signature requirement because students saw them as obstacles to overcome rather than as important people who contributed to student achievement. Therefore, in many places the requirement disappeared, (coincidentally or not) institutions developed increasingly effective means for students to track their own progress toward graduation, and gradually the reason for seeing one's advisor became more difficult to identify.

By seeing advisors as people who help them make sense of their learning, today's students understand the rationale for making advising appointments. As a result, they experience powerful conversations with their advisors and find them sources of intellectual excitement comparable to the best "Aha!" moments in the classroom. Seeing how the parts of one's education fit together can be as stimulating as finally understanding why differential calculus makes sense, or what the various phenomena called the *Renaissance* have in common. Tremendously motivating for students, advising converts all of those boxes on the degree audit into a meaningful pattern; in effect it is what makes an education of various seemingly unconnected classes.

Advisors and Institutions

In this section, I explain more concretely how colleges and universities have facilitated the interaction between students and advisors described in the previous section. Such arrangements cannot be implemented without quite a bit of administrative support.

In fact, some may doubt that they can be undertaken at all, and others will wonder at any possible motive for students to enter into the challenging enterprise of advising with all the other demands on their time and energy.

Plato's *Republic* portrays Socrates describing an ideally organized society. One of his interlocutors, Glaucon, expresses doubts about the viability of such a society, and Socrates in a famous passage says a single step is both necessary and sufficient for such a state to evolve: "Cities will have no respite from evil, my dear Glaucon, nor will the human race, I think, unless philosophers rule as kings in the cities, or those whom we now call kings and rulers study philosophy . . ." (Plato, 1974, p. 133). The point, for purposes of the present discussion, is not to start a debate on Plato or to propose that advisors should be philosophers (though many are). Here, Plato's suggestion serves as an analogy. Just as he thought a single point of leverage (easy to describe but perhaps difficult to implement) could change society, so the accomplishment of the new role for advising depends largely on a relatively simple set of institutional changes.

Advising Is Rightfully a Credit-Bearing Activity

To persuade all stakeholders to view advising as a serious learning experience on par with the classroom, educational leaders reasoned that institutions need to award academic credit for it. This effort turned out to be the single lever that made many other changes possible. The importance is partly symbolic but also very practical. By making advising a credit-bearing activity, the academy communicates that students should expect to experience learning in their advising relationship and that advisors are teachers. The move also suggests that advisors bring considerable knowledge and wisdom to the advising encounter and that students should prepare for it as they do for class. Indeed the mandate implies that the advising relationship has intended learning outcomes such that students bear responsibility for achieving results for which they will be graded! More mundanely, but just as importantly, the students understand that advisors assign homework that students are expected to complete.

The various implications of awarding academic credit for advising reflect the characteristics that make real the vision of advising as a locus of learning. Most important, the new status of advising affects student incentives: People value that for which they have paid (or earned) more highly than that which they get for free. Paying tuition for an experience encourages students to seek value in it. Moreover, the prospect of receiving grades for their work encourages students to take it seriously. (Educators are not so idealistic to suppose that the intrinsic value of the experience is sufficient to put it at the top of students' priority lists; that is, if such a motivator does not inspire writing term papers, it will not encourage appreciation for advising either.)

Students do not receive grades or credits just for visiting their advisors and chatting, even about weighty topics such as those involving life goals and learning about the logic of the curriculum. They must provide concrete evidence of learning. At most institutions students show learning in the context of a course for which they register and complete either every semester or some fixed number of times. Many institutions title this course "Reflective Learning," although other titles apply. Reflective learning, now common in colleges, referred to as *RL*, may be offered on an independent study basis or in a group format. Content is based on a syllabus, a tool evolving from the advising syllabus, which became prominent in the early 21st century. The syllabus lists learning objectives generally, but not exclusively, related to the integrative function of advising. It also indicates the types of assignments students must complete, which include a variety of readings about the purposes of higher education and related topics and writing assignments that reflect these matters as well as structured meetings (some in group format) with the advisor (who is the course instructor).

As the most substantial product of RL, students typically maintain an electronic portfolio to which they add items throughout their years in college. The entries include papers and other assignments appropriate to their studies that illustrate the content of their learning, the patterns it forms, and development over time. The portfolio also includes ongoing reflection on these matters, for which the student primarily earns the grade for each successive RL course. The electronic format allows students to link their reflections to portfolio documents that substantiate their achievements. It also lets them connect topics over time to illustrate altered perspectives or increasingly sophisticated understandings.

Students' RL grades are not earned based on the quantity of learning in a major or general education course. Rather, the RL grade rewards astuteness of reflection on learning across the curriculum and success in constructing connections among learning experiences. It also rewards the cogency with which students document their reflections on their educational progress by citing appropriate papers and other exhibits included in the portfolio.

Colleges and universities do not offer RL grades in addition to the credits that they already provide for undergraduate degrees. Rather, they judge RL as sufficiently important in enhancing learning throughout the students' curricula, making their entire education more effective (including strengthening their ability to make use of the content material from their other courses), that they reduce the number of other required degree credits to ensure that students gain the most from RL.

Advisors Are Faculty Members

If students earn credits toward graduation for their RL courses and pay tuition, then those who teach the courses should earn teaching credit for them as well, and just as institutions consider the credits a worthwhile trade-off for students in meeting degree requirements, they value the advisors' work in RL and treat it as in-load teaching rather than a discretionary extra.

Many institutions that originated this practice immediately encountered a puzzle: Most of their advisors were faculty members with formally defined teaching loads, whether by institutional tradition or union contract, but other advisors were full-time staff who did not otherwise teach, and the teaching load had no meaning in their jobs. That is, they could not teach RL instead of teaching something else.

Initially universities dealt with this problem in ad hoc ways that no one considered really satisfying, but gradually, over a period of years, a solution emerged that revolutionized the institutional role of advisors. Many universities concluded that if advising is teaching (which they had claimed to believe for decades), and if the RL classes offer value, full-time advisors taught just as much as traditional faculty had taught such that the distinction between these two categories of people proved artificial. So the leadership collapsed the distinction altogether and began classifying everyone who taught RL the same—as faculty. Only the distinction between advisors who solely taught in RL and those who teach some RL classes as well as in a specific departmental discipline, such as chemistry, finance, or anthropology, remained.

Everyone understood from the start, however, that merely decreeing the equality of a status does not make it universally appreciated. For the full-time RL teachers truly to be peers of the other faculty, they must hold similar credentials, which is the reason the change in advisor status took a number of years to accomplish. Initially universities instituted large-scale graduate programs to enhance the academic background of advisors while faculty members complemented their terminal disciplinary degrees with in-service programs that helped them explore ways to translate their teaching skills into the RL setting. Ultimately, however, many of the graduate programs that had long prepared teachers in higher education adapted to produce well-prepared professionals for the RL program, and most hired to teach and advise now have similar educational attainments.

Of course, education is not enough: Just as faculty members have traditionally engaged in productive scholarship throughout their careers, full-time advisors now face a similar expectation. They carry out empirical studies of the effectiveness of various teaching and advising techniques and also write about their discoveries in learning gained by working with students.

Not all institutions have adopted the RL model and not all faculty members who can participate choose to do so. Moreover, not all full-time advisors have embraced the possibilities, preferring to keep their traditional role.

In the remainder of this chapter, the word *advisors* continues to appear as the designation for those instructors who teach mostly in RL-type settings. Although the distinction reflects only the number of hours devoted to each type of teaching, *advisors* may be contrasted with *faculty members* who teach mostly non-RL courses.

Advising and Assessment Are Inextricably Linked

The mandate that grew up in the late 20th century that colleges and universities assess student learning and adjust curricula or pedagogies to address any disappointing results remains in force. However, the new role that advising plays in higher education has added at least three new dimensions to assessment.

First, students' portfolios provide superb raw material for assessment. Students know the learning goals they are attempting to reach, and they have intentionally chosen the papers and other items in their portfolios precisely to illustrate their progress toward those goals. Their written reflections describing the reasons for selected items, as well as the items themselves, illustrate the portfolios' usefulness for assessment. Faculty members in degree programs or external stakeholders, such as accreditation teams or employers, find useful evidence here.

Second, the best assessments for advising are more clear than in the past. Advisors define the learning objectives of their work with students—specifically in their RL classes—and the concrete work that students produce provides the best evidence of the amount and applicability of their learning. No longer must evaluators resort to indirect measures of the effectiveness of advising, such as inputs rather than outcomes or compiled satisfaction surveys. (The latter are not useless but they are far from the best available measures of learning.)

When looking at these two aspects of assessment together, one sees the interesting consequence that the assessments of curricular learning and the assessment of learning in the advising setting have converged. The same evidence supports both, and indeed the questions are the same as well.

Finally, students have become active partners with the faculty in the assessment enterprise. Their understanding of learning objectives and of how to marshal evidence of their achievements aligns with the knowledge that the faculty needs for assessment. When department leaders wish to assess learning goals for graduates or university administrators seek a random selection of students to participate in some nationwide test of essential intellectual skills, students come forward to volunteer because they are just as eager as the faculty to learn from the results and to write about their achievements in their portfolios.

Advisors Are Campus Thought Leaders

At most institutions, select people are seen as particularly adept at articulating the institution's mission and at thinking through implications for issues of curriculum and strategy. These individuals likely head task forces to reconfigure general education or serve as key participants in the institutional self-study for regional accreditation. When they rise to speak at faculty senate meetings, others actually listen. They are likely to have written and spoken on their ideas about education for both internal and external audiences, and other institutions have invited them as speakers, evaluators, or consultants.

Historically these thought leaders were employed as discipline-based faculty members, or occasionally as administrators. Now, as advisors have taken a more prominent role in examining learning at their institutions and as they increasingly involve themselves in studying the issues that surround teaching and learning, they too are seen as thought leaders. For example, they play prominent roles on curriculum committees because they have spent more time than other faculty members in studying how students interact with the institutional curriculum as a whole; for the same reason, advisors serve as respected members on assessment committees. When an advisor rises to speak at a faculty senate meeting, others listen.

Advisors Expect and Are Expected to Continue Learning

At most universities, to be an effective teacher one needs to continue learning. In most cases, both the institution and the faculty have understood that the expression of this learning means conducting scholarship in one's discipline. Of course, colleges have always varied in the manifestations of the scholarship expected from the faculty.

Now that advisors have taken on roles increasingly similar to those of traditional faculty members and their institutions understand them to be teachers on par with other faculty members, they face the expectations historically applied to their peers. They are vigorous consumers and producers of the literature on higher education—on curriculum, learning, assessment, and civic engagement as well as the relationships between general education and majors and between learning and the workplace. Their institutions support advisor–scholar work and allocate travel funds, comparable to those given to other faculty members, for them to attend conferences, and they also show that they value these learning efforts by publicizing advisors' achievements and basing promotions partly on accomplishments related to learning.

Admissions Brags about Advising Programs

When recruiting students, admissions personnel show off their fitness centers and computer labs, cite the names of eminent scholars on the faculty, and point out activities available to students. Recently, however, they also boast about the quality of the advising programs. Everyone on campus clearly understands that the success students achieve during and after their enrollment is tied to their advising experience. The students who guide families on campus tours and the student orientation leaders who greet them several months later at registration all brim with enthusiasm about their own experiences with their advisors. The admissions staff add their own voices about advising to the litany of characteristics they like to highlight. Parents, increasingly savvy about the potential impact of advising, have learned to ask questions such as "What kind of reflective learning courses do you offer?" Just as institutions have long sought to enhance their reputations by citing Pulitzer Prize winners or Fulbright scholars on their faculty, they now add prominent advisors to the list as well.

Advisors and Academia

As institutional leaders have recognized and acted upon advisors' importance to student learning, the world of academia as a whole has also come to value advisors in new ways.

Advising Gains High Status as a Career

As befits their co-equal role, advisors enjoy the same career-path opportunities that institutions provide for traditional faculty members, including promotions in rank and tenure. As individuals in the field gain national prominence for their work, especially for their scholarship, they may become attractive targets for recruitment by other institutions, just as has been the case for well-known scholars in other academic disciplines.

Of course, not everyone aspires to a career in academia. Not everyone enjoys the intellectual life or is sufficiently well equipped for it. Not everyone enjoys regular interactions with students. In addition, many people qualified for academic work can demand higher salaries in other walks of life. None of these workplace realities has changed since the early 21st century.

However, for college students excited by ideas, with talent for intellectually demanding work, and stimulated by the prospect of lighting the intellectual spark in the next generation of students, a career in advising is every bit as attractive as one in traditional teaching.

Advising Is Informed by Cutting-Edge Thinking

Higher education continues to play a vital role in society both for its contributions to national economic, social, and political life and for the benefits it brings to individuals who attend college. Therefore, it is a constant subject of study, analysis, and debate. Governments at all levels, accrediting bodies, journalists, and citizens are among the participants in the ongoing discussion. At colleges and universities, top administrators have traditionally been involved, along with a limited number of faculty members, but more recently, advisors have been among the most avid readers of the literature. The most important writing about higher education deals with the purposes of education, the structures and practices most likely to enhance learning, the curriculum, and assessment. These topics are central to the work of advisors.

On individual campuses, advisors get together on a regular basis to exchange ideas gleaned from the higher education journals they read. Of course, they have plenty of other ways and venues for communicating about these matters.

Advising Is Nonpreferentially Informed by Many Disciplines and Paradigms

At one time, the developmental approach to advising enjoyed a semi-official status as the favored, sanctioned approach. Accordingly, most practitioners and leaders in the field assumed that those from disciplines based on the study of student development, namely the behavioral sciences, would possess the best intellectual background for the field. This supposition led to powerful implications for

- the types of educational preparation that administrators expected in potential advisors;

- ○ the preference (in some quarters, see O'Banion, 1974/1994/2009) for professional advisors with such backgrounds over faculty advisors;
- ○ the research methodology, format, and style book that characterized the first leading advising journal; and
- ○ even the types of questions that advisors chose to consider and investigate.

This last point is immensely important. A paradigm of thought not only preferences some kinds of answers over others, but tends to dictate, without adherents even being aware of it, the kinds of questions that seem appropriate to raise.

No one ever intended that one approach to advising, and its accompanying way of knowing, achieve hegemony over others, but *advising* and *developmental advising*, at one time, were practically synonymous. The only alternative to the developmental approach that anyone could name was a straw man named *prescriptive advising*. More recently, however, two mutually reinforcing trends have changed this picture.

First, people from a much wider range of disciplinary backgrounds have entered advising and achieved positions of leadership. Second, the approaches to advising described in this volume have emerged because advisors trained in diverse disciplines brought their own modes of thinking to their work and to their discourse about their work. Why did they pursue advising and how did their ideas converge?

The answers lie in the changed character of advisors' work. The challenge of engaging with students in the integration of their curricula and reflection on the similarities and differences among modes of knowledge calls for individuals with a specific type of intellectual equipment rather than those within any specific area of knowledge specialization. During their own intellectual upbringing, these future advisors tended to explore disciplines broadly and devoted more energy than their classmates to reflection about the ways the elements of knowledge fit together to support and complement each other.

Now that the new paradigm of advising has been in place for some years, many students are graduating from universities with this kind of experience, but in the early years they were difficult to find. Those with the specific interest and skill suited for advising come from many different areas of concentration at both undergraduate and graduate levels. They have less in common in the topics they studied than in how they studied them: intentionally, reflectively, and with an eye on how subject matter is related to other areas of thought.

As the range of advisors' backgrounds broadened, so too did the modes of thought that informed their work. The result was the rich array of approaches to advising that contributors to this book describe and an advising community accustomed to greeting new approaches and increasingly being receptive to them.

Advisors Contribute to Nonadvising Conferences and Journals

No one is more intimately involved in intensive thought about learning than advisors. After all, they spend most of their time discussing learning with students and coaching them to think about learning in new ways. So when they think and write about their work, they think and write about learning. However, learning is equally central to the concerns of classroom faculty and curriculum committee members, assessment officers, deans, provosts, student affairs leaders, and others. So the scholarship that advisors create has become important not only to other advisors but to the wider world of higher education.

National and international higher education journals and conferences invite them to present their ideas, and higher education trade papers send reporters to advising conferences to glean the new and interesting ideas that their (nonadvising) readers will want to know. In general, as an area of scholarship advising has become much less insular.

Advisors Debate Their Ideas about the Future

With so many different intellectual traditions available for consumption, advisors naturally introduce and debate new ideas about advising practice, philosophy, and intellectual foundations. Any such views will affect the future of the profession. No one can predict the ideas that may emerge from this ferment, nor can one guarantee that the next set of ideas will bear any resemblance to those promoted in this chapter.

Reflections: Fantasy and Reality

The future world of advising I have described is quite different from present reality. To be sure some semblances can be found; for example, current discourse on advising is drawing on a wide and growing range of intellectual traditions. However, as it relates to learning, institutions, and higher education at large, advising remains far from the central influence envisioned in this essay. Readers, even those who may find the ideas herein attractive, are likely to believe that they are idealistic, utopian, and impractical.

The two responses to this observation are both important. First, a utopian vision need not be fully realizable to be valuable. An attractive vision can serve practitioners well by serving as a goal, even as those who are striving to reach it understand that they will not quite succeed. Moreover, it can be a standard against which they measure their actual accomplishments. Visions of social utopias or of human goodness can be useful in these ways.

More important, arguably, the vision presented can be accomplished. It will not be easy, but three initial steps lead to the goal.

1. Institutions must pursue the kinds of learning outcomes that academic advising is uniquely able to facilitate. That is, leadership must commit to the goal of students making intentional connections, creating coherence out of the disparate parts of the curriculum, reflecting on the similarities and differences among ways of knowing and how they complement each other, and the other metacognitive learning objectives described in this chapter. Those who make this decision may also realize that the best people on campus to accomplish the goal are advisors.

2. The advising community must learn to think big and aim high in envisioning a role for the profession in higher education. Advisors cannot permit themselves to be characterized as handmaidens to the "real" work of universities, but must insist that they are central to it. Advisors cannot engender this attitude unilaterally: Others in the institution must recognize advisor talents and insights, and therefore, advisor ability and wisdom must be visible outside the advising community. To gain attention and shine in the spotlight, advisors must make themselves heard in the institution on such topics as curriculum and assessment, and in the wider world, they need to participate in conferences and write on higher education in venues not solely addressed to their fellow advisors.

Advisors who have learned to see their potential must convince policymakers that they are best suited to help meet institutional goals. They must call attention to their key role in learning, pointing out that they teach some of the most important lessons at the university and that advising learning outcomes are central to institutional mission. They must also present themselves, not as drones, but as thought leaders from whom faculty and administrators alike have a great deal to learn.

Some of the measures needed to achieve this future are not under the direct control of advisors. However, none of the vision will come to fruition without advisors taking some of the key first steps on their own.

3. Advisors must invoke their personal visions. Early in this chapter, readers were prompted to think about their visions for advising. Specifically I asked whether the profession as described in the chapter looks promising or whether they prefer their own, different visions that lead to a future and profession different than the one presented here.

In reflecting again on the vision for the future, readers should note that it rests on a theory or philosophy of the essential nature and purpose of advising. In the present chapter, the theory presented—sometimes explicitly stated and sometimes implied—suggests that advising is a fundamentally academic activity focused on teaching and learning as well as the integration of each student's curriculum. If taken to its logical conclusion, it is the theory that elevates advising to the pinnacle of importance among academic professions.

Readers who favor a different theory about the essential nature of advising and therefore a different vision for the future of the profession may profit from contrasting it with the ideas presented here. Regardless of the preferred vision, the future of the field will be dictated by advisors. Therefore, individually and collectively, advisors must identify a theory that describes the profession, a vision of where it should go, and a path for getting there.

References

Hagen, P. L. (1994). Academic advising as dialectic, *NACADA Journal, 14*(2), 85–88.

Hemwall, M. K., & Trachte, K.C. (1999). Learning at the Core: Toward a new understanding of academic advising. *NACADA Journal, 19*(1), 5–11.

Hemwall, M. K., & Trachte, K. C. (2005). Academic advising as learning: 10 organizing principles. *NACADA Journal, 25*(2), 75–83.

Lowenstein, M. (2000, April–May). Academic advising and the "logic" of the curriculum. *The Mentor: An Academic Advising Journal.* Retrieved from http://dus.psu.edu/mentor/old/articles/000414ml.htm

Lowenstein, M. (2005). If advising is teaching, what do advisors teach? *NACADA Journal, 25*(2), 65–73.

Lowenstein, M. (2011, September 28). Academic advising at the University of Utopia. *The Mentor: An Academic Advising Journal, 13*(3). Retrieved from http://dus.psu.edu/mentor/2011/09/university-of-utopia/

O'Banion, T. (2009). 1994 (1972): An academic advising model. *29*(1), 83–89. (Reprinted from *Junior College Journal, 42,* 1972, pp. 62, 63, 66–69; *NACADA Journal,* 1994, *14*[2], pp. 10–16)

Plato. (1974). *Plato's Republic* (G.M.A. Grube, Trans.). Indianapolis, IN: Hackett.

Schulenberg, J., & Lindhorst, M. (2010). The historical foundations and scholarly future of academic advising. In P. L. Hagen, T. L. Kuhn, & G. M. Padak (Eds.), *Scholarly inquiry in academic advising* (pp. 17–29). Manhattan, KS: National Academic Advising Association.

NAME INDEX

A

Abelman, R., 139, 142, 143, 144, 146, 152
Abes, E. S., 124
Adamchik, K., 220
Adams, V., 111
Alderman, M. K., 90
Allen, J. M., 141
American Association for Higher Education, 35
American Association of Colleges and Universities (AAC&U), 121, 122, 134
American College Personnel Association, 35
Amrhein, P. C., 68
Amundsen, S. A., 84
Anderman, L., 90
Anderson, E. C., 18, 105, 106, 107, 108, 109, 111, 113
Anderson, M. Z., 159, 160
Angelo, T., 34, 35, 41–42
Appleby, D. C., 18
Aspinwall, L. G., 106
Astin, A. W., 3, 90
Atwood, J. A., 84
Augustine, 224–225

B

Bailey-Taylor, A., 84
Bandura, A., 70, 87, 90, 106
Bane, K. D., 160
Banning, J. H., 7
Barrington, L., 76
Baxter Magolda, M., 39, 121, 122, 123, 124, 125, 126, 128, 134, 165
Bays, C., 220
Bean, J., 10, 12, 13, 90
Beatty, J. D., 4, 143
Benfari, R. C., 160
Bensimon, E. M., 6, 7
Berg, J., 165

Best, S., 220
Binkert, J., 160
Biswas-Diener, R., 106, 107
Bixby, K., 220
Bloland, P. A., 7
Bloom, B. S., 20, 29
Bloom, J., 9, 68, 83–99, 101, 106, 110, 127, 161, 165
Blumer, H., 6
Bobbitt, P. E., 220
Boeree, G., 192
Bolles, R., 76
Bono, J.E., 160
Boss, R. W., 160, 161
Boyatzis, R., 160
Boylan, H. R., 144–145
Bradford, L. P., 166
Bransford, J. D., 41, 110
Brickhouse, B. C., 199
Brophy, 141
Brown, A. L., 110
Brown, S., 24
Brown, V., 220
Bruner, J., 194
Buckingham, M., 106, 107, 108, 115
Burg, J. E., 114
Burkum, K., 83
Bybee, D., 114

C

Cameron, K. S., 106
Campbell, S., 3–15, 18
Cantwell, L. S., 107
Carnevale, A. P., 62
Carroll, L., 3
Casner-Lotto, J., 76
Cate, P., 61–63
Center for Substance Abuse Treatment, 75
Centre for Applied Positive Psychology, 112
Cerabino, K. C., 69
Champlin-Scharff, S., 86, 198, 223–239

259

SUBJECT INDEX

A

AA framework. *See* Appreciative advising framework

Academic advising: academic credits offered for, 249–250; constructivism as basis for, 181–183; contributing to student retention, 10–13; counseling vs., 46–47; developing meaning with, 6, 246, 248; envisioning new role for, 243–248; establishing developmental academic advising, 48–50; fable of future, 243–244; finding learning patterns, 248; foundation of good practice for, xiii; four levels of knowledge in, 9; future career status of, 254; giving meaning to education, 246, 248; helping students take responsibility, 248; hermeneutics approach to, 223–224, 226; influenced by cutting-edge thinking, 254; linking assessment and, 251–252; as locus of learning, 245–246; multiple disciplinary backgrounds in, 254–255; philosophical and sociological basis for, 4–9; philosophy of strengths-based advising, 106–107; pragmatism and, 4–5; prejudgments brought to, 231–233; prescriptive, 46, 47; reversing O'Banion's model of, 61–63; role in student success, 9–13; setting goals for, 4; social science approaches to, 7; Socratic advising approach, 212–214; studying theoretical and philosophical thinking for, 180–181; supporting student success, 3–4; symbolic interactionism in, 5–6; systems theory applied to, 183–191; taking pride in programs for, 253; theories supporting, 180–181, 195; transformational process in, 247; unique for each student, 6, 10; using multiple theories for, 17; year-round, 247. *See*

also Future advising trends; Scenarios; *and specific theories of advising*

Academic Advising (Habley & Grites), 18

"Academic Advising Model, An" (O'Banion), 48

Academic Advising Today, 155–157

Academic Center for Excellence (ACE) program, 84

Academic Improvement Model Advisor Cohort I: applying Socratic advising process, 198, 200, 212–214; assessing advisor learning, 215; measuring student thinking, 202, 204–207; participants in, 198; self-reflection exercise for, 203; Socratic questioning toolbox for advisors, 208–209; traits chosen in, 214; types of thinkers studied, 201–202

Academic performance: effect of AA on, 84; evidence of strengths-based advising in, 106

Academic recovery program (ARP), 102–103

Achievements and expectations, 39

ACPA Developments, 47

Action: basing on pragmatism, 4–5; lessons demonstrating mastery of, 20; reflecting meaning, 6

Action stage, 75

Advising. *See* Academic advising; *and specific theories of advising*

Advising as coaching: applying levels of, 161–168; decision facilitation process in, 165–167; developmental program level of, 161–162; history of, 159–160; individual session, 163–164; levels of, 161–168; overview, 159–161; scenarios for, 168–171

Advising as teaching: about, xv; behaviors for good teachers, 19–22; Crookston's contributions to, 47; demonstrating care for students, 22–24; impact of learning